CHRISTIAN HIGH SCHOOL RELIGION SERIES

God's Old Testament People

Student Book

Prepared by:
Thomas Buck
Margaret and Fred Trinklein

CONCORDIA PUBLISHING HOUSE · SAINT LOUIS

Contents

Concordia
Publishing House

Copyright © 2005 by Concordia Publishing House
3558 S. Jefferson Avenue
St. Louis, MO 63118-3968

1-800-325-3040 • www.cph.org

Unless otherwise indicated, Scripture quotations are taken from the HOLY BIBLE, NEW INTERNATIONAL VERSION®. NIV®. Copyright © 1973, 1978, 1984 by International Bible Society. Used by permission of Zondervan Publishing House. All rights reserved.

Scripture quotations marked "RSV" are taken from the Revised Standard Version of the bible., copyright 1946, 1952, © 1971, 1973 by the Division of Christian Education of the National Council of the Churches of Christ in the U.S.A. Used by permission.

Scripture quotations marked "TEV" are taken from the Good News Bible, the Bible in TODAY'S ENGLISH VERSION. Copyright © American Bible Society 1966, 1971, 1976. Used by permission.

Scripture quotations marked "NASB" are from the NEW AMERICAN STANDARD BIBLE, © The Lockman Foundation 1960, 1962, 1963, 1968, 1971, 1973, and 1975. Used by permission.

This publication may be available in braille, in large print, or on cassette tape for the visually impaired. Please allow 8 to 12 weeks for delivery. Write to Library for the Blind, 7550 Watson Rd., St. Louis, MO 63119-4409; call toll-free 1-888-215-2455; or visit the Web site: www.blindmission.org.

Manufactured in the United States of America

7   8   9   10   11   12   13   14   15   16   14   13   12   11   10   09   08   07   06   05

To the Student

Adam, Eve, Abel, Noah, Abraham, Isaac, Jacob, Joseph, Moses, Joshua, Deborah, Gideon, Samson, Samuel, David, Solomon, Elijah, Hezekiah, Isaiah, Jeremiah, Ezekiel, Daniel, Jonah, Esther, Ezra . . .

"Stop! Who are these people?"

They're some of the people God tells us about in the Old Testament—some of the people you'll learn about in this course.

"Wow! They must have been great! I mean, for God to tell about them in the Bible. Didn't they ever do anything wrong?"

Of course they did. You'll find out that they did some *awful* things. But God still loved them. And they loved Him. They repented of their sins, and God forgave them.

God didn't save these people because they were His good leaders and good servants. He saved them by grace through faith in the Messiah. One whole chapter of the New Testament tells about their faith. Read **Hebrews 11** to get a preview of the people in this course.

The last verses in **Hebrews 11** tell us, **These were all commended for their faith, yet none of them received what had been promised. God had planned something better for us so that only together with us would they be made perfect (verses 39-40).**

"What does that mean?"

It means that God loved those special Old Testament people, but not any more than He loves *you*. They received lots of blessings from God, but God kept them waiting for the final fulfillment of His promises till now! He has honored us by joining us to them that we all might be made perfect together!

God makes us all "one." He keeps His promise of salvation to us all through Jesus' life, death, and resurrection. Together with God's Old Testament people you get to enjoy all the blessings that come with God's love and forgiveness!

Unit 1
Getting Started

For 14 years Jason lived in a small, sleepy town. But last summer his family moved to the coast.

Finally, in September, he visited the big city, 50 miles away. It seemed that he discovered new sights and sounds every minute! The big building project at a major intersection especially impressed him. It looked like complete confusion. Hard-hatted workers directed the operation of huge cranes; steel girders were being placed in strange patterns; cement mixers droned; cavernous excavations were edged with ramps over which strong men pushed wheelbarrows.

Jason could see no rhyme or reason in all this activity, so he walked up to the fence at the edge of the construction site to get a better look. There he saw an architect's drawing of the finished building. It was beautiful! Jason looked up thoughtfully. "Maybe," he thought, "lots of big projects seem to start out with chaos—at least that's what it looks like. But it's really not. An architect and supervisors are planning every bit of that activity. All those people look like they're doing different things. In a way they are, but in a way they're not. Each one is doing something that has to be done in order to finish this neat building!"

That thought made Jason feel better, because his life right now seemed to be a little like that building site. He lived in a new town; he was still getting adjusted to his new school; his older brother, Ryan, had gone off to college a short time ago; the pressures of moving had made his parents short-tempered; his face was breaking out more lately; the attractive girl he had met at the tennis court was dating a football player. His life seemed just as chaotic as that construction project.

But Jason had always trusted God. He knew

UNDER CONSTRUCTION

BE PATIENT

GOD ISN'T FINISHED WITH ME YET

Jason heaved a big sigh of relief. He thought, "I can't see how the parts of my life fit together, but God can. And He loves me so much. Why, He even sent His Son to die for my sins! I *know* He will help me now, too! He has already given me lots of helpers—including the Holy Spirit, the best Helper of all! I'm sure He will keep on giving me all the help I need. I don't need to worry about my life. With God looking out for my future, what more could I want?"

COVENANTS

In this course we will talk about covenants God has made with us. The dictionary defines a covenant as a "contract" or "agreement." It's a kind of blueprint. Contracts are law-oriented; covenants are love-oriented. God has been making covenants with people ever since He created the world. He always keeps His part of the covenant/agreement. Unfortunately, we are unfaithful to God. And if God had not provided a way out of this problem—by sending a Savior—we'd be lost for sure, condemned to an eternity in hell with Satan, who began all our troubles.

In this course you will study God's covenant relationship with His creatures from the time of creation until shortly before Christ's birth. As you consider this record, you will better understand your own relationship with God. As you learn more about God through the study of His Word, He will build your faith, lead you to pray for His guidance, and help you make wise decisions in many areas of life—choosing friends, preparing school assignments, pursuing an occupation or choosing a college, selecting a life partner, finding a home, whatever you do. No structural detail in the building of your life is too small to take to God for help.

After a building has been designed, the people in charge of construction use the best possible materials and the most dependable workers for the project. But they are limited by the amount of money the owner is able and willing to invest in the structure. In much the same way, God has wonderful plans for your life. But He does not force that plan upon you. He calls upon you to devote time and effort to the plan. And He promises to build your life for you.

God really cares! Do you?

Remember, God doesn't make junk!

that God loved him and had already provided helpers for him. Grandma helped him sort out family problems and cheered him when he felt lonely for Ryan. The counselor at his new high school had done her best to make him feel welcome. Several guys on the block had asked him to join their bowling league. He had met the new vicar of the nearby Lutheran church and was surprised how easily they had talked in that first meeting; Jason learned that there was an active youth group at the church. Maybe things weren't all bad.

Session 1

Getting to Know Each Other

Where should we start? Here, now, in this class—how can we encourage each other to build good friendships with each other and a firm relationship with God? What should be our top priority?

A first step in any building project is to choose an architect. Satan is eager to act as our adviser, and he will keep trying to misguide us all through our lives. But Satan is a liar **(John 8:44)**! As God's people, we follow God! He is our **"Refuge and Strength, an ever present help in trouble" (Psalm 46:1)**! He gives us all the guidance we need. We are blessed to know Him and to be His own!

How do we live as Jesus' very own people? Jesus Himself gave us these words, " **'Love the Lord your God with all your heart and with all your soul and with all your mind.' This is the first and greatest commandment. And the second is like it: 'Love your neighbor as yourself.' All the Law and the Prophets hang on these two commandments"** (Matthew 22:37-40).

Jesus also gave us a promise, **"Where two or three come together in My name, there am I with them"** (Matthew 18:20).

So each day as we meet together, Jesus will be here with us and we will listen to Him speak through His Word.

GETTING TO KNOW EACH OTHER

"Love your neighbor as yourself," Jesus said. Who are your neighbors? They certainly include all your classmates. If you don't know everyone, why don't you ask your teacher to help you learn to know them? As friendships develop, you will surely want to learn new ways to show your love to those new friends. What can you do? Here are some examples from God's Word:

Carry each other's burdens. Galatians 6:2

Do not seek revenge or bear a grudge. Leviticus 19:18

A perverse man stirs up dissension, and a gossip separates close friends. Proverbs 16:28

If anyone is in Christ, he is a new creation. 2 Corinthians 5:17

They devoted themselves to the apostles' teaching and to the fellowship, to the breaking of bread and to prayer. Acts 2:42

Let's build each other up!

"Fear not, for I have redeemed you; I have called you by name; you are Mine."

Isaiah 43:1

Session 2

Getting the Message from God's Word

IMPORTANT MESSAGES

Margo frantically searched, first through her purse and then her flight bag. The jet engines were already whining on the plane she was to take to Singapore. All her companions were already on board. But the airport official left no doubt: Margo would have to stay in Java indefinitely if she could not present her passport. It seemed impossible to Margo that such a small thing could so drastically affect her life.

A poor widow barely managed to eke out a living as she awaited her son's return from service in a foreign country. She was puzzled by the strange slips of paper that he included in his letters, and she carefully saved them in a drawer. Little did she know that the mysterious papers were money orders! Her son sent them to support her in ease—even in luxury—during his absence.

As Hans and his father were forcibly separated at the entrance to the concentration camp, the father secretly passed a crumpled piece of paper to his son. The coded message gave the location of the family jewels that had been carefully hidden to keep them from falling into enemy hands. How important it was for Hans to preserve and decipher that message!

You and I possess a message far more important than any of those mentioned in these stories. We find that message in the Bible. There God shows us His plan of salvation. The message in the Bible deals with eternal as well as earthly treasures. For that reason, we study it carefully and frequently. This course will help you to do that.

A MESSAGE-WRITING EXERCISE

Messages come in many different forms, depending on the writer, the recipient, and the purpose of the message. To help you understand this, test your own skill in writing a message. Pretend that you have been asked to make a written report of a dramatic event (such as a violent story). You have been told that your report should be made in a specific style of writing: as a newscast, as a personal experience to be shared with a friend, as a poem that will be printed in a school publication, or as a coded message from a spy to the general of an army that is about to invade the country.

Write your report on the lines that follow. Choose any of the styles of writing mentioned above.

_____

_____

_____

_____

_____

_____

_____

_____

_____

_____

MESSAGE FORMS IN THE BIBLE

Of all the messages that have ever been written, none has been more widely read than the Bible. The Bible is the all-time best-seller among books. It has been translated into more languages than any other written work. People in all parts of the world are reading the Bible right now to find the message that God has put there for them.

The various parts of the Bible were written by different authors in different styles and under different circumstances. See if you can find an example of each of the following styles of writing in the Old Testament. Write the name of an appropriate book in each blank space.

Poetry _____

History _____

Prophecy _____

GOD'S LOVE LETTER

God used many writers, and each wrote in his own style. But God inspired the writers. Though human beings wrote the Bible books, God was the Author. We call that "God-breathed," or "inspired."

Each book of the Bible reveals a part of God's message of love to the human race. The Bible shows God's power; it shows us how sinful we are—that we deserve eternal punishment in hell; it shows how God sent Jesus to save us from our sin; it shows how the Holy Spirit gives us faith, and thus Jesus' salvation becomes our salvation; it shows how we can demonstrate our love to God and to other people; it provides the blueprint for a happy life.

Read the following Bible passages and be prepared to tell what each of them says about the purpose of the Bible. Pay particular attention to what the passages say about the Old Testament.

READING GOD'S WORD

2 Timothy 3:16-17 (KJV): All Scripture is given by inspiration of God, and is profitable for doctrine, for reproof, for correction, for instruction in righteousness: That the man of God may be perfect, throughly furnished unto all good works.

Luke 24:27 (NIV): Beginning with Moses and all the Prophets, He explained to them what was said in all the Scriptures concerning Himself.

John 5:39 (TEV): [Jesus said,] "You study the Scriptures, because you think that in them you will find eternal life. And these very Scriptures speak about Me!"

A WORD OF CAUTION

A Bible passage often becomes more clear when we read it in different translations. In fact each of the passages above comes from a different translation. Today we have access to many English versions of the Bible. Obviously, the version you read should be as accurate as possible. And it should be written by a translator who believes that the Bible is God's Word and that its central message is God's love for us in Jesus Christ.

In the space below make a list of the Bible versions you know about. Then add other versions that your classmates list. After each version, write whether it is a literal (word for word) translation, a paraphrase, or other type of Bible. Ask your school librarian or some other adult to help you with this list. Discuss in class why the version chosen for this course is a good choice.

_____

_____

_____

_____

_____

_____

_____

_____

_____

_____

_____

_____

_____

_____

_____

_____

_____

_____

_____

_____

[Jesus said,] "You diligently study the Scriptures because you think that by them you possess eternal life. These are the Scriptures that testify about Me."

John 5:39

Unit 2
Beginnings

Have you ever experienced chaos and frustration when you start a new activity and no one seems to know what is supposed to happen next—or no one knows who is supposed to do what? Imagine trying to play a football game if no one knows the rules and you have no referees or coaches. Cheerleaders would look pretty silly, too, if none of them would know what to do next, and each of them would lead a different cheer.

We need good direction when we begin a new activity. A capable and fair leader can help an activity succeed, whether it is playing a football game, producing a school paper, taking a class trip, or accomplishing any other of life's many important details. A good leader gives direction, announces the rules, provides the necessary equipment, encourages the participants, and keeps a sharp eye out for any problems. The good leader is *for* the team—each team member individually—as they work together for the common goal.

In this unit we will examine how God dealt with His people before the days of Abraham. During this time of beginnings, God, a very good and very wise leader, created and cared for His people. And He continues to lead His people today in good and wise ways. God knows what is good for His creatures—both here on earth and hereafter in heaven.

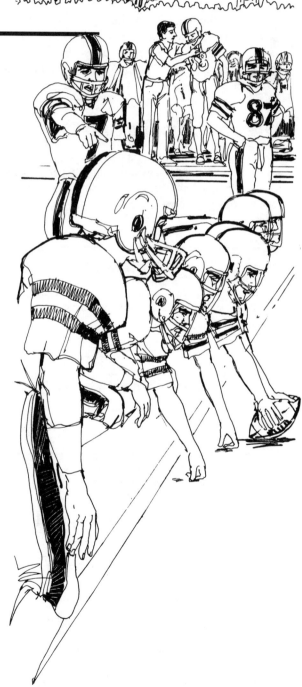

Session 3

The Origin of Everything but God

"In the beginning God created . . ." The first five words of God's love letter to us are simple and direct. No elaborate introductions—no detailed explanations—simply a clear statement of fact that shows that God rules all that exists.

THE JOY OF CREATING

1. What creation of yours has given you the most satisfaction? A tree house? a drawing? a poem? Perhaps it was a drama or a batch of cookies or a model rocket. Write down how you felt while you were actually creating it.

_____

_____

_____

2. How did you feel when your creation was finished?

_____

_____

3. Read **Genesis 1:1-26** and write down how God felt about His creation.

_____

_____

4. What evidence of frustration, if any, do you find on God's part as His creation progressed?

_____

5. Why do we sometimes feel frustrated when we make something? _____

_____

_____

6. Did you ever create something for the purpose of making you feel bad? Of course not. If you wrote a drama in which several people participated, you wanted your work to bring pleasure to you, to the actors, and to the audience. Even if the drama was meant to teach a lesson, the outcome was surely intended for the good

of all. Right? What does this suggest about God's relationship to His creation?

_____

_____

We can almost see the smile of satisfaction on God's "face" as we read **Genesis 1:31.**

WAYS OF TELLING

Read **Genesis 2:4-25** and tell briefly how it differs from **Genesis 1:1—2:3.**

_____

_____

Why does God provide two accounts of the creation of Adam and Eve? We can only speculate. But God does give us some clues. Compare, for example, **Genesis 2:4** with **Genesis 5:1; 6:9; 10:1; 11:10; 11:27; 25:12; 25:19; 36:1;** and **37:2.** What does God say in each of the 10 verses?

_____

_____

Thus we see that **Genesis** begins with the creation of the world **(1:1—2:3)**, and then God provides 10 history accounts. The first history account begins in **2:4.** We can call **2:4—4:26** "The History of the Heavens and the Earth." In **Genesis 2** God provides the transition from creation to the fall into sin **(Genesis 3)**.

For more than 2,500 years God transmitted the events of Genesis through His people—probably by word of mouth in most cases. (See **Deuteronomy 6:6** and **Psalm 78:4.**) One generation after another of fathers and mothers told their children and grandchildren about God's creation. They also told about the other things that happened to God's people and of the promise of salvation. Then God inspired Moses, the human writer of Genesis, to write these accounts, and they have been preserved to this day.

materialism to "pollute" the designated day of worship whenever possible.

Have you ever heard of "blue laws" that limit certain activities on Sundays? Such laws were originally designed to stem the tide of materialism as it began to eat away at the practice of Sunday as a day of church-going and rest. Many of these blue laws have been repealed in recent years.

Of course, many people—such as fire fighters, police, and hospital workers—have always had to work on Sundays, and in such cases they could use another day of the week for rest and worship. God does not demand that we do this on a specific day (**Colossians 2:16-17**). But He does instruct us to rest from our regular work and to spend a part of that time to worship the Creator and to study His Word.

Imagine, for a moment, that you were asked to plan an ideal Sunday for your family. After thinking about what you have just learned about God's day of rest, and after considering the likes and dislikes of the members of the family, briefly outline an ideal day.

_____

_____

_____

_____

_____

_____

In our Lord Jesus, who has conquered Satan and his worldly plans for our time and lives, we have the Christian freedom to arrange our activities according to the Creator's loving plan and to find the joy that He intended for us to have from the very beginning.

Talk to a parent or grandparent about the way Sunday was observed when they were young. Do they think it was a more worshipful or restful day than it is today? Why or why not? Do they have any suggestions as to how the observance of Sunday could be improved today? Summarize your findings here.

_____

_____

_____

_____

_____

God saw all that He had made, and it was very good.
Genesis 1:31

"ON THE SEVENTH DAY HE RESTED"

Both students and teachers are happy when Friday rolls around. Everybody needs time to rest after a period of hard work. People say, "Thank God It's Friday." From the beginning God designed a weekly time of rest.

When God rested (**Genesis 2:2**) it was not because He needed to rest. The almighty God needs no sleep or rest, as **Psalm 121:4** points out. God's "rest" from His creating activity provides an example to His creatures. The day of rest—the Sabbath—also foreshadows the "Sabbath rest" we will enjoy in heaven (**Hebrews 4:4-11**).

God wants us to use the weekly time of rest especially for the worship of the Creator, for the study of His Word, and for the discussion of the marvelous truths it contains. Of course, Satan does not want us to have time for these purposes. He uses human greed and

Session 4

The First People

What do you do when you're lonely—when you feel you don't have a friend in the world? Do you read a book where the characters become your friends? Or maybe you turn to a household pet—a snuggly, purring cat or a faithful, tail-wagging dog, or even a parakeet or hamster. In this high-tech age, some genius might try to make a robot so lifelike that it could pass for a human being. It could even be programmed to say, with enthusiasm, things like "You're terrific!" or "I'm very fond of you." And it would never say or do anything it was not programmed to say and do. What if you could do that? Would that be the best solution to the problem of loneliness? It would certainly eliminate all arguments and disagreements, wouldn't it?

Write down some of the advantages and disadvantages of having a robot friend.

_____

_____

_____

_____

Some people wonder why God didn't make us "sin-proof"—like robots who would do only what He programmed us to do. They wonder why He gave us a free will—the freedom to *choose* to do what He asks or *choose* to disobey. Do you think that perhaps God wants us to *really* love Him rather than just saying "I love you" robot-fashion, because we couldn't say anything else?

SETTING THE STAGE FOR HAPPINESS

Think about **Genesis 1** and **2**. God did not ask Adam what sort of environment he would like. God's wisdom, obviously superior to that of anything He might create, brought forth the ideal setting for Adam and Eve before He created them. God provided everything necessary—plus an infinite number of "fringe benefits"—to make their lives interesting and exciting.

God really went all out for Adam and Eve. What fun He must have had anticipating their reaction to the many different animals He made!

Make a list of things God created that intrigue you most, and tell why.

_____

_____

_____

_____

_____

Did you ever stop to think that God could have made everything in shades of black and white? Or even if they were colored, our eyes might have been made to receive only black and white, just as a black-and-white TV fails to pick up and reflect the colors in a full-color program. Scientists tell us that most animals cannot perceive colors the way humans do. God could have created us that way, but He didn't.

And what about texture? How boring it would be if, instead of fur and bark and sand and flower petals, everything felt like plastic or pine cones! Another "extra" of God's creation makes it possible for us to enjoy music. Messages can be given in monotone, but isn't it much more beautiful to listen to the lilt of laughter and the melodic flow of cultured speech?

CASTING THE CHARACTERS

"Let Us make man in Our image, in Our likeness, and let them rule . . ." (Genesis 1:26). What marvelous plans God had for Adam and Eve—and for us! God created us to be like Him— creative, active in service, eager to communicate honestly, and loving. Yet so many people are consistently destructive, selfish, distrustful of others, noncommunicative, and hateful. What happened to God's image in people to cause them to behave differently from what He created them to be? _____

_____

_____

God created Adam and Eve as rational beings who had a perfect knowledge of Him and by nature desired to live according to His will. Through sin, humanity lost the image of God, but it has been partially restored in Christ. The Holy Spirit empowers Christians to believe in God and to begin to do the good works that demonstrate a saving faith (**Colossians 3:10** and **Ephesians 4:24**).

Genesis 2:7 informs us that God tenderly formed the first man from the dust of the ground. Made in God's image, he would yearn for companionship. So, recognizing that Adam needed a mate, God provided one tailor-made from Adam's rib. Not from his foot, to be stepped on, or from his head, to rule over him, but from his side—near his heart—to be his partner in life and in love.

And God gave these first people the ability to have children. (Many TV programs and magazine articles almost lead us to believe that sex is a recent discovery. Far from it. God Himself "invented" sex and He intended it to be one of the greatest blessings of His creation. But if we do not heed His will regarding this blessing, it can become a curse.)

Look at **Genesis 1:27**. Is "man" a male term, or does it denote both sexes? _____

According to **verse 28**, when God blessed Adam and Eve, what did He tell them to do with their lives?

_____

_____

_____

What a challenge! Adam and Eve were to be "creators" of many more people like themselves, "subduers" of their environment (which would involve the arts and sciences), and "rulers" of every living creature. Zoology, oceanography, geology, and many, many other areas of learning were theirs to study and enjoy. And remember, they were created perfect and so had full use of their marvelous bodies and minds!

Physiologists tell us that, at most, we use only about 10% of our brain's capacity in a lifetime. And even that small fraction is capable of processing and storing more information than any modern computer. Can you imagine what the capabilities of Eve's and Adam's brains must have been? According to **Genesis 2:19-20**, Adam was able to name all the animals God had created.

Doesn't that seem like a lot of work? And wouldn't it have been hard to take care of the whole Garden of Eden **(2:15)**? Yes, for us it surely would be. But remember, Adam was perfect, unspoiled by sin. In Adam before the Fall we see the perfect image of God.

HAPPINESS TOGETHER

Together Adam and Eve enjoyed this image of God. Together they obeyed God's command, "**You are free to eat from any tree in the garden; but you must not eat from the tree of the knowledge of good and evil, for when you eat of it you will surely die**" (**Genesis 2:16-17**). Together they enjoyed life as husband and wife in accordance with God's words in **2:24**, **For this reason** [because God instituted marriage] **a man will leave his father and mother and be united to his wife, and they will become one flesh** [united in the closest blood-relationship possible here on earth, in which the entire inner attitude becomes one].

The relationship of these sinless people provides further evidence of God's grace. When Adam looked at Eve, he could see the very image of God in her! And when Eve looked at Adam, she could see this same perfect holiness of God in him!

Adam and Eve were united into one supernatural body. No amount of rationalization can change this. Nor can living together or having sex without a marriage ceremony affect the validity of God's pronouncement. The two were united. Is it any wonder that so much pain is caused when marriage is ended by divorce? It involves supernatural surgery that leaves scars. St. Paul underscores this when he writes in **Ephesians 5:28-30, "Husbands ought to love their wives as their own bodies. He who loves his wife loves himself. After all, no one ever hated his own body, but he feeds and cares for it, just as Christ does the church—for we are members of His body."**

The last part of this passage refers to a relationship that joins all believers to Christ Jesus through faith. In your own words describe the love God has for us.

_____

_____

_____

Look at **Genesis 1:27**. Is "man" a male term, or does it denote both sexes? _____

Then God said, "Let Us make man in Our image, in Our likeness, and let them rule over the fish of the sea and the birds of the air, over the livestock, over all the earth, and over all the creatures that move along the ground."

Genesis 1:26

Session 5

Satan and the Beginning of Evil

Read **Genesis 3.**
Have you ever heard a serpent speak? Why would a snake want Eve to eat the forbidden fruit?

1. Someone who is reading the Bible for the first time might not immediately recognize the true identity of the source of all evil, but the Scriptures answer the riddle for us. Read **Revelation 20:2** and write down the three names that the devil is called in that verse.

_____ _____ _____

2. What other names do you know for the devil? (See, for example, **Mark 5:9; John 8:44; John 16:11; Ephesians 6:16; 1 Peter 5:8;** and **Revelation 9:11.**)

_____ _____ _____

THE SOURCE OF EVIL

1. Satan is an angel who sinned and fell away from God, along with the other wicked angels. This occurred sometime before Satan tempted Adam and Eve. God does not provide the details about those events in His Word, but He does tell us all we need to know. Read **2 Peter 2:1-12.** What did God do to the evil angels (**verse 4**)? _____

_____

2. What promise does God make to the godly (**verse 9**)? _____

_____

3. Why is there so much pain and sorrow in the world **(1 John 5:19)?** _____

_____

Have you heard the saying, "Misery loves company"? Satan went from being an angel of light (which is what Lucifer means) to being the prince of devils and darkness. Hell was created for these evil angels **(Matthew 25:41).** Because he was cast out of heaven, Satan hates God and wants to drag everyone away from God and to him. He knows that those who believe in God through Jesus will experience all the joys of heaven forever. Satan's goal is to have lots of company

in hell. The evil angels who were thrown out of heaven with Satan are his helpers, and he has many of them **(Mark 5:9).**

3. The pictures of Satan with horns, red suit, and forked tail make clever cartoons, but they are far from the truth. If Satan appeared like that, it would be easy to resist him. We would immediately recognize him for what he is—the enemy. In **2 Corinthians 11:14** St. Paul tells how Satan disguises himself. Describe it.

_____

4. Whom did Satan use as his spokesperson in **Matthew 16:23?** _____

In the account in **Genesis 3**, Satan used a serpent. Let's take a closer look at Satan in action.

HOW TEMPTATION WORKS

1. God does not maliciously paint the worst picture of His creatures. Nor does He "whitewash" His heroes and heroines, leaving the impression that they are superhuman (and we inferior by comparison). He lovingly and mercifully "tells it like it is," warts and all, so that we may have His power against the forces of evil. What would be a good subtitle for **Genesis 3?**

_____

2. Look at the first four words Satan spoke. Was this honest curiosity or did he have another purpose when he asked the question? What was the purpose?

_____

3. Have you ever heard subtle taunts or questions from unbelievers that sound similar to Satan's? Or even from someone who claims to follow Jesus? Perhaps they began with "You don't mean to tell me that your parents (or church or teachers) won't let you . . .!" They are implying, as Satan did to Eve, "How unfair! What right do they have to restrict your freedom?" Write down one way you've heard people ridicule or be ridiculed. Be ready to share it in class.

_____

In these instances, Satan uses the people through whom he is speaking to get as many "fall guys" as possible into his kingdom.

Satan did not start out by introducing himself with "Hi, I'm Public Enemy Number One—Satan—and I want to go to hell!" If he had, Eve would certainly have avoided him.

Recognizing the "Evil Force"

1. Do you ever exaggerate you parents' rules and restrictions? (For example, "They won't let me do *anything* that's fun!") When we do this, we often show self-pity and lack of respect for God's appointed "rule makers"—our parents. What did Eve say in **Genesis 3:3** that sounds like this kind of exaggeration?

_____

Satan answered by saying, in effect, "That's ridiculous!" He moved very quickly from a doubt-raising question to an outright lie—or, at best, a statement with a double meaning. He might even defend his reply by saying, "I meant that she wouldn't drop dead right on the spot." But the death that results from sin is far more terrible than physical death.

2. Then Satan played his trump card. What did he really imply about God and His love in **Genesis 3:5**?

_____

_____

3. What three things did Satan promise Eve if she ate the forbidden fruit?

_____

_____

He made it sound like she would be much better off, didn't he? People don't say, when it comes to sinning, "Come on, do this because it is going to wreck your life!" Satan's approach hasn't changed one bit over the years.

Were Adam and Eve stupid in falling for Satan's lies? Were they "sitting ducks" in this encounter with evil? Before passing judgment, remember that we still get fooled by Satan's lies today, even though we have Adam and Eve's experience, all of Holy Scripture, and world history to warn us about Satan's trickery.

4. What can we learn from the temptation of Eve—about Satan?

_____

about doubting God's Word?

_____

about an accurate knowledge of God's Word?

_____

about the importance of Christian friends?

_____

about statements that flatly deny God's Word?

_____

about the source of lies?

LIVING WITH JESUS

We should always be on our guard when we speak *and* when we listen. We, like St. Peter, can speak for God or we can speak for Satan. We speak with our voice, our conduct, and our personality. When God is our guide, we speak the truth and build each other up in Christ. When Satan speaks through us, we lie, or at best speak half-truths, which ultimately hurt us and others.

Satan knows that if he can get us to rebel against God, we will be the losers. Satan loves to cause us misery.

1. Look at **Hebrews 2:14-15**. What power belonged to Satan? _____

2. What is it that gives us victory? _____

3. Which is that victory? _____

4. As powerful as Satan is, he is still under the control of God, as we can see in the story of Job, especially in **Job 1:12** and **2:6**. In **1 Peter 5:8-9** we see the attitude that we have toward Satan now that we know that Jesus has destroyed his power over death. How would you describe that attitude? _____

5. Read **1 Corinthians 15:55-57**. How can we hope to win over Satan? _____

_____

That is why the writer of the hymn, "What a Friend We Have in Jesus," exclaimed:

Have we trials and temptations?
Is there trouble anywhere?
We should never be discouraged—
Take it to the Lord in prayer.
Can we find a friend so faithful
Who will all our sorrows share?
Jesus knows our every weakness—
Take it to the Lord in prayer.

I am convinced that neither death nor life, neither angels nor demons, neither the present nor the future, nor any powers, neither height nor depth, nor anything else in all creation, will be able to separate us from the love of God that is in Christ Jesus our Lord.
Romans 8:38-39

Session 6

Saved—by the Grace of God

The flashing red lights and wailing sirens seemed like backdrops to a TV show as Kurt sat, dazed, at the side of the road. But the blood and the pain were real—and so were the demolished car and the fact that Nancy was being rushed away in a police ambulance! Kurt's head spun as he tried to recall the events before the crash. It had been such a great evening—up to then. The homecoming game, the bonfire, Nancy's eyes glowing with excitement, the unexpected offer of the use of the family car by his proud dad when the team planned a victory celebration at Mark's house, the exuberance at poolside as they relived the events of the day.

Some of the older guys had brought rum to add to the coke. Kurt didn't care much for the taste, but he drank one glassful rather than look like a "do-gooder." He was glad, later, that he had refused the second drink, because he already felt a little light-headed. Soon after, Kurt and Nancy left the party. It was a beautiful autumn evening and life was going great! Mark lived in a hilly, wooded area and the road was full of curves, but there was no traffic and Nancy said it was almost like a roller-coaster ride, only slower. Kurt responded by accelerating a bit—and that's when it happened: A dog on the road, a swerve, a cement abutment, and the crash! How could he face his dad . . . and Nancy's family? What if she died? What a mess he had made of things!

Maybe you've never made mistakes with such serious consequences as Kurt's, but we've all felt that sickening hollow in the pit of the stomach when we've said or done something we deeply regretted. We wonder how the people we've wronged will respond. With acts of retaliation and vengeance? with the cold shoulder? with gossip? Fear grips us.

Adam and Eve had disobeyed God's command. Now, for the first time, they knew what it was like to fear. The life of Paradise was over. They now had—permanently—the "knowledge of good and evil" that Satan painted so enticingly and from which the Lord wanted to protect them.

DEAD IS DEAD

The instant they sinned, Adam and Eve died spiritually. They lived in rebellion against God and became followers of Satan. And humanity has lived in this hopeless spiritual condition ever since. We are spiritually dead, hopelessly and helplessly dead. Read **Ephesians 2:1-3**. Briefly summarize these verses.

_____

_____

_____

Be ready to discuss the parallels between "gratifying the cravings of our sinful nature" and the encouragement of those secular humanists who say, "If it feels good, do it!" or "It's *your* body to do with as you choose." Give other examples of this kind of thinking.

GOD'S LOVE NEVER WAVERS

Sometimes people ask, "How do you know about something if you haven't tried it? Find out what it's all about. You'll have a real eye-opening experience!"

Read **Genesis 3:4-13**. The eyes of Adam and Eve were opened all right! Wholesome thoughts were invaded by shameful ones and Adam and Eve tried to cover their nakedness. Fear replaced their eagerness for God's companionship, and they tried to hide from Him.

Now look at God's response in **verse 9**. God obviously knew exactly where Adam and Eve were and could have appeared suddenly with a clap of thunder and an "Aha! Hide from me, will you!?" But He didn't. In *love* He *called* to them. As the story unfolds, we can see the progression of sin and the unchanging love of God.

1. Adam first responded to God with a sort of "plea bargaining." What was he guilty of? _____

2. What did he admit to? _____

3. God did not say, "Don't lie to me! The real reason you're hiding is . . ." Instead, how did God direct Adam's attention to Satan, the root cause of his troubles? _____

4. How did He invite Adam to face and confess to his rebellion—that he had listened to Satan rather than to God?

Unfortunately, Adam tried to shift the burden of guilt to Eve and, ultimately, to God by saying, "The woman *You* put here with me . . ." When God confronted Eve, she at least admitted having been deceived as she pointed an accusing finger at the serpent. But she still tried to pass the buck. Neither one repented. They both failed the test.

THE RESULTS OF SIN

Read **Genesis 3:14-19.**

1. God addressed the serpent first. It had served as Satan's tool. What effect did the Fall have on it?

2. Next, God addressed Eve. What were some of the effects of sin on human lives?

The privilege of being "fruitful," cocreators with God, would now be tainted with pain—spiritual, mental, and physical pain. Pregnancy, birth, and child-rearing would have been entirely joyful processes in Paradise. Marriage had existed without tension. But, in Satan's world, physical pain, stress, jealousy, and bitterness would be constant companions. Now, for the first time, the natural organization of family that God designed as a blessing would take on the flavor of coercion because sin had polluted the human psyche and human motives were no longer pure.

Then God turned to Adam. Under this new, evil-infested system much of Eve's time would be taken up by the bearing and rearing of children (it is obvious from **Genesis 5:4** that they had many children), and Adam would need to work in an unpleasant environment to provide food for the family's survival. Work, which had been a pleasant experience, now became tedious and frustrating. The great adventure had turned into a nightmare—just as Satan knew it would.

3. Sin still creates pain for people today as they raise children and do their work. Give examples of this.

THE FIRST TASTE OF DEATH

1. Read **Genesis 3:19.** Lest Adam and Eve think that God was mistaken about sin resulting in death,

God told them very directly, "**Dust you are and to dust you will return.**" Adam and Eve had begun to age. From **Genesis 4:25** and **5:3-4** we know that Eve lived more than 130 years. According to **5:5**, how long did Adam live? _____

2. By contrast, today's average life span is less than 100. How often do you think about your own death? _____

3. It seems pretty far away for most of us, doesn't it? Have you witnessed death? Perhaps it was only the death of a pet or an animal along the highway. How did it affect you? _____

To Adam and Eve, death was an abstract idea. They had never witnessed it. Perhaps that is why God chose to clothe them with skins **(Genesis 3:21).** Can you imagine how Adam and Eve felt when they saw that an animal had been slaughtered? They saw God demonstrate the awful consequences of sin. Through the sacrifice of animals, God clothed Adam and Eve. In this act God also foreshadowed the sacrifice of Christ and demonstrated His love for His children.

NEW LIFE IN CHRIST

Now look at **Genesis 3:15.** What a love-filled, power-packed verse that is! Notice that even before God enumerated the miseries that Adam and Eve had brought upon themselves as followers of Satan, He graciously and mercifully announced His plan of salvation. He didn't let Adam and Eve "sweat it out" for a few centuries. He didn't gloat over them at all. God simply announced a new promise, one with no strings attached! Adam and Eve and all their descendants would live in a corrupted world, but God would provide a way out of the slavery that sin and death brought.

Addressing Satan, God promised to "**put enmity between**" the offspring of Satan and the offspring of woman. "**He** [Jesus, the Messiah, born of woman with no human father] **will crush your** [Satan's] **head and you** [Satan] **will strike His heel.**" Jesus would suffer in the process, but He would emerge victorious. Salvation was thus assured right in the Garden of Eden! Adam and Eve may not have understood the specific details, but they understood enough to realize that God was the Source of their blessings, as you can see in **Genesis 4:1** and **25.**

To see how God's promise in **Genesis 3:15** was fulfilled, read **Ephesians 2:4-10.** Summarize these verses on another sheet of paper.

"I will put enmity between you and the woman, and between your offspring and hers; He will crush your head, and you will strike His heel."

Genesis 3:15

Session 7

Preserving the Promise

Did you ever get a message that was distorted or failed to provide some important details? Perhaps somebody told you that the principal wanted to see you but didn't tell you when or where. Or maybe someone failed to deliver an important message, and you missed a doctor's appointment or a practice for a baseball game or the school play.

Sometimes the failure to transmit a message is a matter of life and death for a great many people. That happened in Hawaii on the morning of Dec. 7, 1941. A large squadron of Japanese planes was on its way to attack the American fleet at Pearl Harbor. The success of the attack depended upon the elements of secrecy and surprise. An American radar operator spotted the planes on his scope when they first approached the islands. He couldn't tell whether the planes were American or Japanese, so he telephoned the radar information center and said, "A large squadron of planes is coming in from the north, three degrees east." The man who answered the phone gave the message to the officer in charge of the center. The phone call raised questions in the officer's mind. Should he alert Pearl Harbor? What if the planes were not enemy planes? What if the radar was malfunctioning? Would he get in trouble for delivering an unimportant message? Finally, instead of calling Pearl Harbor, he called the radar operator back and said, "Don't worry about it." Because one man decided that the message was not important, thousands of lives were lost!

HOW GOD KEPT THE MESSAGE STRAIGHT

God gave His messages to Adam and Eve orally, long before people had a system for keeping written records. How important it was for all humanity that those commands and promises should be transmitted accurately and completely from parents to children during the succeeding centuries.

The Patriarchs from Adam to Abraham are listed in **Genesis 5** and **Genesis 11:10-26**. As you read these sections of Scripture, fill in columns A and C in the table below. (Column A refers to the son mentioned next in Genesis. Dates on the chart will be "After Creation.")

	A Age When Son Was Born	B Date of Birth	C Age at Death	D Date of Death
Adam	130	0	930	930
Seth	_____	130	912	1042
Enosh	_____	_____	_____	_____
Kenan	_____	_____	_____	_____
Mahalalel	_____	_____	_____	_____
Jared	_____	_____	_____	_____
Enoch	_____	_____	_____	_____
Methuselah	_____	_____	_____	_____
Lamech	_____	_____	_____	_____
Noah	_____	_____	_____	_____
Shem	_____	_____	_____	_____
Arphaxad	_____	_____	_____	_____
Shelah	_____	_____	_____	_____
Eber	_____	_____	_____	_____
Peleg	_____	_____	_____	_____
Reu	_____	_____	_____	_____
Serug	_____	_____	_____	_____
Nahor	_____	_____	_____	_____
Terah	_____	_____	_____	_____
Abram	_____	_____	_____	_____

Columns B and D in the table require math skills. You will fill these columns in as a class. You may want to enter your own figures in pencil in advance and share with the class how you arrived at them.

Now let's take a closer look at the figures in the table. Skeptics have suggested that the numbers refer to months rather than years. Can you find a serious flaw in that hypothesis? What are your own conclusions? Be ready to share your views and insights in class.

After discussing this lesson in class, complete the graph on the next page. You may be surprised at the conclusions you can draw when the graph is completed.

The grass withers and the flowers fall, but the Word of the Lord stands forever.

1 Peter 1:24-25

Patriarch	0	100	200	300	400	500	600	700	800	900	1000	1100	1200	1300	1400	1500	1600	1700	1800	1900	2000	2100	2200	2300
Adam																								
Seth																								
Enos																								
Kenan																								
Mahalalel																								
Jared																								
Enoch																								
Methuselah																								
Lamech																								
Noah																								
Shem																								
Arphaxad																								
Shelah																								
Eber																								
Peleg																								
Reu																								
Serug																								
Nahor																								
Terah																								
Abram																								

Session 8

Sin Grows and Grows (Cain and Abel)

Have you ever watched a TV show or movie in which the villain tried to dash across an open area toward a safe spot on the other side—but got mired in quicksand instead? At first he didn't seem scared, because he had been in several inches of sand many times. But the more he struggled, the deeper he sank. Finally he was hopelessly mired, and the hero captured him easily.

SIN—AGAIN!

After Adam and Eve left the Garden of Eden, Eve gave birth to the first two children ever born, Cain and Abel. The first family undoubtedly spent lots of happy times together. But Satan would continue to fan the flames of pride and rebellion in their sinful nature, using every deceitful means to lead them away from God and to their own sorrow and grief—mired deeply in the quicksand of sin.

Nothing, of course, could change God's love for His creatures. He had already determined to send His only Son to live, suffer, die, and rise again so that eternal life with Him would be available to all. But God does not force anyone into heaven. He lovingly and repeatedly invites us, and He creates the faith that will save us. Heaven is ours unless we deliberately turn our backs on God's invitation.

Read **Genesis 4:1-16**. This sin occurred one day when Cain and Abel brought offerings to God.

1. What was Cain's occupation? _____
2. What was Abel's occupation? _____
3. Who was older? _____
4. What made Cain angry? _____

_____

5. **Hebrews 11:4** tells why God accepted Abel's offering. What was the reason?

_____

_____

6. What does **1 John 3:12** tell us about Cain?

_____

_____

A number of questions are not answered in this story. For example: How did Cain and Abel know whose offering was "looked on with favor"? Why did they bring an offering in the first place? What was wrong with Cain's offering? It seems obvious that, at some time, God let it be known that He wanted His people to bring offerings to Him. In some way, He also let His children know whether or not their offerings were pleasing to Him.

Obviously, if Abel's offering demonstrated his faith, Cain's offering must have demonstrated lack of faith.

7. Notice in **Genesis 4:3-4** that Cain brought "some" of his grain while Abel brought "some of the **firstborn**." If you have any gardening experience, you know that the firstfruits are the biggest, best, and most flavorful, whereas the last of the crop is often stunted. What further information on this point do you find in **Exodus 13:12** and **23:19** and in **Leviticus 22:20?**

_____

_____

_____

_____

8. Even though God did not accept Cain's offering, He reached out to him with loving concern. Look at **Genesis 4:6-7**. God continually reaches to us just as He did to Cain. Give some examples of how He does this. _____

_____

9. Like Cain, we can either accept these reminders or ignore them. Cain lost no time making his decision. What was the result **(verse 8)**?

_____

10. Now look at God's reaction. He could have zapped Cain dead with a bolt of lightning! Do you think God really didn't know where Abel was? _____

11. Why do you think He asked Cain the question in **verse 9**? _____

12. Where in the previous lessons have you come across a similar question? _____

13. What excuses have you heard people make to keep from admitting their sin? (Include excuses *you* have made.) _____

_____

_____

SIN BRINGS SORROW

1. In **verses 10-12** God confronted Cain with his sin. Cain had disobeyed God's command, and it was useless to deny it. What did God say would be the results of Cain's action?

a. _____

b. _____

Has your conscience ever made you feel restless after you did something wrong? That is one sure result of disobeying God's commands: we lose the peace He offers us. What a blessing it is to know that when we repent and confess, we have peace again because of Jesus!

2. Instead of repenting, what was Cain's attitude in **verses 13** and **14**?

_____

3. How did God respond to Cain's "pity party"?

_____

_____

Notice in **verses 14-16** that when we remain unrepentant, we are turning our backs on God; we're "out of the Lord's presence" and our relationship with Him is broken through our own deliberate choice.

4. From an earthly viewpoint, Cain didn't suffer very much **(verses 17-24).** Perhaps you know someone who keeps running away from God and still seems to prosper. What does Jesus have to say about this in **Matthew 5:44-45?** _____

_____

in **Luke 12:15-21?** _____

_____

in **Matthew 16:26?** _____

_____

5. What does Paul say about this in **Romans 8:5-6?** _____

_____

GOD BRINGS PEACE

The newspapers are full of stories of apparently successful people who find no peace in possessions, power, or pleasure. Broken homes, drug addiction, and suicide are all too prevalent among such people.

1. Read **John 16:33.** Who would give peace to the disciples?

_____

2. Why could they (and we) take heart?

_____

_____

3. Now read **Philippians 4:4-7.** What do these verses say about peace? _____

_____

_____

We cannot buy peace of mind—not at any price. It is God's free gift to His followers. What a wonderful gift it is! In thankfulness we will surely want to learn and follow God's commands.

By faith Abel offered God a better sacrifice than Cain did. By faith he was commended as a righteous man, when God spoke well of his offerings. And by faith he still speaks, even though he is dead.

Hebrews 11:4

Session 9

New Courage (Noah)

Hans squirmed uncomfortably. He preferred to wear jeans and sneakers, but it wasn't his suit and tie that were making him uneasy. In fact, they made him feel very grown up—"one of the guys"—around the beautifully set wedding reception tables. Why did his mom have to go out of her way to spoil it all? Another boy his age was allowed to have champagne! Then he noticed a couple of younger girls looking his way and giggling. He was sure they were making fun of him.

Hans really liked his mother, and he knew that she tried to do what was best for her family. But did she have to be such a complete square?! Why did he and his younger sister and brother have to be the only ones with no champagne?

Did you ever have an experience like Hans's? He knew he was too young to be served alcohol legally, but if the *other* kids were allowed . . .

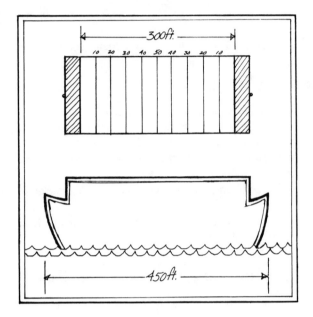

PEER PRESSURES IN NOAH'S DAY

Read **Genesis 6:9-22.**

1. Now look at **Genesis 5:32.** Noah was at least how old when Shem, Ham, and Japheth were born

_____

2. According to **Genesis 6:11-12,** what were most of the people like at that time? _____

3. How do most people today compare to them?

_____

_____

4. If Noah was "righteous" and "blameless" and "walked with God" **(verse 9),** what do you suppose the other people thought about him and his family?

_____

5. To make matters worse—at least that's what his sons may have thought—Noah planned to build an ark to save his family from something called a flood. God told Noah He would send a flood to destroy the whole earth because everyone was so wicked. Noah's sons no doubt hoped that their dad would at least try to do his work inconspicuously, but no such luck. What does Peter call Noah in **2 Peter 2:5?** _____

Nobody else's dad heard God talk to him! Why theirs?

6. To get an idea of the magnitude of Noah's assignment, compare the size of the ark **(Genesis 6:15)** with a football field. Do you think that Noah could have built it single-handedly? _____

7. Who had to help him? _____

Try to imagine yourself in Shem, Ham, or Japheth's "sandals": Your dad is telling everyone that God talks to him and they're all so wicked that they're going to be wiped out. Then he insists that *you* should help him build a huge, ugly boat on dry land! It's not just an embarrassing, temporary thing either—this goes on for *years.* Your family becomes the laughing stock of the century. Talk about peer pressure—everyone else is on their way to the local orgy and you're stuck smearing something called pitch all over the inside and outside of a three-story houseboat!

Noah's boys must have been very loyal and *very* courageous. They had feelings like everyone else, and the odds were surely against them, but they believed the message God sent through their dad. In spite of their situation, they managed to convince three girls to become their wives (which says something about the wisdom and courage of those girls as well). Noah's sons must have become discouraged when no one else would take their father seriously—even when the ark was all finished and they were loading it with tons of food. And especially when the animals started coming voluntarily, two by two, into the ark!

PEER PRESSURE TODAY

Read **Genesis 7.** Satan continues to deceive those who refuse to take God's word seriously. Scoffers today make fun of those who believe the Biblical story of the Flood. Three objections they frequently raise are:

1. No boat could have held all those animals—and the babies that were born during a whole year.

2. There isn't enough water in the whole world to cover mountains—much less to a depth of 20 feet!

3. It was just a local flood.

Be prepared to examine these statements more closely in class. What can you find in the Bible to help make your witness to such scoffers more knowledgeable? Begin by looking at the following passages and making notes about them: **Genesis 1:6-7; 6:19-20; 7:11-12;** and **7:18-24.**

_____

_____

NOAH'S FAITH

1. In **Genesis 2:5-6** God tells us that He did not use rain to water the ground at first. Perhaps Noah had never seen rain, much less a flood. Yet he believed God and was obedient. How obedient was he **(Genesis 6:22** and **7:5)?**

_____

2. Picture yourself as one of Noah's sons or daughters-in-law. Can you hear the noise? Imagine all those animals locked inside; the voices of the people outside, first laughing and jeering, then screaming and pleading as they beat on the sides of the ark trying to get in; the deafening roar of water rushing up from the bowels of the earth and pouring down from the windows of heaven—for 40 days and nights! Can you see yourself groping around the lower decks, bringing appropriate food to each pair of animals? Can you sense the rocking and pitching of the ark as the waters lift it higher and higher off the ground? Do you suppose anyone got seasick? Can you imagine what the stench was like after several months? Remember, no one knew how long they would be cooped up in there! How does **Matthew 24:36-42** apply here?

_____

_____

GOD'S LOVE NEVER FAILS

Read **Genesis 8.** During the months they were floating on the water, Noah and his family must have occasionally wondered whether God had forgotten about them. Imagine their relief, then, when the breezes began to blow to dry up the water. And think of the joy they must have experienced when they felt that the ark had stopped drifting and had come to rest on land! And then, about six weeks later, they could see some mountaintops above the water's surface!

1. How much time passed between the day the flood began and the day they left the ark **(Genesis 7:11; 8:13-14)?** _____

2. What was the first thing Noah and his family did **(Genesis 8:20)?** _____

Once again, God had provided the means for His people to express love to their God. He had instructed Noah to take seven of every clean animal; now Noah's family could bring appropriate offerings and worship God.

3. God responded to the worship of Noah's family with another promise **(Genesis 8:22).** Copy that promise in the space below.

_____

_____

What a patient and loving God we have! How worthy He is to be worshiped and obeyed.

NOAH IN THE NEW TESTAMENT

1. Several times in the New Testament God compares the days of Noah with the days before the end of the world. Read **Matthew 24:37-39.** What style of life did Jesus say would exist at the end of time?

_____

2. Noah warned the people about the Flood. Who warns us about the end of the world? _____

3. How is Noah mentioned in **Luke 3:36?**

_____

4. We find a comparison between the water of the Flood and the water of Baptism in **1 Peter 3:20-21.** What gives Baptism its power? _____

"I will establish My covenant with you, and you will enter the ark—you and your sons and your wife and your sons' wives with you."

Genesis 6:18

Session 10

A New Day Dawns

"Mom, what's a vegetarian?" asked Nick, as he burst into the kitchen. "Why do you ask that, Nick?" replied Mrs. Delius.

"Well, I offered to buy that new kid in my class a hamburger after school today, and he turned thumbs down. He says he's a vegetarian!"

"Vegetarians are people who don't eat meat," said Mrs. Delius. "Sometimes it's a moral conviction and sometimes it's just a nutritional preference."

"Meat is healthy, isn't it?" protested Nick. "We learned in class last year that it has lots of protein."

"That's true," agreed Mrs. Delius, "but many other foods such as beans and lentils are high in protein too. You studied about Daniel in your youth group a few weeks ago. Do you remember that he and his three friends asked to be served only vegetables and water instead of the rich foods and wine that the others had?"

"Hey—that's right! And those four guys were healthier than all the others," remembered Nick. "Did people always eat meat?"

"No," answered Nick's mother. "As I recall, Noah's family was the first to eat meat, and God specifically suggested it. Let's look it up to be sure." Mrs. Delius reached for the Bible on the ledge that served as her desk.

LIFE IN A NEW ERA
A New Life Span

1. Look again at the graph you made on page 19. At what point do the life lines change most drastically?

_____

2. What reasons can you think of to explain why this might have happened?

_____

_____

3. Read **Genesis 6:3.** Who determined that life should be shorter? _____

4. God frequently acts in response to the actions of people. He sent the Flood because of wickedness (**Genesis 6:5-7**). What activity described in **Genesis 9:20-21** and **Proverbs 23:20-21** often contributes to shortened life? _____(Also note **Isaiah 5:10-12, Ephesians 5:18** and **Luke 21:34.**)

Read **Genesis 7:11-12**. We already considered the Canopy Theory in Session 9. Although this theory cannot answer all questions, it certainly presents a very plausible idea. According to this theory, the Flood brought with it some life-shortening side effects like these:

a. Greatly increased amounts of ultraviolet, X-ray, cosmic, and other radiation reached the earth because of the reduction of water vapor in the atmosphere. (If *no* water vapor filtered these rays today, life on earth would cease entirely.)

b. Atmospheric pressure decreased unfavorably. (Data from aquanaut experiments indicate that wounds heal much more quickly under higher oxygen pressure.)

c. Temperatures became extreme; winds and rains resulting from these variations also threaten life.

Another theory suggests that all radioactive materials and other pollutants were safely buried in the bowels of the earth before the terrestrial upheaval that took place when the springs of the deep "burst forth." Obviously, when God decides that the human life span should change, He has many ways at His disposal to bring it about!

New Food

1. Read **Genesis 1:29-30** and **2:16.** What kinds of food had God permitted people to eat before the Flood? _____

2. After the Flood God gave Noah and his family a new kind of food (**Genesis 9:1-5**). What was it?

_____

"Old" Love

1. Compare **Genesis 9:1** and **7** with **1:22.** How was God's blessing of Noah the same as His blessing of Adam and Eve?

_____

2. God continued to show respect for life. How had He shown this respect in the Cain and Abel episode (**Gen. 4:8-16**)?

_____

_____

3. How did He show this respect in **Gen. 9:5-6?**

_____

_____

4. What sign in **Genesis 9:12-17** showed God's respect for life? _____

5. After Adam and Eve sinned, God drove them from the Garden of Eden, but He gave them children and promised them a Savior.

After the great wickedness described in **Genesis 6:5**, God sent the Flood, but He saved eight people and promised that He would never again destroy the world with a flood.

Use **2 Peter 3:9** to finish this sentence: After all the rebellion that has occurred and still occurs on earth, God will destroy the world with fire **(2 Peter 3:3-13)**, but _____

_____

SIN—AGAIN!

Humanly speaking, one would think that Noah and his children should have learned their lesson! They knew of Adam and Eve's fall into sin. They knew of Cain's sins. They knew of the sins that led God to send the Flood. They experienced God's deliverance from the Flood. They heard His covenant and saw its sign, the rainbow. So what did they do? They fell victim to Satan's temptations. We read in **Genesis 9:21** that Noah got drunk! Then **(9:22)** his son Ham told his brothers about their father, apparently as gossip **(9:24-25)**.

WHAT IS GOSSIP?

1. Have you ever been the target of gossip? Is gossiping one of your hobbies? Write a dictionary definition of gossip: _____

Gossips often pass along wrong information or deliberate lies. Can a true statement be considered gossip? Be ready to discuss what you feel constitutes gossip.

2. Ham's actions seem more like that of an impish little boy when he spies a nude female statue. Sure, Ham told Shem and Japheth the truth, but was it helpful? Luther sums up the Biblical attitude toward acceptable conversation in the last part of his explanation to the Eighth Commandment, which says

_____

_____

GOD SPEAKS THROUGH NOAH

If Noah had reacted to Ham's mockery completely

on his own, surely he would have "cursed" Ham, not Canaan. Noah's remarks, however, were a prophetic message given to him by God Himself. We see God's judgment on those who wallow in sexual perversion.

To understand this prophecy better, write the names of Noah's descendants, specifically the sons of Canaan, as given in **Genesis 10:15-18.** _____

_____

Notice where they settled **(verse 19)**. Now turn to Joshua **3:9-10**. Compare the names given there with the names of Canaan's sons.

In later lessons we will be reminded that the two chief sins of Canaanites were idolatry and adultery. Sexual perversion was rampant!

By saying, "Cursed be Canaan," God did not predestine these people to be adulterous. Rather, their preoccupation with sex brought about the curse described. Notice that not all of Canaan's sons are mentioned in the list of wicked nations to be destroyed. Perhaps the others heeded the warning and avoided the errors of their pornographic relatives who were exemplified by the citizens of Sodom and Gomorrah.

RAINBOWS

1. The most clearly worded prophecy in **Genesis 9** has to do with rainbows. How do you react to rainbows? Perhaps you have seen brightly colored rainbows and fluffy white clouds used as a decorating theme. What message does a rainbow usually convey?

_____

2. Why do you think so many people consider the rainbow a Christian symbol?

_____

_____

3. What two things are necessary to produce a rainbow?

_____ and _____

The next time you have a psychologically "rainy day," bring this light of God's loving promise into your consciousness by quoting **John 3:16-17** and **8:12**. They will help you to experience the private, personal rainbow that is caused by the interaction of tears and "Sonshine."

"Whenever the rainbow appears in the clouds, I will see it and remember the everlasting covenant between God and all the living creatures of every kind on the earth."

Genesis 9:16

Session 11

Concluding Activities for Units 1 and 2

Answer the following questions. They will help you review the first two units.

TERMS

On a separate sheet of paper write definitions of the following terms:

1. Bible
2. creation
3. tree of knowledge of good and evil
4. Satan
5. Adam
6. Eve
7. patriarch
8. The Flood
9. Canopy Theory
10. ark
11. marriage
12. rainbow

SHORT ANSWER

Write a short answer to each of the following questions:

1. What is the main purpose of the Bible?

_____

_____

_____

2. What are some kinds of writing that you will find in the Bible?

_____

3. Why did God create Eve?

_____

_____

4. Describe life in the Garden of Eden.

_____

_____

_____

5. Describe the fall into sin.

_____

_____

_____

_____

_____

6. What are some ways God showed His love after the Fall?

_____

_____

_____

7. Describe the faith of Cain and Abel.

_____

_____

_____

_____

8. Why did God send the Flood?

_____

_____

9. What signs of God's love do you find in the description of the Flood and the events just after it?

_____

_____

_____

_____

10. Describe one of the promises from God in unit 1 or unit 2. What does this promise mean to you today?

_____

_____

Unit 3
God's Covenant with Abraham

The Flood demonstrates an awesome way God intervenes supernaturally when sin rears its ugly head. But already in Session 10 we saw an example of sin following the Flood.

In the years that followed, sin continued to grow. The narrative of the tower of Babel, which opens this unit, describes another supernatural event—one also brought about by the deliberate human disobedience.

People were ignoring God's commands. In **Genesis 12** we learn of a new plan. God made a special covenant with one man. He promised that through this one man He would bless the whole world. This covenant with Abram is so important that the rest of the Bible focuses on how God carried it out to its ultimate fulfillment in Jesus Christ, the descendant of Abram, through whom all nations are blessed.

Session 12

Tongues and Races (Babel)

PRIDE VERSUS HUMILITY

1. When people want to glorify themselves instead of God, they are guilty of pride. Pride is one of the most common of sins—and God speaks clearly about it in the Bible. Briefly state what God says about pride in the following passages:

Isaiah 2:17 _____

Proverbs 3:34 _____

Proverbs 16:18 _____

Luke 1:51-52 _____

1 Corinthians 1:31 _____

1 John 2:16 _____

2. The opposite of pride is humility. What do the following passages say about humility?

2 Chronicles 34:27 _____

Proverbs 22:4 _____

Matthew 18:3-4 _____

Matthew 23:12 _____

James 4:10 _____

1 Peter 5:5-6 _____

Another word for pride is conceit. How do you react to someone who acts conceited? Do you think we sometimes mistake shyness for conceit? Are braggarts sometimes unsure of themselves? Be ready to talk about this.

PRIDE AT BABEL

1. Read **Genesis 11:1-9.** What did the people in the story plan to build? _____
2. What reason did they give for doing it?

_____

3. Whose name did Seth's family proclaim in **Genesis 4:26?** _____
4. According to **Joshua 7:19** and **1 Chronicles 16:28-29,** and **Psalm 29,** who should be given glory?

_____

5. What was the angel's message on the night that Jesus was born **(Luke 2:14)?**

_____

6. Whom did Jesus want to glorify **(John 17:1)?**

_____

7. The people of Babel were guilty of self-centeredness and pride. As so often happens, this sin led to other sins. The people deliberately disobeyed the command of God to Noah and his descendants in **Genesis 9:1.** What was this command?

_____

8. Read **Acts 17:24-28** to learn what Paul has to say about this topic. What does he give as God's reason for populating the whole earth?

_____

9. Where did we first read about Satan encouraging someone to live for "self"?

_____

10. This is still one of Satan's favorite approaches today. Can you give some examples? What does Jesus say about living for oneself in **Matthew 16:24-27?**

_____

11. The world may try to make fun of those who live unselfishly. Paul, who went through many hardships for the sake of spreading the Gospel, records his feelings in **Romans 8:18.** What were they?

_____

Living for God is a real adventure!

GOD INTERVENES

When God's people ignore His will, they suffer. God lets us go on our chosen way, but He uses many different circumstances to help bring us closer to Him again. Usually the special circumstances seem so "natural" that we hardly notice them. Occasionally they are so unusual that we can't explain how they came about, as in the events at the tower of Babel.

About 100 years after the Flood, God saw that unless He intervened, the people would continue to let pride keep them from obeying His command to "fill the earth." He used a very simple but supernatural tactic: He disrupted their language! A worker who wanted to say, "Hand me another brick," may have heard himself saying something like, "Gib mir noch einen Backstein," while another worker may have requested, "Dame otro ladrillo."

Can you imagine the chaos that resulted? Sin caused the chaos, and our loving, powerful God used this event to populate the whole earth and prevent anarchy. How wisely God was dealing with His creatures! And how wisely God still holds nations in check today when they try to replace Him as the ultimate authority! They find themselves in contention with other nations and are thus held in check in their schemes.

We are not told just how many languages came into being that day in Babel, but people in the world today speak an estimated 6,000 different languages and dialects—727 of them in Papua, New Guinea alone!

1. This mass migration also helps to account for the different races in the world today. When people move to another climate, the adaptation to new conditions and the resulting intermarriages with other people result in distinctly different physical characteristics. Climate also affects a person's emotional makeup. Where would you expect to find a more easy-going, laid-back type of lifestyle—in a tropical or an arctic climate? Which can stand long periods of heat more comfortably—black skin or white skin? When we realize that we are all descendants of Noah, how should each of us treat people from other races?

_____   _____

2. What do the following passages say about racism?

Acts 10:28 _____ _____

Acts 17:25-26 ___ _____

Colossians 3:11 _____

Isaiah 66:18 _____

Revelation 14:6 _____

GOD STILL INTERVENES

In the story of Babel, God used supernaturally provided languages to divide peoples. Can you think of another time when He acted in much the same way to bring about unity?

1. Read **Acts 2:1-21.** What country were "they" in **verse 1** from? _____

2. How many different nationalities hear their own language being spoken? _____

3. Who had prophesied that this sort of thing would happen **(verse 16)?** _____

4. When did He say it would happen **(verse 17)?**

_____

If Pentecost was in "the last days," are we also in "the last days"? Isn't it wonderful to know that God still works naturally and supernaturally when and where He chooses? Be ready to share ways in which God has worked in your family or among your friends in these "last days."

Notice the contrast between Babel and Pentecost:

Babel	Pentecost
Lack of communication	Communication
Disunity	Unity
Pride	Repentance
Prejudice and hatred	Love

Do lack of communication, disunity, pride, and prejudice still trouble you? How can you drive them away? First of all, recognize them as the sins that they are. Then call on God for forgiveness and appreciate His power in your lives. Gathered around the Word, you can be united with your brothers and sisters in the love and blessing Jesus came to bring to all people!

"As surely as I live," says the Lord, *"every knee will bow before Me; every tongue will confess to God."*

Romans 14:11

Session 13

Abram—Spiritual Giant with Clay Feet

How does God "call" someone to serve Him in a special way? Does He still call people today? How will we answer when He calls us?

Trevor Ferrell is a teenager who lives in Philadelphia. When Trevor was 11, he and his family were watching TV one winter evening. The program included pictures of homeless people huddled and shivering in downtown Philadelphia. No one knows how many thousands of people who saw that same program "heard" God's call to "love your neighbor as yourself." But in Trevor Ferrell God found the kind of love that acts.

Trevor persuaded his parents to drive him from their comfortable suburban home to the downtown area so that he could give a blanket and a pillow from his bed to one of those unfortunate people. And that was only the beginning. Next came nightly tours through the downtown streets to deliver soup and sandwiches and to distribute clothing and blankets. Soon Trevor realized that he and his family would need more help. He canvassed suburban neighborhoods for help. He and his father visited churches.

When the newspapers began to tell this story, Trevor's Campaign, as it was now called, began to grow as donations poured in from sympathetic readers. One person donated an old house that is now being renovated with the help of volunteers and the residents of this new home-for-the-homeless called Trevor's Place. Among other developments, Trevor received an international award that included a grant of $10,000.

But it has not been easy. Trevor had to repeat the sixth grade because of the long hours he spent helping others. His dad closed his successful TV repair shop when the demands of the campaign overwhelmed him. His mom admits that she often feels tired after washing so many pots and pans. But the family feels that they are doing the Lord's will, and many others who are also convinced support them with donations, encouragement, and prayer. What a difference the response of one young boy to God's call is making!

ABRAM'S ROOTS

1. Read **Genesis 11:27—12:20**. The setting for this story is referred to as the Fertile Crescent. It arches up the northern tip of the Persian Gulf, along the Tigris and Euphrates rivers, and down the east coast of the Mediterranean Sea. Ur **(Genesis 11:28)** is in the eastern tip of the crescent; Haran **(11:32)** was probably named after Terah's dead son and is near the top of the crescent; Shechem and Bethel **(12:6-8)** are near the western tip.

Ur was a major center of moon worship. **Joshua 24:2** gives us some insight into Terah's character. Describe it.

_____

_____

2. Do you know anyone who believes in horoscopes? What does God say in the following passages about predicting the future?

Isaiah 47:13-14 _____

Deuteronomy 4:19 _____

2 Kings 17:16 and **21:2-3** _____

Jeremiah 19:13 _____

3. Jewish tradition states that Abram's father was an idol-maker and that Abram became disillusioned with these lifeless gods when he was still a child. We know that Abram was already married when Terah's family left Ur. Perhaps Abram encouraged that move. Unfortunately, Terah did not go any farther than Haran, which was also a center for moon worship. Abram stayed there also until his father died. Then God asked him to leave three things **(Genesis 12:1)**. What were they?

_____

_____

4. Where did God tell Abram to go?

_____

That's not very definite, is it?

5. What did Abram do? _____

_____

6. How old was Abram? _____

Put yourself in Abram's "sandals." Suppose God told you to do what He told Abram. How would you feel? What would you do?

BLESSED TO BE A BLESSING

1. Read **Genesis 12:2-3** and list all the promises you can find.

_____

_____

_____

Notice how both verses end. Who were to be the final benefactors of Abram's blessings? As you continue your Bible study, watch how God moves to bring this about.

Abram took God at His word. He obeyed. He left all his friends and the comforts of civilization in Haran to go to an unknown land. Notice that he did not "settle" anywhere. But as he wandered he shared his knowledge of the one true God by openly building altars and boldly worshiping even though he was in Canaanite country and among idolators.

2. Like Abram, we are the recipients of God's blessings of family, prosperity, purpose, encouragement, and protection. What does God expect us to do with these blessings?

_____

_____

3. Is Trevor Ferrell on the right track? _____
4. Will such activities earn heaven for us? _____
5. Quote a Bible passage to support your answer.

_____

_____

If each of us would use our blessings to bless others, how would the world be different from the way it is today?

6. Is there a project you could undertake, individually or collectively, that would make you a blessing to others? List some suggestions.

_____

CLAY FEET

1. Read **Genesis 12:10-20.** Where did Abram go?

_____

2. Why?

_____

3. From what you know about the geography of Egypt and Canaan, why is the water supply more reliable for crops in Egypt?

_____

4. How would you describe Abram's actions in **verses 11-13?**

_____

5. How did the Lord intervene to stop this immorality?

_____

6. How did God use even Abram's deception to bring blessings on him?

_____

_____

AMAZING GRACE

Did you ever build a sand castle on the beach and watch what happens when waves lap at the base? If you have, you know that the castle soon falls. Clay is a bit finer than sand, but it is not much stronger. Abram had "clay feet," and God mercifully shows them to us so that we will not despair when we make mistakes.

1. Read **Romans 4:1-5** and **Hebrews 11:8-10.** Did God pick Abram because Abram was so "good"? No. Abram's goodness had nothing to do with God's action. God picked Abram because He loved him. And then Abram received God's blessings by

_____

Do you know people who feel that they are "too far gone, too sinful" for God to forgive them and claim them as His children? Why not share the story of Abram with them?

2. Read the story of the thief who was crucified with Jesus and who asked for forgiveness in the midst of his pain and suffering **(Luke 23:39-43).** How did Jesus answer the question of whether a person is ever "too far gone" to become a child of God?

_____

Amazing grace! How sweet the sound
That saved a wretch like me!
I once was lost but now am found,
Was blind but now I see!

Lutheran Worship 509

If, in fact, Abraham was justified by works, he had something to boast about—but not before God. What does the Scripture say? "Abraham believed God, and it was credited to him as righteousness."

Romans 4:2-3

Session 14

God's Chosen People

During a safari through the beautiful wilderness country of Kenya, a Jewish member of a tour group said to his fellow tourists one evening, "If the Jews were *really* God's chosen people, He would have given them a beautiful land like Kenya instead of that God-forsaken strip of land at the east end of the Mediterranean Sea." He was surprised, however, when another member of the safari group answered by saying, "Oh, no! The Jews *had* to be in Palestine because the trade routes of the ancient world passed through that land and in that way all the world would hear about God and His mighty acts."

The first speaker did not understand what the Jews were chosen *for*. God did not choose them to be "teacher's pets"—for their own prestige and pleasure—but to serve as channels through whom God could bless the whole world. They were blessed to be a blessing.

Just what does it mean to be "chosen"? A soldier who is chosen to carry out a difficult and dangerous mission is thereby recognized as a capable person and may even receive honors for his bravery, but his mission will probably involve a large element of risk and discomfort. The football player who is chosen to be captain of the team enjoys the attention and popularity that his position carries with it, but he also experiences great responsibilities and makes difficult decisions. He cannot do as he pleases, because he is accountable to his coach and to his team.

CAPTAIN, PLAYER, OR SPECTATOR?

Just as a team captain has a certain amount of flexibility under his coach (as do all the players), so we, as Christians, enjoy a great deal of freedom under God. In this lesson, we will identify wise and foolish uses of this freedom as we compare the lives of Abram and Lot. God has recorded these stories to help us play our own "game of life."

1. Read **Genesis 13**. What was the blood relationship between Abram and Lot (see **Genesis 12:5)?**

_____

2. Was Lot with Abram in Egypt? _____

3. What does **13:6-8** tell us about the day-to-day relationship of the two men?

_____

4. Who quarreled? _____

5. Who was the first to try to make peace?

_____

6. What does **verse 9** tell us about Abram's character?

_____

7. What do **verses 10-13** say about Lot?

_____

8. After the two men parted, with Lot choosing the most attractive area of Canaan for his home, did Abram show any signs of jealousy or resentment? _____ (Read **Genesis 14:8-16** and **18:20-33** for clues.)

9. We learn more about Lot in **Chapter 19.** Read it and tell in which verse you find the answers to the following:

Was he polite? _____

Was he hospitable? _____

Did he recognize the Sodomites' way of life as wicked? _____

What widespread sin caused God to destroy the whole valley? _____

Were Lot's future sons-in-law accustomed to hearing him speak about the Lord and His ways? _____

10. What sort of character trait do **verses 18-20** suggest? _____

11. What weakness is alluded to in **verses 32-34?** _____

And that is the last we read about Lot! How sad.

12. Abram and Lot were in the same household most of their lives—in Ur, in Haran, in Canaan, and in Egypt. What made them so different? What do we find Abram doing in Shechem (**Genesis 12:7**)?

_____

_____

In Bethel **(12:8)?**

_____

Between Bethel and Ai **(13:4)?**

_____

In Hebron in **13:18?**

_____

13. Can you find a verse that says that Lot was doing any of these things? _____

14. What would you say was Abram's top priority?

_____

_____

15. What seemed to be Lot's top priority?

_____

_____

GOD'S COVENANT WITH ABRAM

1. After Abram had unselfishly offered Lot his choice of land and the two households had separated, God appeared to Abram again. What promise did He make **(13:14-17)?**

_____

Can you imagine what this meant to a man who was over 75 years old and who was a childless nomad?

2. **Chapter 15** records God's covenant with Abram. In **verses 2-3**, we see that Abram began to panic. He questioned what would come of God's promise of an heir—a son. How did God reply **(verse 4)?**

_____

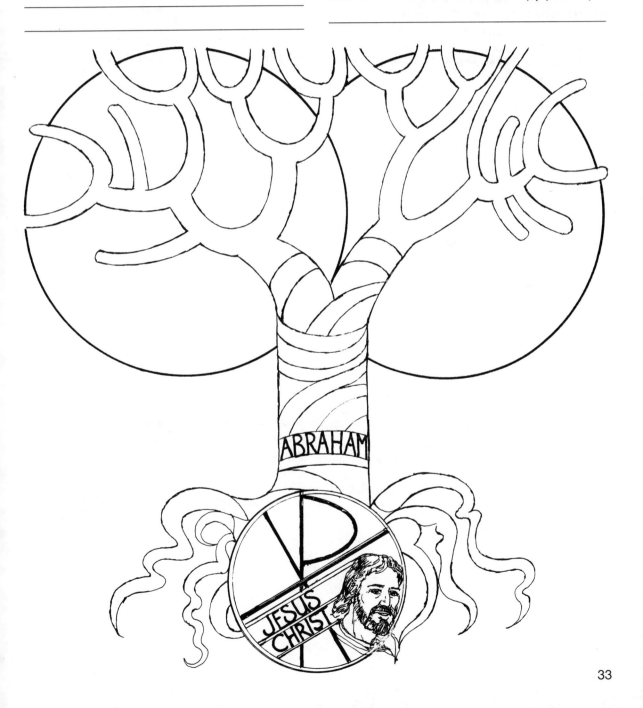

3. How did Abram react **(verse 6)?**

_____

4. What new information did God give in **verses 13** and **14?**

_____

_____

_____

How would you have felt in Abram's sandals? In this age of instant gratification, we would probably expect to have God's promises fulfilled within a few short years, at most!

5. When Abram's wife, Sarai, was 90, she still did not have a child. Then God appeared to Abram again. Read **Chapter 17**. Notice that God summarized His part of the covenant in **verses 4-8** and reemphasized descendants, nations, land, and His blessing and protection as their God. He also gave new names to Abram and Sarai. What were they?

_____

6. As part of the covenant, what did God ask Abraham and his descendants to do **(verses 9-14)?**

_____

_____

This was to be the sign of their relationship with God.

7. According to **verses 17-18**, what were Abraham's conclusions about his son, Ishmael?

_____

8. What did God say about this in **verses 15, 16,** and **19?**

_____

9. How long did Abraham wait to carry out his covenant responsibilities **(verses 23-27)?**

_____

In our comparison of Abram and Lot, we saw that Abram was committed to God and was richly blessed. God chose him to be a "captain." Lot, a "player," was blessed too—because of his association with Abram. They both came back from Egypt with great wealth. When they separated, Lot's troubles began. He was captured by enemy kings, and Abram rescued him. He even rescued all the unbelievers and their families, the "spectators" in this game of life.

Later, when Abraham learned of God's plan to destroy Sodom and Gomorrah, he interceded for Lot and any other "righteous people" who lived there. God agreed to spare the whole city if only 10 such people could be found there! What a blessing believers are to their companions in life.

CHILDREN OF ABRAHAM THROUGH JESUS

Do you know any people who are completely dedicated to serving God? If you do, you will find that they, like Abraham, are eager to worship, ready to help those in trouble, persistent in their prayers for others, obedient to God's guidance, quick to make peace where there is quarreling, unselfish, and strong in faith.

God offers every Christian the power to display such dedication. Unfortunately, many resist this power from God and are content, like Lot, to ride the coattails of the Abrahams in their midst. They are "lukewarm" in the faith. What does the Bible have to say about this condition in **Revelation 3:14-16?**

_____

The "children of Abraham" are God's chosen people. **Galatians 3** tells how one becomes such a person. Summarize it in your own words.

_____

_____

_____

_____

_____

_____

_____

_____

Understand, then, that those who believe are children of Abraham. The Scriptures foresaw that God would justify the Gentiles by faith, and announced the Gospel in advance to Abraham: "All nations will be blessed through you." So those who have faith are blessed with Abraham, the man of faith.
Galatians 3:7-9

Session 15

No Rejects with God (Abraham and Isaac)

There are many versions of the story of Aladdin's lamp, but they all have the same basic plot: a creature appears by magic and offers to fulfill one or more wishes of some fortunate person. As you recall this story, what kind of relationship exists between the "genie" and the "master"? Isn't it true that the "master" thinks of the "genie" only as a tool to be used for selfish purposes?

Many people think of God as their own personal genie. But the story of Abraham shows us a better attitude.

SARAI'S IMPATIENCE

When Sarai and Abram had been in Canaan for 10 years and Sarai was still childless, she concluded that God needed help in carrying out His plan. So she suggested a compromise to Abram. Abram went along with the plan—and the course of history was changed for all time.

1. Read **Genesis 16.** Sarai and Abram's attempt to "help God out" resulted in strained relationships, bitterness, and unhappiness. When today do we face similar temptations?

_____

_____

2. What advice can you give to someone who thinks God is just too slow in responding to some special need? (See, for example, **Romans 8:26-39** and **Isaiah 40:28-31.**)

_____

_____

3. Put yourself in the place of Hagar, the female slave of Abram and Sarai. You are pregnant; your jealous mistress mistreats you so badly that you run away; you think that it's probably your own fault for showing how pleased you were to be the pregnant one instead of your mistress; you're tired, frightened, and hungry. Suddenly a voice asks who you are and what you are doing. (Remember that slaves were often severely

beaten or put to death for running away!) What would you do?

Hagar told the truth. The voice told her to return to her mistress. The voice did not promise that her mistress would now treat her well. But what promise did Hagar receive **(Genesis 16:10-11)?**

_____

_____

4. How do we know that she told her experience to Abram **(verse 15)?** _____

About 15 years after Ishmael's birth, Abraham and Sarah got some surprise company. It seems that the visitors were on their way to Sodom and Gomorrah. But hospitable Abraham convinced them to stay a while. Sarah knew that the strangers were there, but she busied herself baking some fresh bread.

5. Read **18:9-15.** If someone told you that a 90-year-old woman was going to have a baby, what would *your* reaction be? Memorize the first part of **verse 14** and say it to yourself or to someone else when an "impossible" situation arises.

6. Read **21:1-7.** Isaac's name served as a reminder to Sarah of how she felt when she heard God's promise and of the joy she and Abraham knew when Isaac was born. In spite of Sarah's impatience, how did God deal with her?

_____

FAITH TESTED, PRESERVED, AND STRENGTHENED

Genesis 22:1-14 tells the dramatic story of the ultimate test of Abraham's faith and obedience. (You probably know the story well, but God frequently provides new insights when you read His Word again and again.) Reread that familiar story now and expect to be blessed by it.

1. The sacrificing of children was not uncommon in Canaan at the time of Abraham, but it is certainly not something that we would expect God to ask anyone to do. Why did He ask Abraham to do it **(verses 1-2)?**

_____

2. God's relationship with Abraham was such a close one that Abraham knew that it was God who was speaking to him; this was not some kind of hallucination. How long did Abraham wait before doing what God asked? _____

3. Why do you think Abraham left the servants and the donkey behind when they got near Mt. Moriah?

_____

_____

4. Who did Abraham say would return? _____

5. **Hebrews 11:17-19** gives us some insight into Abraham's thinking at this point. Summarize the passage.

_____

_____

We all know the wonderful ending of the story.

6. Read **1 Corinthians 10:13.** How does the **Genesis 22** incident demonstrate the truth of these words?

_____

_____

7. Do you think Abraham's faith was stronger before or after this incident? _____

8. Who was responsible for faith so strong that Abraham was willing to sacrifice Isaac—Abraham or God? _____

9. When Isaac was about 37, his mother died. Then Abraham purchased the only piece of land in Canaan that he would ever call his own. Read **Genesis 23:17-20** and tell what that land was.

_____

10. Both Abraham and Isaac were important parts of God's great plan of salvation. What phrase did God use in **Genesis 22:15-18** to indicate how sure and unconditional his covenant with Abraham was?

_____

More than once in later years, that promise was the very thing that prevented God from completely destroying the rebellious, idolatrous nation of Israel.

GOD'S HEARTACHE FORESHADOWED

In the moving story of Abraham and young Isaac, God shows His great love for the sinful human race. There are many similarities between the lives of Isaac and Jesus, as you will see by completing the following statements.

1. Isaac was the son of promise. Jesus is the promised _____

2. Isaac was the _only_ son of Abraham and Sarah. Jesus is the _____

3. Isaac carried the wood for the sacrifice. Jesus carried His _____

4. Isaac willingly submitted to being offered as a sacrifice for sin. Jesus willingly gave His life as a

_____

Here the similarity ends. Isaac's life was spared by the substitution of a ram. No one else—nothing else—could be a substitute for Jesus.

We feel Abraham's heartache as he climbs the mountain and prepares to sacrifice his precious son. Do we also "feel" the heartache of God as He "gave His only begotten Son" **(John 3:16 KJV)?** How dearly God must love us to make such a sacrifice! How disappointed He must be when somebody refuses the gift of salvation that was purchased by the shedding of the precious blood of His only Son, Jesus!

The great joy that Abraham felt when Isaac was saved from death is only a pale image of the "rejoicing in the presence of angels of God over one sinner who repents," which Jesus describes in **Luke 15:10.**

By faith Abraham, when God tested him, offered Isaac as a sacrifice. . . . Abraham reasoned that God could raise the dead, and figuratively speaking, he did receive Isaac back from death.

Hebrews 11:17 and 19

Session 16

Slave or Free?
(Isaac and Ishmael)

Have you ever watched a potter sit at a wheel and change a muddy glob of clay into a beautiful, symmetrical vase or bowl? This gradual process requires gentle pressure. The color and consistency of clay varies. The potter chooses raw material carefully. Coarse, grainy clay could never become a fine piece of china; smooth-textured, pale clay would not be the right choice for fashioning a heavy, primitive-type urn. The master potter knows how to use any of the available materials for maximum beauty and utility.

In **Jeremiah 18**, God tells us that people are like the clay and that He is like the potter. God decides what we are best suited for, and He will mold us into our best possible form if we do not resist His gentle pressure.

ISHMAEL AND ISAAC

1. In some ways, Ishmael and Isaac were alike. Look up the following passages and jot down the similarities.

Ishmael	Isaac	Similarity
Genesis 16:11	**Genesis 17:19**	_____
Genesis 16:15	**Genesis 21:3**	_____
Galatians 4:1-2	**Galatians 4:1-2**	_____
Genesis 17:26	**Genesis 21:4**	_____
Genesis 25:9	**Genesis 25:9**	_____
Genesis 17:20	**Genesis 26:3-4**	_____
		_____
		_____

Clearly, God loved and blessed both Isaac and Ishmael.

2. In other respects, Ishmael and Isaac were very different. What great difference is mentioned in **21:10** and **25:5?**

_____

_____

3. Ishmael's wife came from **(21:21)** _____ , while Isaac's wife came from **(24:4)**

_____

_____

4. What type of personality did Ishmael have **(16:12)?** _____
What was Isaac's personality like **(24:63; 25:21; 26:16,17,** and **25)?**

_____

_____

5. Who was Ishmael's mother? _____
Isaac's mother? _____
What was the relationship between the two women?

_____

6. With whom did God renew His covenant?

_____

Isaac was chosen to serve a special role in God's plan of salvation. What special blessings did that bring **(26:12-14)?**

_____

7. Isaac's 12 grandsons by Jacob occupied the land of Canaan and were the forefathers of all Jewish people. Ishmael's 12 sons **(25:12-18)** settled in what is now Arabia. In Bible times they were known as Ishmaelites. Today all Arabs, following Mohammed's pronouncement, claim Ishmael as their forefather. How do the present conflicts in the Middle East reflect the Biblical description of Ishmael and his sons in **16:12** and **25:18?** Which nations or groups of nations are at odds? Who objected to the Camp David agreement between Israel and Egypt in 1978? Be prepared to discuss these questions in class.

8. Imagine—bitterness that began between Sarah and Hagar has continued for almost 4,000 years, and still goes on! How could this bitterness be stopped? How can any bitterness and hatred end?

Read **1 John 4:7-21.** What's the key to ending any bitterness and conflict? _____

9. What steps can you take when you find yourself in a position of conflict with someone?

_____

_____

ARE YOU SLAVE OR FREE?

Many centuries after the time of Isaac and Ishmael, a group of Christians in the Roman province of Galatia were being confused by false teachers called Judaizers, who were Law-oriented and insisted that it was necessary to follow all the old Jewish rules in order to attain salvation. The apostle Paul heard about this and wrote a letter to the Galatians in which he used Isaac and Ishmael as examples to help explain what faith in Jesus does for us. Read **Galatians 3:26—4:31** carefully and keep in mind all you have learned about Isaac and Ishmael. Then answer the following questions:

1. How are the lives of a slave and an heir similar during childhood **(Galatians 4:1-2)?**

_____

What do you think Ishmael's childhood was like?

_____

What was the only real difference between Ishmael and Isaac?

_____

2. When we are born, are we slaves or free **(verse 8)?**_____
Why is this?

_____

(For help, see **Genesis 3** and **Romans 5:12.**)

3. **Galatians 4:23** says that Ishmael was born "in an ordinary way." So were we. What does Jesus say in **John 3:6?**

_____

4. What does God say about this in **Ephesians 2:1-3?**

_____

5. As dead slaves, what chance do we have to help ourselves? _____

6. How, then, can we become reborn, free of sin, and heirs of God **(Galatians 4:4-8)?** _____
So now, like Isaac, we are children of God by virtue of the promise given to Eve that was passed along through all the succeeding centuries.

7. According to **Romans 8:17,** if we are children, what are we also?

_____

What does this include?

_____

Why **(Hebrews 12:7-11)?**

_____

8. How did the apostles feel about sharing in Christ's suffering **(Acts 5:41)?**

_____

(James 1:2-3)?_____

9. How much are you willing to suffer for Jesus? What does the apostle John say about this in **1 John 3:16-24?**

_____

What does St. Paul say about suffering in **Romans 8:18?**

_____

10. When John and Paul, inspired by the Holy Spirit, wrote the above words, their faith was strong. But what if someone's faith is weak? **Mark 9:24** gives the answer through a distressed father:

_____

Isaiah 42:1-3 says:

_____

St. Paul says in **Romans 12:3:**

_____

11. How about you? Is your faith strong? Look at the following passages. What do they say about a strong faith?

John 13:35 _____

Matthew 25:34-40 _____

Matthew 7:1-2 _____

Hebrews 13:15-16 _____

James 1:27 _____

Galatians 5:19-26 _____

12. Would you like your faith to become stronger? What do these passages say you should do?

Romans 10:17 _____

Luke 17:5 _____

James 1:17 _____

Ephesians 2:8 _____

What a marvelous message! We don't *earn* heaven. We *can't.* In fact, trying to earn heaven is really an insult to God, because it ignores the great sacrifice that Jesus made for us.

We are not children of the slave woman, but of the free woman. It is for freedom that Christ has set us free. Stand firm, then, and do not let yourselves be burdened again by a yoke of slavery.

Galatians 4:31—5:1

Session 17

A Cheat Becomes a Champion (Jacob)

Did you ever watch a chick hatching? If you did, you know how it has to struggle. The whole egg trembles as the crowded chick strains to pierce the hard shell with its tiny beak. Often it makes several brief attempts separated by longer resting periods before a hole appears in the shell. Then, in continuing bursts of desperation, the entire chick—exhausted, wet, and bedraggled—emerges victorious. Still later, it blossoms into the bright-eyed, fuzzy little creature we see in children's picture books and on Easter cards.

Sometimes a child, out of sympathy for the struggling chick, tries to help by removing the shell *for* the chick—only to learn, too late, that the very process of struggling is necessary to develop the strength the chick needs to survive outside its previous environment. If a chick that has been helped out of the egg lives at all, its growth is usually stunted.

JACOB'S YOUTH

After 20 years of marriage and fervent prayer, Isaac and Rebekah had twin sons, Jacob and Esau. Only one of them would inherit the covenant. Even before they were born, God indicated to Rebekah that "the older will serve the younger."

As young men, neither of them showed too much promise. Esau, the firstborn, was a "macho" type and was brash; Jacob was a cheat and what some might call a "mamma's boy." Jacob was well aware that the firstborn son was automatically entitled to a double portion of his father's estate and became head of the clan. Esau knew this too, but he was so irresponsible that he traded Jacob his birthright for the equivalent of one deluxe pizza!

Genesis 27 tells the familiar story of Isaac blessing his sons. Rebekah, like her mother-in-law, Sarah, decided that God needed help in carrying out His plans. So she helped Jacob masquerade as Esau to trick Isaac into giving him the blessing that he had intended for Esau. The plot worked—and then backfired. In fear of Esau, Jacob fled the country—and never saw his mother again. Isaac told him to go to his uncle Laban to find a wife among Rebekah's relatives.

To use the language of our introductory story, Rebekah and Jacob nearly "killed the chick" in their impatience. Esau remained at home with all the family wealth, and Jacob left with only the clothes on his back and a walking stick! He had to struggle just to survive.

GOD TRAINS JACOB

1. Heartsick and homesick, Jacob must have been thrilled over the encouragement that he received on that first night away from home. Angels appeared to him on a ladder that reached from earth to heaven, and God told him that he would indeed be the bearer of the covenant. Read **28:16-22.** What was Jacob's response to God? _____

2. Read **29:1-12.** When Jacob approached Haran, whom did he meet first? _____

3. Whom did he see in the distance soon afterward? _____

4. Read **29:12-20.** What was Laban's reaction to Jacob's arrival? _____

5. After a month's visit, the two men became employer and employee. What wages did Jacob ask?

_____

6. Over what period of time? _____

7. What shows that Jacob's love for Rachel remained strong during all that time? _____

8. What weakness in Jacob's character did God deal with in this case? _____

9. Read **29:21-30.** The wedding day finally arrived. What spoiled the celebration for Jacob?

_____

10. What compromise did Laban propose?

_____

11. So now Jacob had two wives and their personal maids. But how much income did he have?

_____

12. When Jacob recognized that this could not go on, he made a request of Laban **(30:25-43).** What was it?

_____

13. What does **verse 27** tell you about Laban's religion?

_____

14. Could he have figured out what the diviners told him just using his own reason? _____

15. What bargain did Laban and Jacob now make? _____

16. As you think about pictures of flocks of sheep that you have seen, who stood to gain more from this deal, Jacob or Laban? _____

17. But by means of a special breeding method and through God's blessing, what happened?

_____

18. Read **31:1-13.** Give some of the reasons Jacob had for leaving Laban:

_____

You can imagine Laban's dismay when he lost a major part of his household! He pursued Jacob, but through God's intervention Laban begrudgingly allowed Jacob and his party to continue on their way.

JACOB TRANSFORMED

1. Read **32:1-6.** What encouragement did Jacob receive? _____

2. What bad news?

_____

3. Why should Jacob fear Esau?

_____

4. Once Jacob had done what he could to safeguard his possessions, he turned to God in prayer. Then he sent five separate herds of animals to Esau as gifts of peace and friendship. What character change did this show? _____

_____

5. Read **32:22-32.** After Jacob got his wives and children safely across the Jabbok River, what happened?

_____

_____

Jacob had finally reached the place in his life where, in his loneliness and fear, he recognized his deep need for God. The transforming process culminated in a new man with a new name (Israel)—and a permanent limp to remind him of his role as God's covenant-bearer.

6. After a tension-filled reunion with Esau, Jacob diplomatically arranged for Esau to return to his home with Jacob's gifts while Jacob crossed over into Canaan and set up an altar to worship his God. After a brief stay near Shechem, Jacob was reminded of the vow he made more than 20 years earlier and he returned to Bethel. Who met with him there **(35:9)**?

_____

7. Why?

_____

The "cheat" became a "champion." Take a look at the prayer he spoke earlier **(32:9-12),** at a time when he recognized that he needed to depend completely on God instead of himself. What does each of the following parts of Jacob's prayer say when you "read between the lines"?

a. **"O God of my father Abraham, God of my father Isaac.**

b. **"O Lord**

c. **". . . who said to me, 'Go back to your country and your relatives and I will make you prosper,'**

d. **"I am unworthy of all the kindness and faithfulness You have shown Your servant."**

e. **"I had only my staff when I crossed this Jordan, but now I have become two groups.**

f. **"Save me, I pray, from the hand of my brother, Esau,**

g. **"For I am afraid he will come and attack me, and also the mothers and their children.**

h. **"But You have said,**

i. **" 'I will surely make you prosper and will make your descendants like the sand of the sea, which cannot be counted.' "**

How do your prayers compare with that of Jacob? Have you become a champion by "giving in" to the lordship of the Triune God?

God said to him, "I am God Almighty; be fruitful and increase in number. A nation and a community of nations will come from you, and kings will come from your body. The land I gave to Abraham and Isaac I also give to you, and I will give this land to your descendants after you."

Genesis 35:11-12

Session 18

What About Dreams? (Joseph at Home)

We all have dreams, especially if we eat hard-to-digest food just before bedtime! But some dreams really get our attention—like Jacob's ladder. And like Lillian's dream.

Fifteen-year-old Lillian was beside herself with grief. Her younger brother, Walter, had died as the result of an auto accident and the negligence of a doctor. She tried and tried and tried, but she just couldn't regain her peace of mind. She lay awake night after night reliving the awful days before Walter's death. The doctors had told her that, even if he had lived, the high fever would have resulted in brain damage. But that was small comfort. She loved him so dearly.

Then one night Lillian had a dream. She saw herself in one of the stalls of the horse barn on their farm. She heard a horrible, snarling sound and she spun around to see her brother—his eyes rolled back and his face contorted with pain as he strained to break the

chains that shackled him to the rough partition. When Walter shrieked, Lillian woke with a start and sat straight up in bed.

What did it all mean? Lillian felt that God was speaking to her through her dream. Tears of gratitude streamed down her cheeks. She now actually thanked God for Walter's death. It seemed to her that it was far better for her brother than what could have happened, had he lived.

Do you think Lillian's dream had any spiritual significance? Just think about it now, and be prepared to talk about it later in the session.

JOSEPH'S DREAMS

Genesis 35:23-26 names Jacob's 12 sons. In **37:2-4** we learn that he had one favorite—Joseph—and that this caused Joseph's brothers to hate him. Immediately after this, in **37:5-11**, we read about some dreams Joseph had.

1. Were Joseph's dreams sent by God? _____
2. What did the dreams mean?

_____

_____

_____

3. From what you know about Joseph's later life, when were these dreams especially meaningful to him?

_____

_____

4. Joseph told the dreams to his brothers. How did this fact affect his relationship with them?

_____

_____

Apparently Joseph felt that God had given him a special revelation. Perhaps he thought God wanted him to share this revelation with his family. Perhaps he felt proud about this revelation and shared it in sinful pride—and that's the way his brothers (and his father) interpreted Joseph's actions.

DREAMS TODAY

Many times the Bible explains the meanings of events that happened back then. But what about things that happen today? How can we know what they mean?

1. Look again at the story about Lillian at the beginning of this session. Let's assume that Lillian and Walter were Christians. Lillian tried and tried to feel peaceful after Walter died. But she kept looking at the problem. What do you think would have happened if she had spent her time thinking and reading about Jesus, about His forgiveness, about the joy Walter was experiencing in heaven—things that God has revealed to us in His Word?

_____

_____

2. After the dream, Lillian seemed to base her faith on one dream rather than the sure revelation of God in Christ. What does **Hebrews 1:1-2** say about this?

_____

_____

3. What (or who) caused Lillian's dream? Talk about the following possibilities:

a. Lillian had thought about her brother so often that the dream occurred from the power of suggestion in her subconscious mind.

b. God gave this dream to Lillian.

c. Satan gave this dream to Lillian.

4. Lillian's story did not end there. For a long time she did not share her dream with anyone lest people would think her conceited for feeling that God had sent the dream just for her. But one day she met somebody else who was struggling with a similar grief, and then she shared her story. And then she felt that she had been blessed to be a blessing.

Discuss the following possible meanings to the end of Lillian's story:

a. God led Lillian to use a "natural circumstance" to comfort her friend.

b. God had sent the dream and now led Lillian to use it in the way He intended.

c. An unbeliever could have had the same experiences and reacted in similar ways. This was a "natural" event, and we read too much into it when we try to figure out how God or Satan was acting through it.

d. The friend wasn't "comforted" at all—or had false comfort—because the friend wasn't reminded of the eternal salvation Christians enjoy after death.

5. Compare (a) the comfort you would give by sharing Lillian's story with (b) the comfort you would give if you shared 1 **Thessalonians 4:13-18** with a bereaved person

_____

_____

_____

6. "What if something like this would happen to me? How should I respond?" Christians ought to follow these guidelines:

a. God speaks to us through His Word. His Word is reliable. We need to learn more and more about it so we *know* who is speaking and what He means by what He says.

b. Wanting something more than the Word is a subtle denial of the all-sufficiency of the Word. We already have Christ and forgiveness; God talking to us in His Word, the Bible; God even giving us His love through special Sacraments that address our senses of touch and taste. Why should we want more? In one sense, craving for "more" or "special" revelations through dreams and the like is similar to the temptation that came in the Garden of Eden. The devil's temptation there was for "more"—a special knowledge of God *beyond* what God had promised. (In **2 Thessalonians 2:9-10** God foretold how Satan will attempt to use signs to deceive us today.)

c. Dreams, like emotions, are not usually very reliable.

d. Wishing for revelations through means like dreams may damage our relationship with God. Consider, for example, the response, "God must not hold me as a very special person, because I've never had a special dream or a special revelation." In His Word God tells us that each of us is important to Him—so important that if any of us would have been the only person in the world, Jesus still would have died for us! *We don't need special dreams or special revelations to know we're important to God!*

e. When we experience something "unusual," we should measure our interpretation of it in light of God's Word. Does it *support* or *ignore* God's revelation in Jesus? See **Jeremiah 23:25-32.**

These are written that you may believe that Jesus is the Christ, the Son of God, and that by believing you may have life in His name.

John 20:31

Session 19

Concluding Activities for Unit 3

Answer the following questions to help you review unit 3.

TERMS

On a separate sheet of paper write a definition of the following terms:

1. pride
2. justification
3. the Fertile Crescent
4. covenant
5. Hagar
6. Israel
7. Sodom
8. Babel
9. Leah
10. Rachel
11. dreams

SHORT ANSWER

Write a short answer to each of the following questions.

1. How can pride lead a person away from God?

2. What covenant did God make with Abraham?

3. How did Abraham arrange for Isaac to marry a godly girl?

4. Describe God's love for Abraham.

5. How did Abraham show love for Lot?

6. How do we get faith?

7. How did Joseph's dreams affect his relationships with his brothers?

8. Do you think dreams today have special meanings? Explain your answer.

9. Describe the relationship between works and faith.

10. How do you become a "child of Abraham"?

11. Compare the sacrifice of Isaac and the sacrifice of Jesus.

Unit 4

The Covenant Family Multiplies

In this unit you will see how God kept His promises to Abraham, Isaac, and Jacob. Seventy descendants emigrated to Egypt to escape starvation during the great famine. There they multiplied rapidly. In His faithfulness God made them a strong people and delivered them exactly when He had said He would—*and* with great possessions.

Surely there is no other god like our mighty and faithful Yahweh **(Exodus 3:14)!**

Session 20

Slave to Sovereign (Joseph in Egypt)

It was Nancy's first day at Broadhollow High School. Her dad's transfer from the Southwest to the East Coast had made big changes in her life. The family had moved from a relaxed rural environment to a suburban community near a big amusement park. As an only child, Nancy had always made friends easily, but now she was scared. All the kids at her new school seemed so sophisticated and sure of themselves. Even their clothes seemed "far out" by the standards of her home town.

The girl who sat behind her in math class invited Nancy to join her group for a Friday night "blast" at the amusement park. It sounded like fun—but would she fit in? She felt so *different*—so out of it! Then she remembered the advice of one of her teachers before she left her old school: "When in Rome, do as the Romans do." But how many of the "Roman" activities should she go along with?

JOSEPH IS DIFFERENT

1. Read **Genesis 39:1-8** and watch for ways Joseph (who was about 17 years old) was different from the people around him. How was his nationality, or race, different from the people around him?

_____

_____

2. What difference did Potiphar notice in **verse 3**?

_____

3. How was Joseph's response to Potiphar's wife different from what she expected?

_____

4. What three things did Joseph mention in **verse 9** that set him apart and helped him to arrive at his decisions?

a. _____

b. _____

c. _____

5. We can easily transpose Joseph's experience into the 20th century. The story line (plot) occurs again and again in today's soap operas, both daytime and prime time. Suppose that a modern Joseph, perhaps a rising young executive in his 20s, would write to a personal-advice column about his dilemma. What kind of answer do you think he would get?

_____

_____

6. If you asked the typical man on the street what he would do in Joseph's sandals, what response might you get?

_____

_____

7. What did Joseph do **(verse 10)?**

_____

_____

8. Read **verses 11-20.** How was this meeting "ideal" for promoting an affair?

_____

9. What shows that Joseph's reaction was quick, decisive—and not overly concerned with diplomacy?

_____

_____

10. What did Solomon, one of the wisest man who ever lived, advise in **Proverbs 1:10?** _____

_____

11. What did the apostles say about sinful desires in **1 Peter 2:11** and **2 Timothy 2:22-26?** _____

_____

12. How did Potiphar's wife demonstrate the true nature of her attraction to Joseph? _____

_____

13. What would be your reaction at this point if you were Joseph? You had done your very best even

in difficult circumstances. Now you find yourself moving from slavery into prison—for doing right! When you feel that life is unfair to you, how do you react? Be ready to talk about it.

14. Read **Genesis 39:21-23.** If Joseph had been angry, sullen, and bitter, do you think he would have "found favor" in the eyes of the prison warden? How did Joseph's "career" as a convict parallel his "career" as a slave? Why? Be ready to discuss how Joseph's "being different" contributed to his success in both instances.

15. What was the key to Joseph's success and to his ability to withstand temptation **(39:2 and 21)?**

_____

16. What promise does God make to you (**Hebrews 13:5-6**)? _____

SOME DREAMS COME TRUE

Now Joseph experienced another great disappointment. He showed interest in the problems of his fellow convicts and shared his faith in God as he correctly interpreted their dreams. As a result, Pharaoh's cupbearer promised that he would try to get Joseph released from prison. But the cupbearer "forgot." Again, Joseph must have wondered, "Why? Will I be here for the rest of my life?"

But God's perfect timing for Joseph had not yet arrived. When it did—two full years later—Joseph's patience was richly rewarded. Pharaoh had dreams that foreshadowed seven years of plentiful harvests and seven years of famine, and he decided to call for Joseph to interpret the dreams.

1. How does **Genesis 41:15-16** show that Joseph was not a self-seeking opportunist? _____

_____

2. What did Pharaoh conclude in **41:38-40?**

_____

Who could have imagined such a turn of events: a poor Hebrew slave became the leader of a world power!

Of course, all the predictions that God gave to Joseph with regard to Pharaoh's dreams came true: Seven bountiful years were followed by seven years of famine. And, in fulfillment of Joseph's boyhood dreams, his brothers bowed down to him when they came to Egypt to buy food. After a careful study of their condition and personalities, Joseph invited his brothers to bring Jacob's entire household to Egypt, where food was plentiful and where he was in a position to protect them and help them to prosper.

"CURSED" TO BE A BLESSING?

1. Read **Genesis 45:1-11.** What do you think caused Joseph's brothers to be terrified (**verse 3**)?

_____

2. How did Joseph view his experiences?

_____

3. Why did God allow Joseph to be sold?

_____

4. God had promised Abraham that his descendants would become a great nation. How did God use Joseph to fulfill this promise?

_____

5. Being blessed to be a blessing is not difficult. But being willing to suffer so that others will be blessed takes the kind of courage that comes with spiritual maturity. It's the kind of courage that only God can provide.

Read what King David wrote about trust in God and perseverance in **Psalm 37** (especially **verses 1-7** and **39-40**) and summarize it: _____

_____

_____

_____

6. Like Nancy in the opening story, you have probably heard the saying, "When in Rome, do as the Romans do." What does St. Paul say about this in his letter to the **Romans (12:1-2)?**

_____

_____

7. How is Joseph a good example of what Paul encourages us to do?

_____

Why not rededicate your life to God right now? Then ask Him to make you bold in your obedience to Him and faithful in the tasks He gives you to do—large or small. Read His Word regularly and trust Him to guide and bless you, and to lift you up with His forgiveness when you fail Him. Then, like Joseph, you can take your turn at being a blessing to others.

The salvation of the righteous comes from the Lord; He is their stronghold in time of trouble. The Lord helps them and delivers them; He delivers them from the wicked and saves them, because they take refuge in Him.

Psalm 37:39-40

Session 21

A Family Becomes a Nation (Israel in Egypt)

In your mind create an imaginary family from England who settled in Virginia in 1641. Make it a large family—maybe about as large as Jacob's family when they moved to Egypt. Did all the people in your family stay in Virginia? Did they develop a successful tobacco or cotton plantation? What kinds of relationships did they have with the people around them? Whom did the children marry? Did the grandchildren and great-grandchildren still think of themselves as members of that family?

Now let your mind jump to today, less than 400 years later. What do you think has happened to that family? _____

_____

_____

_____

CHOSEN FOR *THIS?*

1. God chose Abram and his family to play a special role in world history. Innumerable descendants, a unique nation, a covenant relationship, their own land, and spiritual prominence were all included in God's promise. But God did not say life would always be easy. Read **Genesis 15:13-14**. What had God predicted would happen to Abram's family?

_____

_____

2. Undoubtedly Joseph and his brothers did not know it, but God was now fulfilling part of that prophecy. Their father, Jacob, really did not want to go to Egypt. Why did he go **(Genesis 45:11 and 28)?**

_____

_____

3. Certainly Jacob felt frightened as he traveled to Egypt. Maybe this is why God appeared to him **(46:1-4).** The Bible calls this a vision rather than a dream.

Notice that God called to Jacob, and Jacob answered Him. How did God identify Himself?

_____

4. This must have reassured Jacob that God still cared about His covenant people and their whereabouts. What four things did God promise Jacob?

a. _____

b. _____

c. _____

d. _____

5. What did this first promise indicate about the length of time that Jacob's family would be in Egypt?

_____

6. How did Joseph's promise to Jacob **(47:30)** ensure parts of the promise?

_____

With the promise that God would go with him, Jacob was willing to go anywhere—even to Egypt, and at the age of 130!

THE GOOD LIFE IN EGYPT

1. Read **Genesis 46:5-27**. How many of Jacob's family were descendants of Leah? _____ How many of Zilpah, her maid? _____ How many of Rachel? _____ How many of Bilhah, her maid? _____ How many "Israelites" lived in Egypt altogether at this time? _____

2. Read **46:28-34**. The annual flooding of the Nile kept adding rich alluvial deposits to the river valley and the delta region. Goshen is located in the eastern part of the delta. Lush and fertile, but vulnerable to attack, it was not occupied by the Egyptians. Joseph was eager to keep his family isolated from the Egyptian culture. What kind of prejudice **(verse 34)** was a source of blessing for the Israelites? _____

_____

_____

3. Who apparently felt that allowing the Israelites to live in Goshen was his own idea **(Genesis 47:5-6)?**

_____

4. Read **Genesis 47:7-11.** Can you picture the incongruity of this scene? Jacob, a 130-year-old foreigner in the full beard and coarse clothing of the detested shepherd people was presented to the clean-shaven, regally robed Pharaoh, who was probably the most powerful man in the world at that time. Jacob gave Pharaoh the one thing that all of Pharaoh's wealth could not buy. What was it **(verses 7** and **10)?**

_____

For the time being, at least, life for the Israelites was beautiful!

5. With Joseph's weighty administrative duties and the distances involved, Jacob probably saw very little of his son Joseph. What brought Joseph to Goshen in **48:1?** _____

6. Read 4**8:3-6.** After reminding Joseph that it was the destiny of Jacob's family to occupy and rule Canaan, Jacob made legal promises that, in effect, gave Joseph the "double portion" that rightfully belonged to the firstborn son. How did Jacob accomplish this?

_____

7. What did Jacob promise Joseph in **48:21?**

___

Jacob used this opportunity to give his final blessing to all his sons **(Genesis 49)**. With food and the promise of God's blessing, Jacob's children must have felt happy to stay right where they were.

JACOB CROSSES THE FINISH LINE

1. Notice in **49:29-33** how calmly and simply death was faced and accomplished. Did Jacob sound terrified? _____ Do you get the impression from **verse 33** that he struggled or pleaded to prolong his life for a few more weeks or even days?

___

2. Look at **47:9** for a hint at Jacob's secret. What is a pilgrimage? _____

3. How long had Jacob been on his pilgrimage?

___

4. Where was he going? _____
So death marked his arrival at his destination.

THE FAMILY BECOMES A NATION

What happened to your imaginary family at the beginning of this session? Did they intermarry with other families, first of all in Virginia and finally throughout the United States and beyond? Could you imagine that family still existing as a family throughout all these years? Probably not.

1. Now go back to **Genesis**. Recall that Abraham did not want Isaac to marry one of the local girls **(24:2-4)**. Isaac, in turn, had given the same advice to Jacob **(28:1-2)**. When you think of the sinfulness that existed also in Jacob's family, what do you think would have happened to Jacob's descendants if they had remained in Canaan? _____

___

2. Read **46:34** again. Why would Jacob's descendants likely not intermarry with their new neighbors, the Egyptians?

___

3. Of course, God could have used other means to keep His people separate from other people. And He accomplished other purposes through this episode. (For example, He showed His mighty power at the Red Sea during the Exodus—the return of His people to Canaan 400 years later.) The point is, however, that God *did* work through this event in history. He *did* change a family of 70 **(Genesis 46:27; Exodus 1:5)** into a large nation **(Exodus 1:7)**. What does this show about God? _____

___

4. But God's people could not always see that God was keeping His promises. Read **Exodus 1:8-14**. Describe some of the reasons why you think Jacob's family (now called "Israel") must have wondered whether God was still with them. _____

___

5. How did the Israelites react to their misery **(Exodus 2:23)?**

___

6. What does **2:24-25** tell about God?

___

7. Talk together with your classmates about some times when people today wonder whether God really is with them.

a. Tell about your own doubts, listen to the doubts of others, and tell about the doubts of people you know.

b. Roleplay conversations in which you discuss these doubts. Suggest ways to deal with the doubts, tell about promises from God (be sure to quote Bible verses whenever possible), and tell of ways you will help the person (prayer, longer discussions about God's promises, etc).

"I am God, the God of your father," He said. *"Do not be afraid to go down to Egypt, for I will make you into a great nation there. "I will go down to Egypt with you, and I will surely bring you back again. And Joseph's own hand will close your eyes."*

Genesis 46:3-4

Session 22

Retrofitting a Reject (Moses' First 80 Years)

Fritz was a high-school student who had all the qualifications for a career in scientific research—and that was his goal. Imagine his disappointment when the only option open to him financially was a Lutheran teachers college that did not offer a science major! Undaunted, he resolved to work hard and eventually earn a degree in science later, while he worked as a teacher. But his bachelor's degree with majors in education and English literature and a minor in religion produced a chuckle when he applied for graduate work in science at a major university. He was forced to settle for a master's degree in the *teaching* of science instead of scientific research.

As a scientist, Fritz felt like a reject. But God had a plan. Fritz's undergraduate training in English, education, and religion and his graduate work in a prestigious university were ideal for the avocation that God had in mind for him: writing textbooks in science and religion! By devoting weekends and vacations to painstaking writing and library research, he was rewarded with international professional recognition and many other unexpected blessings as well—including numerous lecture opportunities, worldwide travel, and financial success. God had retrofitted a reject would-be scientist into a powerful worker and witness to His people.

A "BORN LEADER" IS REJECTED

Moses is undoubtedly one of the best-known heroes in all of secular and religious literature. At the time of his birth, Egypt was a world power and was famed for its center of learning at Heliopolis (north of what is now the city of Cairo). The reigning Pharaoh felt no obligation to favor the Israelites for Joseph's sake. In fact, he saw them as an asset only as slave laborers. But they became so strong and so numerous (through God's blessings) that Pharaoh also considered them to be a threat to national security.

Even though he regarded himself as a god, Pharaoh had a gut sense of insecurity and ordered the massacre of all Israelite baby boys at birth—for the national

welfare! (This action easily reminds one of the abhorrent practice of abortion today.)

Through the courageous initiative of his mother Jochebed, Moses lived. Read **Exodus 2:1-10** for an overview of the first 40 years of his life. List two things from these verses that seem most significant to you.

_____

_____

_____

Read **Acts 7:21.** What did Stephen say about the training of Moses at this time?

_____

_____

With his character formed in his early years by his God-fearing family, and his mind and body trained in the royal court, Moses appeared to be the ideal candidate for Israelite leadership. But his self-confident effort to exert this leadership led to rejection and exile. How old was he and to what country was he exiled **(Acts 7:23** and **29)?**

_____

RETROFITTING A LEADER IN THE DESERT

1. Read **Exodus 2:16-22.** How did Moses gain the respect and admiration of a priest's family?

_____

2. What was the name of the priest **(verse 18)?** _____ This name means "Friend of God." Do you think it was just a "coincidence" that Moses came to this family?

3. What nationality did they assume Moses to be?

_____

4. Who became the wife of Moses?

_____

5. Why did Moses name his first son Gershom?

_____

6. According to **Exodus 3:1**, what was Moses' occupation now? _____

7. What is the name of Moses' father-in-law in this verse? _____ This is really a title; it means "his excellency." Perhaps he had been "promoted" in the years that passed between **2:18** and **3:1.**

8. According to **Acts 7:30**, how many years did Moses spend in Midian? _____

9. Finding enough food for the flocks probably took Moses over a good part of the southern end of the Sinai peninsula. (Many Bible scholars think that Mount Horeb and Mount Sinai are the same place.) How did this fit into God's plan for Moses? _____

_____

THE RELUCTANT LEADER

1. In **Exodus 3** and **4** we find the familiar story of Moses and the burning bush. Contentedly grazing his flocks, 80-year-old Moses was called by God to do what Moses had wanted to do 40 years earlier! How did God identify Himself? **(3:6)?**

_____

2. Obviously, the Israelites had kept the covenant promise alive as they gathered together to encourage one another during their difficult years of slavery. What comforting term did God use to describe Israel in **3:7?**

_____

3. Compare **3:8** with **Genesis 15:18-21.** Did God seem to be describing the same general area of the world to both Moses and Abram? _____ What might account for some of the differences in the names of the listed countries?

_____

4. Moses gave five negative responses to God. What were they?

3:11 _____

3:13 _____

4:1 _____

4:10 _____

4:13 _____

5. How did God respond?

3:12 _____

3:14 _____

3:15 _____

3:18 _____

3:19-20 _____

3:21-22 _____

4:2-9 _____

4:12 _____

4:14-15 _____

7. To whom did God speak in **Exodus 4:27?**

_____

We are not told about Aaron's response. He may have had some reservations, too. Certainly it would not have been a simple matter for a slave to decide to go traveling! But the obedience of these God-fearing brothers brought about a joyful reunion and they began to function as a team to serve the purposes of God for His people. Note their response **(4:31).** Read what Stephen had to say about this in **Acts 7:35.**

8. So the rejected military leader was now accepted as God's ordained spiritual leader. What parallels can you find between Moses and Jesus? Be ready to share these in class.

9. God knows that there are times when each of us feels rejected, times when we feel inadequate and don't know what to say. That is why He wants to help and comfort us (through our knowledge of Scripture) with examples like Joseph and Moses and Stephen and with direct words of comfort. One of these passages is **Romans 8:26-39.** Summarize that reading below and think about how to apply it in your own life.

_____

_____

_____

_____

10. Sometimes roadblocks—including roadblocks that occur because we "mess up"—keep us from accomplishing the goals we have set for our lives. What comfort do God's love and forgiveness provide for us at times like this?

_____

_____

_____

The Lord said, "I have indeed seen the misery of My people in Egypt. . . . So I have come down to rescue them from the hand of the Egyptians and to bring them up out of that land into a good and spacious land, a land flowing with milk and honey."
Exodus 3:7-8

Session 23

I AM for Everyone (Moses Confronts Pharaoh)

Psalm 90, which was written by Moses, is probably the oldest of the Psalms. Because he was chosen by God to lead the Israelites out of captivity, one might expect Moses to be isolationistic and nationalistic in his thinking, but this was not the case. Perhaps his broadbased training in Egypt gave Moses his world view, or perhaps he learned of the universality of God's love at his mother's knee during his early childhood. At any rate, God gave Moses a global perception of His concern and involvement.

What can you find in the latter part of the psalm that might apply specifically to the Israelites as Moses and Aaron prepared to confront the mighty Pharaoh?

_____

_____

DARKNESS BEFORE DAWN

1. Read **Exodus 5.** When Moses and Aaron appeared before Pharaoh, whom did they quote in their request to "Let My people go"?

_____

2. What was Pharaoh's response?

_____

3. What problems was the presence of Moses causing for Pharaoh **(5:5)?**

_____

4. Whom did the Israelites blame for their predicament **(5:20—21)?** _____ Imagine Moses' feelings as he realized that the Israelites were much worse off now than they were before his return to Egypt!

5. Often it seems darkest just before the dawn. But God overcomes darkness. Read **Exodus 6:1-10.** After identifying Himself as the God of Abraham, Isaac, and Jacob, of what agreement did God remind Moses **(verse 4)?**

6. What promises did God make?

(verse 6) _____

_____

(verse 7) _____

_____

(verse 8) _____

_____

7. How did the Israelites respond to these promises **(verse 9)?**

_____

Why?

_____

MIGHTY ACTS AND A HARDENED HEART

1. Pharaoh considered himself to be a god. He had refused to listen to Moses' message from God in **Exodus 5:1-5.** Now God told Moses how He would go about freeing the Israelites **(Exodus 7:1-5).** The Egyptians had *many* gods: Pharaoh, the Nile, the vulture-goddess Nekhbet, the sun-god Re, the frog-goddess Hape, the fly-god Uatchit, the protector-god Serapis, and many other gods represented by animals—especially the bull.

Now look at the plagues that God used **(Exodus 7—11).** List them.

_____

_____

_____

_____

2. Why do you suppose God selected these particular plagues?

_____

3. Notice the progression in the plagues. The first four were repulsive and bothersome; the fifth caused the death of cattle; the sixth was painful for the people; the seventh and eighth destroyed their food supply; the ninth surely brought psychological distress; and the tenth brought death to every household. Beginning with the fourth plague, what made the Egyptians even more aware of God's special concern for the Israelites (8:22; 9:6, 11, 26; 10:15, 23; 11:6-7)?

_____

4. Imagine the distress the Egyptians must have felt. *They* were the powerful nation. People regarded *their gods* as the most powerful gods in the world— certainly much more powerful than any god of a slave nation of shepherds! Pharaoh hardened his heart to the true God—the God of Israel. But even through the hardening of the heart, we can see the power of God. Read the following verses and summarize four results of God's action.

Exodus 7:16-17; 8:10, 22-23 _____

_____

Exodus 7:5; 11:9; 14:18, 25 _____

_____

Exodus 9:16; Joshua 4:24a _____

_____

Exodus 10:1-2; Joshua 4:24b _____

5. Did God's plan work? Tell what you find in the following.

Exodus 8:8, 28; 9:27-28; 10:16-17 _____

_____

Exodus 8:19; 9:20; 11:3 _____

_____

Joshua 2:8-11 _____

_____

Exodus 14:31 _____

_____

6. In what way were the terrible plagues evidences of God's love, rather than His anger?

_____

7. How do the plagues demonstrate God's love for you?

_____

GOD'S NEVER-CHANGING MESSAGE

1. How does God speak to us today (**Hebrews 1:1-2**)? _____

2. What is the message (**Hebrews 1:3**)?

_____

3. Is this a message of revenge or of love?

_____

4. How does God give authority to His message today (**Hebrews 2:1-4**)?

_____

_____

5. What is God's purpose according to **Hebrews 2:10-11?**

_____

6. Whose family do we then become?

_____

7. So whose brothers and sisters are we?

_____

8. **Hebrews 3** tells us what our next step should be. Summarize **verses 1-14.**

_____

_____

_____

_____

9. Not only do we have the mighty works of the Old Testament to build up our faith, but we also have all the miracles of the New Testament! And we have the record of the saving work which Jesus our Savior accomplished for us.

Read **Hebrews 4:16.** God tells us to approach the throne of grace. How should we approach it?

_____

What benefits will we receive? _____

_____

Let us then approach the throne of grace with confidence, so that we may receive mercy and find grace to help us in our time of need.

Hebrews 4:16

Session 24

I AM—a Key to God's Word

WHAT'S IN A NAME?

1. Do you know the meaning of your name? Parents sometimes choose their children's names just for the pleasant sound, but sometimes they place great emphasis on the meaning of the name as well. The Bible stresses the meanings of names. What are some meaningful names we have already studied?

_____

_____

What does a name like "Superman" imply? What sort of person do you visualize when you hear the name "Rockefeller"? "Hitler"? "Houdini"?

2. Read **Exodus 3:13-15** again. Moses recognized the importance of presenting his message to the Israelites with the proper "credentials." They had flatly rejected him when he tried to be their leader 40 years earlier. He wanted to be sure to do it right this time. Read **Exodus 6:3.** By what name did Abraham, Isaac, and Jacob know God? _____

3. Now, at this turning point in history—just as a new nation was about to be born—He gave them a new name for Himself. What was it? _____

In Hebrew, this name is spelled YHWH, which is translated Jehovah or Yahweh. This name was considered to be so holy by the Jews that they never uttered it aloud. Instead, they substituted the word *Lord.* Bible translators, for the most part, have followed this example. In some Bibles, **Exodus 6:3** reads, "**. . . by my name Jehovah was I not known to them**" (KJV).

4. God must want to convey a very special meaning with His new name. What do you suppose it is? The name seems so simple. Read **John 8:56-58.** Here Jesus uses the phrase *I AM* to describe Himself. What was He trying to teach the skeptical Jews?

_____

5. How does the divine author's description of Jesus in **Hebrews 13:8** echo this idea?

_____

6. Perhaps you have run across the term *primal cause* in a science book, which means the origin of

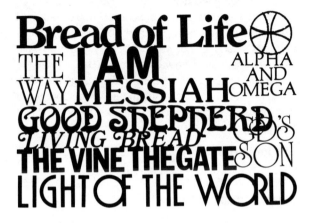

matter or of the universe. St. Paul spoke about the primal cause when he wrote to the Colossians. Read what Paul says about Jesus in **Colossians 1:15-17.** Notice how meaningful and profound God's name, I AM, really is. What does that name say about Him?

_____

_____

THE POWER OF GOD'S NAME

1. Because God wants *everyone* to recognize His great love and mercy, He acts to protect and glorify His name. He used the plagues, as we learned, to make His name known all over the earth. For the sake of His name, what did God do in the instances that are referred to in the following passages?

1 Samuel 17:45-50 _____

Isaiah 48:9 _____

Ezekiel 20:9-10 _____

Ezekiel 36:22-24 _____

Acts 3:1-7; 4:7, 10 _____

2. Who instructed the Israelites to use God's name as a battle cry in **Judges 7:15-18?**

_____

3. What was the result (**Judges 7:19-22**)?

_____

4. What three-word phrase, spoken by Jesus in the Garden of Gethsemane, knocked the tough soldiers right off their feet (**John 18:6**)?

_____

5. What name is given to Jesus in **Philippians 2:9-11?**

_____

To whose glory?

_____

6. In **John 17:11**, Jesus asked His Father to protect all believers. By what power?

_____

By which name?

_____

7. During His life on earth, how did Jesus protect His disciples according to **John 17:12?**

_____

_____

"I AM" REVEALED

1. When God gave us His name, I AM, He told us more about His nature than we knew before. He continued to reveal His nature through Scripture, through His mighty acts, and most especially through Jesus, who is the physical embodiment of I AM. What did Jesus say to His disciples about who He is in **John 15:23?** _____
In **John 14:7-10?**

_____

2. What did Paul say about Jesus in **Colossians 2:9?**

_____

3. So as Jesus made Himself known, He made His Father known. Jesus often used the phrase *I AM.* Look up the following passages and write (a) what Jesus called Himself in each of them and (b) what the passage means to you.

Name and Meaning

John 4:25-26 I AM _____

John 6:35 I AM _____

John 6:51 I AM _____

John 8:12 I AM _____

John 10:7 I AM _____

John 10:11 I AM _____

John 10:36 I AM _____

John 11:25 I AM _____

John 14:6 I AM _____

John 15:1 I AM _____

John 18:37 I AM _____

Revelation 1:8 I AM _____

Revelation 22:16 I AM _____

Revelation 22:20 I AM _____

4. Read **John 20:30-31.** Why does God reveal all these things—and more—about Jesus?

_____

_____

5. Isn't it beautiful—this covenant name, I AM—and the way that God uses it to unite all Scripture into a grand picture of His holiness, power, grace, mercy, and love? In the spaces below, list the numbers and titles of hymns in your hymnal that refer to Yahweh (Jehovah) or to the power of Jesus' name. Discuss and expand the list in class.

Number Title

_____ _____

_____ _____

_____ _____

_____ _____

_____ _____

_____ _____

_____ _____

_____ _____

[Jesus] is the image of the invisible God, the first-born over all creation. For by Him all things were created: things in heaven and on earth, visible and invisible, whether thrones or powers or rulers or authorities; all things were created by Him and for Him. He is before all things, and in Him all things hold together.

Colossians 1:15-17

Session 25

A Night to Remember—Passover

Have you ever attended a Seder in a Christian church? ("Seder" is a modern name for the Passover meal.) Christian churches sometimes sponsor Seders to promote a greater understanding of the setting in which Jesus instituted the Lord's Supper. If there is a Jewish Christian agency in your community, you might ask them (or someone trained by The Lutheran Church—Missouri Synod's Task Force on Witnessing to Jewish People) to help your church arrange such a Seder and to explain the Passover traditions that have developed over the centuries.

THE FIRST PASSOVER

1. God Himself instituted the very first Passover for a very special purpose. According to **Exodus 11:5**, what was about to happen?

_____

2. It's hard to imagine such a horrible thing. Why did God do it? What answers do the following passages provide?

12:12 _____

11:7-8; 12:31 _____

3. What instructions did God give to the Israelites?

12:3-5 _____

_____

12:6 _____

12:7 _____

12:8-9 _____

_____

12:10 _____

12:11 _____

12:22 _____

4. How does **Exodus 12:28** show that the Lord was accomplishing His purposes—that the Israelites were growing in faith?

_____

5. If one of the Israelite fathers refused to put blood on the door frame of his house, what do you think happened, according to **Exodus 12:23?**

_____

PASSOVER CELEBRATIONS TODAY

A Jewish book of liturgy called the Haggadah contains the prescribed service for the Seder for Jewish people. Several days before the Passover, the house is thoroughly cleaned to make sure that there is no leaven (yeast) left **(Exodus 12:15)**. On the day of Passover, the family attends services in the synagogue or temple and then returns to the house, which is brightly lit. This reminds them of the light in the houses of the Israelites when darkness descended upon the Egyptians.

Dressed in holiday finery, the family members sit around the table, on which the elements of the Passover meal are spread. They leave an extra chair empty for the prophet Elijah, who they believe will come on a Passover night to announce the good news of the coming Messiah.

Following are the elements of the meal. The sections in parentheses suggest a symbolic meaning for the elements.

Four glasses of wine (Four expressions of redemption in **Exodus 6:6-7**; the blood of the lamb on the doorpost)

Shank bone of a lamb (A reminder of the sacrifice of the lamb)

Three matzos (Reminder of the unleavened bread that was prepared for the first Passover)

Bowl of salt water (Tears of the Israelites during slavery)

A boiled egg (Eternal life)

Celery or parsley (New life)

Bitter herb—horseradish (Bitterness and sorrow of slavery)

Chopped apples, nuts, raisins (Mortar used to make bricks for Egyptians)

As the leader relates the story of the first Passover, he explains the meaning of each element of the Seder. Early in the meal, he breaks the middle matzo of a stack of three matzos in half and hides one of the halves. At the end of the meal, the children look for the hidden matzo half. When they find it, it is returned to the other half, and then they are broken and shared with everyone. The family eats no more food that evening. The celebration ends with the reading or singing of a psalm from the Hallel **(Psalms 113—118.)**

THE SYMBOLISM OF THE SACRIFICIAL LAMB

The unique relationship between sin and the shedding of blood—the sacrifice of life—is a sobering but beautifully unifying thread in Scripture. The first sin, in Eden, resulted in the shedding of blood to provide clothing to cover Adam and Eve's nakedness. Abel sacrificed the firstborn of his flock in his acceptable act of worship. Noah preserved more than one pair of the "clean" animals that he sacrificed after leaving the ark.

On Mount Moriah God provided a ram to be sacrificed in Isaac's place.

And now, during Passover, the lamb became the sacrifice that provided deliverance from bondage and death. God used dramatic picture language to reveal both the seriousness of sin and the means of escape from its grasp. Let's examine some of the ways in which the Passover lamb became a picture or "type" of the coming Messiah, the ultimate sacrifice for sin whom John the Baptizer identified in **John 1:29** and **36.**

Passover Lamb	The Lamb of God
A lamb	**John 1:29** _____
Without blemish	**1 Peter 1:19** _____
Set apart	**Hebrews 7:26** _____
Blood preserved lives	**1 John 1:7** _____
No bones broken	**John 19:31-36** _____

Isaiah, in prophesying about Jesus 700 years before His birth, called attention to another similarity. Read Isaiah 53:7. Then find a New Testament passage that speaks of that aspect of Jesus' life.

_____

_____

THE LAST SUPPER

1. Read **Luke 22:1-30.** What festival were Jesus and His disciples celebrating? _____

2. How can you tell that this was not just a boring tradition for Jesus? _____

3. What kind of bread was used at the meal?

_____

4. What beverage was served? _____

5. What Sacrament did Jesus institute here?

_____

6. How can you explain the use of the term *the new covenant in My blood* by Jesus in **verse 20?**

_____

_____

7. What did St. Paul call Jesus in **1 Corinthians 5:7?** _____

Read **Hebrews 9:26-28** and **10:17-18** for further clarification of the role of Jesus as the Sacrificial Lamb.

8. What does **Hebrews 9:22** say about blood?

_____

1 John 1:7? _____

9. When we receive the Lord's Supper, we receive the blessings of Jesus' blood—forgiveness of sins, increased faith, eternal life. The blessings we receive lead most Christians to receive the Lord's Supper frequently. In what ways can our frequent participation in this Sacrament also be a blessing to others (**1 Corinthians 11:23-26)?**

_____

_____

10. What warning does Paul give in **1 Corinthians 11:27-32?**

_____

_____

Clearly, God wants us to take Communion seriously and to make sure that all who take it understand what they are doing so that they can benefit from it.

Jesus, our Passover Lamb, not only maintains physical life but He also offers eternal life. In **Revelation 5** and **7** we find vivid symbolism of the awesome majesty of the Lamb. One of the most beautiful of these descriptive passages is **7:9-17.** Be ready to discuss these selections in class. In the space below, copy **7:15-17** so that you can reread it often and take comfort from it.

_____

_____

_____

_____

_____

John saw Jesus coming toward him and said, "Look, the Lamb of God, who takes away the sin of the world!"

John 1:29

Session 26

Free at Last (The Exodus)

On the evening of Nov. 9, 1965, as thousands of workers in the New York metropolitan area were going home, a power outage plunged the entire area into sudden darkness. The blackout trapped some people in subways, others in elevators. Even those fortunate enough to be at home had to grope their way around without even a street light to break the blanket of blackness. And the crisis continued for hours—in some areas for days.

What a comfort it must have been for the children to hear a familiar voice during the blackout, or to feel a comforting arm. And then, when a candle was lit or a flashlight turned on, the whole world must have suddenly seemed more friendly again!

Do you remember a frightening experience in your own life? What were some things that helped you feel better?

THE COVENANT PROMISE FULFILLED

When someone makes a promise to you, how do you know if he or she will keep it? If it's that person's very first promise, you may not be too sure. If several years have passed since the promise, you might be even less sure. God made His covenant with Abraham *hundreds* of years before the time of Moses. Read what God said to Abram in **Genesis 15:13-14** and to Moses in **Exodus 3:18-22.** Now read **Exodus 12:31-41.** Surely Moses and those families who took God's words seriously and taught them faithfully to their children were filled with awe as they—former slaves—left Egypt loaded with silver, gold, clothing, and livestock!

1. Do you recall the size of Jacob's family when they moved into the land of Goshen? See **Genesis 46:26-27.**

2. What did God promise Jacob in **Genesis 46:3?**

_____

3. According to **Exodus 12:37**, how many Israelites left Egypt in the great **Exodus?** _____

4. According to **verse 38**, who left with them?

_____

5. So a conservative estimate of the total number

of people leaving Egypt is two million or more. Add to this the "large droves of livestock," and you have a truly *awesome* multitude! If the people walked 10 abreast and left two feet of space between rows, how long was the line of refugees? _____

6. If you were Moses and Aaron, how would you go about leading this procession? Keep in mind that there were no automobiles, helicopters, mounted police, or walkie-talkies to help you. Read **Exodus 13:21-22.** How did the Lord help these people?

_____

_____

7. What kind of terrain were the Israelites traveling through **(13:20)?**

_____

8. What probably caused a problem during daylight hours? _____
At night? _____

Can you see how much God blessed the people by the form of leadership He selected? Imagine what large "pillars" God created so all the people could see them! Think, for example, how small the goalposts on a football field must look next to those pillars! They were surely a very welcome and reassuring sight to that poor, homeless mass of slaves who had never had the freedom to travel anywhere on their own before and probably had no idea where they were going.

MISSION IMPOSSIBLE

1. Did you ever wonder what happens when an irresistible force meets an immovable object? This is the situation the Israelites faced soon after they left Egypt. Read **Exodus 14:1-14.** Who was responsible for putting the Israelites in this predicament?

_____

2. Why did God let Pharaoh send his army **(verses 4** and **18)?**

_____

Because the Israelites didn't know the end of the story, as we do, they panicked **(verses 10-12).** Moses *sounded* calm **(verses 13-14),** but **verse 15** shows that on the inside he was crying out to God for help.

59

Sometimes God places us in seemingly impossible and very uncomfortable situations. How do we react in such cases? Do we panic like the Israelites did, or do we remain calm as we cry out to God, as Moses did?

Once the sea parted and the water stood in walls to form a corridor of dry land **(verses 21-22)**, would you have been eager to be the first person to walk through? The fear of the Egyptian army was no doubt largely responsible for the people's "bravery." But they also needed faith in Yahweh, as we read in **Hebrews 11:29.** Moses held up his staff, stretched it out over the sea, and commanded the people to walk through the Red Sea. They obeyed because they believed in God. The Egyptian army lacked that faith and entered the corridor to their destruction.

3. When we look back on times of difficulty that we have faced with faith, we can identify them as faith-strengthening times. What was the result of the harrowing experience at the Red Sea for the Israelites **(Exodus 14:30-31)**? _____

Compare **14:13-14** with **verses 24-28.** Surely Yahweh keeps His promises faithfully!

4. The Exodus points us to the deliverance Christ accomplished for us. Without this deliverance, we would continue to live in the slavery of sin, death, and hell. What do we receive instead **(John 3:16)**?

PRAISE AS A FORM OF APPRECIATION

Can you imagine yourself among those thousands and thousands of relieved and joy-filled people whom God had so miraculously rescued from the wrath of Pharaoh? How would you have shown your thanks and praise to the Lord? Maybe with a festive parade like one of those that went down Wall Street in New York City to celebrate military victories or successful space voyages? **Exodus 15:1-21** describes the victory celebration of the jubilant Israelites. If you are familiar with Hebrew music, you have some idea of the zest and syncopation, the fervor and animation of this victory song and dance.

1. Down through the ages, stories of the freeing of slaves, deliverance from abuse and oppression, and victory over evil have inspired and encouraged people in situations similar to that of the fleeing Israelites. Asaph, an accomplished musician who lived at King David's time, recognized the importance of remembering God's mighty deliverance. Read **Psalm 78:1-7, 12-14,** and **52-53.** According to **verses 5-7,** what was the purpose of this remembering?

2. Hundreds of years later, the prophet Isaiah echoed these thoughts in **Isaiah 63:7-9** and **64:4-5.** Paraphrase the prophet's message:

_____

_____

3. These promises of protection apply to our physical enemies as well as to our spiritual foes. According to **Ephesians 6:10-12,** against whom do Christians struggle?

_____

_____

4. Whose power does God give us for this battle (**Ephesians 1:18-21**)?

_____

5. How do we "plug into" that power **(Colossians 2:8-10)**?

_____

6. According to **Romans 8:38-39,** what are our chances for victory?

_____

7. In **Revelation 15** God showed visions of the end of the world to the apostle John. Read **verses 2-4.** Who was singing?

_____

Whose song were they singing?

_____

8. Why will all nations worship Yahweh **(verse 4)**?

_____

Be prepared to discuss how we, in the 20th century, have been freed from slavery, oppression, and from the forces of evil.

9. God gives us the stories of His mighty acts to move us to enthusiastic praise, worship, and acts of witnessing. How can we best encourage one another to join Moses, Miriam, Asaph, Isaiah, and all the saints in praising Almighty God for keeping His covenants and delivering us from evil?

_____

_____

Moses and the Israelites sang this song to the Lord, "I will sing to the Lord, for He is highly exalted. The horse and its rider He has hurled into the sea. The Lord is my strength and my song; He has become my salvation. He is my God, and I will praise Him, my father's God, and I will exalt Him."

Exodus 15:1-2

Session 27

Concluding Activities for Unit 4

Answer the following questions to help you review unit 4.

TERMS

On a separate sheet of paper write definitions of the following terms:

1. Goshen
2. I AM
3. Alpha and Omega
4. Passover
5. Seder
6. plagues
7. Pharaoh
8. Exodus
9. Jethro
10. Jochebed

SHORT ANSWER

Write a short answer to each of the following questions:

1. How did God bless the Israelites during the years they lived in Egypt?

_____

_____

2. What were some things that caused the Israelites to feel unhappy in Egypt?

_____

_____

_____

3. Describe the call of Moses.

_____

_____

_____

_____

_____

4. What in the New Testament did the following foreshadow?

a. the Passover lamb

_____

b. the slavery in Egypt

_____

c. the Exodus

_____

d. the Passover

_____

5. What about the Exodus would cause later people to talk about God's deliverance of Israel "by His mighty hand"?

_____

_____

_____

6. What are some good ways to show our appreciation for the blessings God has given us?

_____

_____

_____

7. What signs of God's love can you find in Joseph's life?

_____

_____

_____

_____

Unit 5

The Covenant Nation Is Nursed and Nurtured

For as long as the Israelites could remember, they had been slaves in the land of Egypt. God protected them and provided for their physical needs in Goshen. While their forefathers served as shepherds, their families grew and multiplied. Conditions became increasingly uncomfortable as God, through their surrogate mother, Egypt, brought them to their birth as a nation. We can compare the path through the Red Sea to a birth canal. The millions of people were virtually forced through the narrow passageway and emerged on the other side as the infant nation of Israel. But their obvious source of sustenance was also cut off as the waters of the Red Sea crashed together over Pharaoh's armies, forever severing Israel's umbilical cord to Egypt. They were now a separate and distinct people.

But it takes considerably more than large numbers of people to make a united, functioning nation. Some form of governing principles would have to be drawn up, leadership established, and goals set.

If you have ever tried to organize a camping trip, a bike hike, or a sophisticated club activity, you have some idea of the enormity of the task facing Moses as Israel's leader. In this unit we will see how he became a ready tool in the hand of the almighty God to accomplish His purposes. At times, however, disobedience and lack of faith complicated and delayed the path of the blessings that God had planned for His covenant people.

Session 28

Infant Israel Begins to Walk

How long do you think newborn babies could survive on their own? What are their needs? How do they become self-sufficient? How can parents help? Can they be a hindrance? How? How can growing children help in this process? Can *they* be a hindrance? How? Be ready to talk about this in class. Think of examples you can share from the point of view of a child and of an adult—a baby-sitter, for instance.

ISRAEL IS TAUGHT HOW TO WALK WITH GOD

Infant Israel had many needs. The baby was delivered by faith, and now had to learn to walk by faith.

1. Read **Exodus 15:22-27.** After they crossed the Red Sea, where did the people of Israel find themselves? _____

2. What was the first thing they needed?

_____

_____

3. When they found it, what was wrong with it?

_____

4. To whom did they complain? _____

5. To whom did Moses turn? _____

6. What did God use to perform a miracle?

_____

7. This miracle strengthened the faith of the Israelites. God supplied their needs, and He called upon them to follow a comprehensive rule for success as He continued to build their faith. What rule did God give them? _____

_____

8. What faith-strengthening promise did God make? _____

_____

9. Thus far God had provided the infant Israel with pure drinking water and foolproof medical insurance. Now He gave the people the perfect spot for rest and rehabilitation—an oasis with palm trees and 12 springs! Where did Moses find water the next time **(17:5-6)?**

_____

10. What did God tell Moses to do to cause the water to flow?

_____

YAHWEH PROVIDES

1. In **Exodus 16** we learn how God provided another lesson. The Israelites were moving through the desert toward Sinai. What did the people need this time?

2. To whom do they complain?_____

3. After being reassured by God, what two things did Moses promise the people **(verse 8)?** _____

_____

4. According to **verse 4,** what was one purpose of these miracles?

_____

5. According to **verse 12,** what was another purpose of these miracles?

_____

6. To get some idea of the magnitude of the ongoing miracle of manna, it helps to realize that 150 railroad boxcars of food and 1,000 tank cars of water would not have been enough to provide for even one day for so many people. God supplied all their needs, including some 2,000,000 pounds of manna, every day for how many years **(verse 35)?**

_____

7. What parallel can you find between **Exodus 16** and the Fourth Petition of the Lord's Prayer?

_____

_____

YAHWEH PROTECTS

1. The Sinai Peninsula was not entirely uninhabited. Read **Exodus 17:8-16.** What need arose next?

_____

2. Who attacked Israel? _____
3. What was the name of Moses' general?

_____

4. How did God demonstrate that it was His power that was winning the battle and not the cleverness or strength of the Israelites?

_____

_____

GOOD ADVICE

1. How did Moses spend most of his time according to **Exodus 18:13-16?**

_____

2. What did Jethro think about this **(Exodus 18:17-18)?** _____

3. What did he advise **(verses 19-23)?**

_____

_____

4. What did Moses think of this advice **(verse 24)?**

_____

5. How do *you* react when someone tries to give you advice? Have you ever seen a situation where someone who is running a large operation almost single-handedly was advised to share his or her authority with others? What was his or her response? How do personal pride and humility enter into these situations? Be ready to discuss this in class.

THE JOY OF BEING AT GOD'S MERCY

Yahweh was encouraging infant Israel to rely on Him for all its needs. He wanted the people to rely on his love and mercy. He wanted to sustain them in any and every adversity. He yearned for their expressions of gratitude and praise.

1. Who are God's chosen people today (**1 Peter 2:9)?**

_____

2. What does God want to teach them? What does He want in return? Read **Matthew 6:25-34** and paraphrase its message.

_____

_____

3. What attitude does the Bible take toward laziness?

_____

4. What do you think happened when an Israelite refused to go out to collect manna on a given day?

_____

5. Summarize what the following passages say about this topic.

1 Thessalonians 4:11-12 _____

_____

2 Thessalonians 3:10 _____

6. Summarize what the Bible says about worry and work.

_____

_____

"Tell them, 'At twilight you will eat meat, and in the morning you will be filled with bread. Then you will know that I am the Lord your God.' "
Exodus 16:12

Session 29

Schooling at Sinai

You probably know something about eagles. They usually build their nests, called *aeries*, in the tops of tall trees or on high cliffs. Eaglets leave the aerie when they are about 11 or 12 weeks old. They can't fly very well at first, so they stay near the aerie. When the eaglet begins to fly, the mother will hover nearby. She will swoop down and let it rest on her wings when its wings get tired. Moses used this picture when he compared God's care to **an eagle that stirs up its nest and hovers over its young, that spreads its wings to catch them and carries them on its pinions (Deuteronomy 32:11).**

Eventually the eaglet will fly away on its own. The mother will have provided the care and schooling necessary for an eaglet to become an eagle.

NOW WHAT?

1. Moses knew that Yahweh was the real Leader and that he was really a figurehead. So Moses reported to God for further instructions. Read **Exodus 19:3-8.** What do you think the words, **"I carried you on eagles' wings" (verse 4)** meant to Moses and the people?

_____

_____

2. What relationship did God establish with the people? _____

_____

3. As a kingdom of priests, God expected Israel to share the Gospel with the nations around them. They also foreshadowed the relationship we have with God. Describe that relationship **(1 Peter 2:9-10).**

_____

_____

4. What did God demand of the people as His "treasured possesion" **(Exodus 19:5)?**

_____

5. How did the people respond **(verse 8)?**

_____

_____

_____

6. Read **19:9—20:21.** What was the atmosphere like at this time?

_____

7. What name do we give to the basic rules that God speaks here?

_____

8. Do you know another name for them?

_____

9. These rules teach us how we can express the new relationship with God, which the Holy Spirit has brought us. The first rules **(20:1-11)** deal with and define our proper relationship with _____and the remaining rules **(20:12-17)** guide our relationships with

_____

OF WHAT VALUE IS THE LAW?

1. Read **Romans 4:15.** What does the Law show us? _____

2. Because of our sin, we cannot hope to be saved on our own. And the Law keeps on making us seem more and more sinful. What word from **Romans 5:20** tells how we can hope to be saved? _____

3. **Hebrews 9:15** calls the Law the first covenant. How are we saved from the sins committed under the first covenant?

_____

_____

4. Read **Galatians 3:15-25.** God gave His covenant to Abraham 430 years before He gave the Law. Describe the relationship the Law had to the covenant.

_____

_____

5. Explain why Jesus is called the "Seed of the promise."

_____

6. According to **verses 19** and **24**, what was the purpose of the Law?

_____

_____

7. Read **1 Corinthians 15:56-57.** What does Paul call the Law?

_____

8. Who gives us the victory over sin? _____

NEW GROUND RULES

1. Try to imagine living with your family—including aunts, uncles, cousins, and all their pets, plus flocks of sheep, chickens, and cattle—in the wilderness with two million other campers. What are the chances that arguments will start? What might the arguments be about? _____

_____

2. In **Exodus 21—23** God gave some detailed instructions on civil and social problems that the Israelites would be dealing with as they learned to live and work together as a nation. We call our nation—of the people, by the people, and for the people—a democracy. What name do we give to a nation that is ruled directly by God?

_____

3. After each of the following passages, write the part of living that was governed by the passage:

Exodus 21:12 _____

Exodus 21:16 _____

Exodus 21:17 _____

Exodus 21:18-19 _____

Exodus 22:2-3 _____

Exodus 22:16 _____

Exodus 22:21 _____

Exodus 23:4-5 _____

A COVENANT IS RATIFIED

1. Read **Exodus 23:20-33.** What did God require of those who wanted to remain in the covenant community?

v. 22 _____

vv. 24-25 _____

v. 32 _____

v. 33 _____

2. Briefly describe what God promised to do if the people kept their part of this covenant.

_____

_____

3. Now Moses took this more detailed information to the people. How did they respond **(24:3)?**

_____

4. After writing all this down, what did Moses call these laws **(24:7)?** _____

5. Then, after the people promised a third time to obey, Moses sprinkled them with blood from the sacrificial bulls to seal the agreement. What did this foreshadow **(Hebrews 9:11-14)?**

_____

6. When today do we receive the blood of Christ?

_____

7. Some people in Jesus and Paul's day believed that they could keep the laws God gave at Sinai. They hoped that keeping those laws would save them. How does Paul respond to that hope in **Galatians 5:4-6?**

_____

_____

CLOSER TO GOD

1. New commitments often draw us closer to God. Many people feel self-satisfied if they have committed one hour each Sunday morning to Him. Others see their involvement in Sunday school or choir as examples of exceptionally generous commitment. God wants to be Lord of all of our lives—24 hours a day—not to spoil our fun, but to increase our joy. What does Jesus say about this in **John 10:10?**

_____

_____

2. It's hard to imagine a life more adventuresome than a life that is God-oriented. Satan, however, throws up a smoke screen of lies to prevent us from increasing our commitment to God. We need to turn to God for the help that will empower us to make a commitment to Him. List one commitment you would like to make to God.

_____

You yourselves have seen what I did to Egypt, and how I carried you on eagles' wings and brought you to Myself. Now if you obey Me fully and keep My covenant, then out of all nations you will be My treasured possession. Although the whole earth is Mine, you will be for Me a kingdom of priests and a holy nation.

Exodus 19:4-6

Session 30

New Relationships Are Formed (Ceremonial Laws)

Not long ago, the world's largest uncut diamond was on display at the Smithsonian Institution in Washington, D.C., for six weeks. The gem-in-the-rough weighed 6-1/4 ounces. News reporters stated that it would take the most skilled diamond cutter in the world 18 months to study and ultimately to shape the stone into a gem of approximately 550 carats.

The first cutting of a diamond, called the cleaving, is the most important. If the brittle stone is struck exactly right, it will split naturally in the desired direction. If it is struck incorrectly, it will shatter. And then, after the gem has been roughly cut in this manner, great care and precise planning must continue. Only then can one achieve the ideal angle and number of facets that will bring out the brilliant, multihued flashes of light for which diamonds are so famous and which make them so desirable as jewelry.

We can compare the people of Israel to diamonds. Sin caused them to be the rough, uncut diamonds. But God had rescued them **(Genesis 3:15).** He had brought Abraham, Isaac, Jacob, and now the nation of Israel into a covenant relationship with Himself. Carefully God showed them they could trust Him—at the Red Sea, in the wilderness, and at Sinai. Now He was about to continue the "cutting and shaping" process. During this session you will see how God:

1. Assured the people daily that He was with them

2. Instructed them how to express and acknowledge their covenant relationship with Him in rituals and forms of worship

PRE-SINAI WORSHIP

God used worship as one of the means by which He cut and shaped this diamond in the rough. Let's review what we have learned about worship so far in our study of the Old Testament.

Scripture Section	Worship Principle Demonstrated or Stated
Genesis 4:3-4	_____
Genesis 4:26	_____
Genesis 8:20-21	_____
Genesis 24:26, 48	_____
Exodus 20:4-5	_____
Exodus 20:25	_____
Exodus 33:7-11	_____

They were relatively simple, basic rules for worship, and anyone could carry them out anywhere. But now God was about to give worship a more definite form and a new setting—a form and setting that would daily remind the people of God's covenant with them.

A NEW SETTING FOR WORSHIP

1. For 40 days and 40 nights, on the top of Mount Sinai, the almighty God described the new setting for national worship. According to **Exodus 25:8**, what did the tabernacle show the people about their invisible God?

_____

2. The tabernacle would become the central structure of the Israelite community and the focus of its life and activities. God gave very explicit instructions **(Exodus 25:9** and **40; 27:8; 31:11)** for the ark of the covenant with its mercy seat, the portable house of worship, its courtyard and furnishings, the priestly garments to be worn by those who conduct the worship, and how all these things are to be consecrated and used. In **Hebrews 8:5** we learn why God wanted Moses to follow His instructions so closely. Why?

_____

3. Read **Exodus 25:10-22.** Describe the first and most important part of the worship setting **(verses 10-11).**

_____

4. What were the rings and poles for **(verse 14)?**

_____

5. God told Moses to place inside something that would give permanent testimony to God's commands that Israel be a holy people and abstain from breaking the commandments. What was it **(verse 16)?**

_____

6. What was the cover called **(verse 17)?**

_____

Describe it briefly.

_____

7. What important purpose was this ark to serve **(verse 22)?**

_____

8. What were the two rooms of the tabernacle called **(26:30-35)?**

_____

9. What was inside each room?

_____

_____

10. What was the area around the tabernacle called **(27:9)?**

_____

A NEW ORDER

Next, the Lord gave Moses instructions about those who would be responsible for carrying out the worship requirements. God chose and ordained the priests for that special office.

1. What was the purpose of their priestly robes **(Exodus 28:2)?**

_____

of the breastpiece **(28:29)?**

_____

of the Urim and Thummim **(28:30)?**

_____

2. How long did the ordination process take **(29:35)?**

_____

3. What offerings were to be made daily **(29:38-41)?**

_____

4. What other daily duty did Aaron, as high priest, have **(30:7-8)?**

_____

5. How was the service of the tent of meeting to be financed **(30:11-16)?**

_____

6. What two large objects stood in the courtyard **(27:1; 30:18)?**

_____

7. Making all these beautiful and costly items required exceptional skill. How could an Israelite slave know how to do all this **(28:3)?**

_____

8. What weekly religious observation served as a sign between God and His covenant people **(31:12)?**

_____

9. How were these sacred items and ceremonies a blessing to the nation of Israel throughout the Old Testament **(29:45-46)?**

_____

_____

THE FOCUS OF ISRAEL'S WORSHIP

1. What tool was used to inscribe the tablets of stone that God gave to Moses **(31:18)?**

_____

Those were the very tablets that the ark of testimony was built to house. God made certain that the Israelites would recognize the importance of the covenant promise they made with Him **(24:3).**

2. The cover for the ark is also known as the "mercy seat." The high priest sprinkled blood on the golden lid of the ark to signify that the people's sins against the commandments (which were lying below the lid) had been removed from God's sight. Who met with the people at the mercy seat **(25:22)?** _____

3. The service of the priests reminded Israel that the people needed an intermediary between themselves and God. Who became the New Testament intermediary for all time, thus eliminating the need for the Old Testament priestly ceremonies **(Hebrews 7:22-25)?** _____

4. How does God describe _us_ in **1 Peter 2:9?**

_____

_____

5. We see that all the sacred items and ceremonies were rich in symbolism. God designed them to foreshadow the work of the Messiah in restoring God's people to perfect fellowship with Him. Now that the "real thing" has come, we no longer need the shadow.

WORSHIP IN OUR TIME

Copy **Colossians 2:16-17:**

_____

_____

_____

_____

Now summarize **Colossians 3:1-17**, which tells us what _our_ worship of God involves:

_____

_____

_____

_____

So I will consecrate the Tent of Meeting and the altar and will consecrate Aaron and his sons to serve Me as priests. Then I will dwell among the Israelites and be their God. They will know that I am the Lord their God, who brought them out of Egypt so that I might dwell among them. I am the Lord their God.

Exodus 29:44-46

Session 31

Rebellion and Recommitment (Israel's Adolescence)

When Maria's mother noticed the gusts of wind as the rain got heavier, she quickly began closing windows. When she got to Maria's room, she found her lying across her bed crying.

"Why, Maria! Whatever is the matter?" she asked as she sat down on the bed beside her.

"Oh, Mom, I'm so confused! Some days I feel so grown up, and other days I feel so dumb! For instance, I promised myself that I would quit eating chocolate—all sweets—so I can clear my skin and lose some weight. Then after school, when my friends suggested stopping at the Sweet Shop, guess who ordered a double fudge sundae! Why can't I control myself?"

"We all have lapses like that, Maria. It's not just you," Maria's mother soothed. Then she suggested, "Maybe it would help if you would not carry enough money to buy sundaes."

"There you go, treating me like a child again! Not carry money! The kids would make fun of me then for sure. You just don't understand," she sobbed.

Do you ever feel like Maria? Do you find yourself rebelling against your parents and needing their love all at the same time? This is very common during the teen years. It's part of growing up.

Israel's actions, as described in **Exodus 32**, were like that. They did not recognize that what God asked of them was not designed to interfere with their happiness but came from His sure knowledge of what would bring them lasting joy and undreamed-of blessings.

REBELLION

1. Review the events that happened before Moses' trip up the mountain. Summarize each of the following in one sentence:

Exodus 19:3-9_____

Exodus 20:18-21 _____

Exodus 24:17-18 _____

2. You probably know the story of the golden calf in **Exodus 32.** In spite of all the miracles God had performed for His people, they forgot His power and love. They went back to the idol worship they had experienced in Egypt! How did God react to their disloyalty **(Exodus 32:9-10)?**

_____

_____

3. Put yourself in Moses' sandals. God was offering to release him from the responsibility of leading these rebellious people. The Promised Land might have been called the Land of Moses! How profoundly God tested Moses' integrity as a leader! But God also gave Moses the power to pass the test with flying colors. Read **Exodus 32:11-14** and write two reasons Moses gave for urging God to spare the Israelites:

_____

_____

Clearly, Moses valued God's glory more than his own.

4. How did Moses react when he discovered the extent of Israel's rebellion?

(32:19)? _____

(32:20)? _____

5. What was the "last straw" as far as Moses was concerned **(verse 25)?**

_____

_____

6. It was time for strong leadership. What decision did Moses ask the people to make **(verse 26)?**

_____

7. Who rallied to Moses' side on the basis of this decision?

_____

8. These were the descendants of Jacob's son, Levi. It seems likely that they had worshiped the golden calf along with the others. But now they turned to God in repentance (perhaps because Moses was from their tribe—but so was Aaron). Then they put their loyalty into action by following Moses' directions to kill 3,000 of their fellow Israelites. When they obeyed, what did Moses say to them (verse 29)?

_____

_____

From this point on, the Levites would have a place of honor among their people.

9. Having disciplined his people, Moses went back to God with an ardent plea. What shows his great compassion for the people (verse 32)?

_____

10. Because of this action (and others), some people refer to Moses as a ''type of Christ.'' What do you think this means?

_____

11. In mercy God spared the lives of the remaining Israelites, but He disciplined them. How (verse 35)?

_____

12. The final blow came when God told Moses to lead the people to the Promised Land but that He would not go with them. The people responded by mourning and repentance (33:4-6). What was Moses' plea to God (verse 15)?

_____

13. What ''argument'' did Moses use with God (verse 16)?

_____

_____

14. How did our merciful God answer Moses (verse 17)?

_____

_____

MERCY AND RECOMMITMENT

1. Moses, now more than 80 years old, chiseled out two more stone tablets and carried them up the steep slopes of Mount Sinai, where God appeared to him again. How did God describe Himself in **Exodus 34:6-7?**

_____

_____

Moses again pleaded with God to come with the Israelites, to forgive them and accept them back as His inheritance—and God did (34:10, 27). New tablets of stone (verse 28) represented the restored covenant.

2. What did the Israelites do that showed they made a new commitment to their covenant with Yahweh (35:21-29; 36:3-7)?

_____

_____

_____

3. The remainder of **Exodus** describes the way the people meticulously carried out God's instructions for His house of worship. We know they worked fast. When was the tabernacle set up (40:17)?

_____

GOD'S HOUSE VALIDATED

1. In **Exodus 40:34-38**, how did God show the people that He was pleased with their work and accepted the completed tabernacle?

_____

_____

2. What was the relationship between the cloud and the Israelites during their troubles?

_____

_____

The cloud must have been a truly thrilling sight and a source of constant comfort for all Israel! Do you sometimes wish you had been living back then as an Israelite?

3. Where does God live now (**1 Corinthians 6:19-20)?**

_____

Study the ways God is asking us to relate to Him as His chosen people today. Be ready to talk about it in class. How very blessed we are! How thrilling and comforting it is to know that God now lives *in each believer!*

All the skilled craftsmen who were doing all the work on the sanctuary left their work and said to Moses, "The people are bringing more than enough for doing the work the Lord commanded to be done."

Exodus 36:4-5

Session 32

Atonement/Justification

LIFE WITH GOD: PRODUCED AND DIRECTED BY GOD HIMSELF

God has prepared an unforgettable, fantastic, mind-boggling, bigger-than-life experience that will remain as the unsurpassed triumph of all eternity. Because it has not had its premiere, critics can only speculate what it may feature. Inside sources have alluded to settings composed of pure gold and precious stones, a cast of thousands upon thousands of supernatural beings, as well as audience participation. Attendance is optional, and tickets will be presented to any individual free of charge upon request. No group arrangements are available.

Have you ever seen tickets to a very expensive play or concert? They usually don't look very impressive, do they? They're just ordinary heavy paper, sometimes colored and printed with the name of the performance, the location, the date, and the seat number. Yet whoever holds that ticket—old or young, rich or poor, famous or unknown—will be allowed to occupy that seat and enjoy all the privileges that the ticket allows.

Let's suppose that you and your friend receive two tickets for front-row seats at the most popular play on Broadway. But you decide that the tickets are too ordinary looking. So you proceed to design very elegant, hand-lettered tickets on fine parchment. Your tickets include all the information that is printed on the original tickets—plus a border design. Aesthetically they're far superior to the originals.

What will happen if you present these beautiful tickets to the usher as you enter the performance hall? Why? What makes the drab-looking tickets more acceptable?

VALID TICKETS VS. COUNTERFEITS

Margaret Mead, the famous anthropologist and writer, once said that she abandoned her agnosticism because she found that every culture, no matter how primitive or sophisticated, worshiped a higher power. Every human being created hungers to know God. That search is what we call religion. Many religions involve a multitude of gods. Hinduism, for example, acknowledges millions of gods.

All cultures recognize their lack of holiness, a condition that we call sin. They all devise some sort of system to overcome their feelings of guilt and provide the "tickets" that will provide entrance into peaceful existence with their higher power. Some offer animal sacrifices; some offer human sacrifices; some believe in a system of reincarnation that allows individuals to gradually work their way toward greater and greater perfection.

Once we accept the idea that there *is* a God, it is obvious that no one but God Himself has the authority to decide what must be done to remove the guilt that we all share. But only Christianity, of all the world's religions, does not rely on the performance of certain rituals in order to cleanse us. The Bible reveals the only acceptable solution to sin: faith in a God-given Messiah. Christians recognize Jesus Christ as that Messiah, whose blood was shed to wash away our sins.

ATONEMENT IN THE OLD TESTAMENT

1. The process of reconciling sinners with a holy God is called *atonement*—AT-ONE-MENT. What happens when something clean comes into contact with something dirty? _____

The holy God, because of what and who He is, cannot accept sin into His presence. It would be like matter coming into contact with antimatter. They cannot coexist.

2. Let's review briefly. How did we become sinful **(Psalm 51:5)?**

_____

_____

3. How universal is this condition? Are there any exceptions? See **Psalm 14:3.** _____

4. Why can't we cleanse ourselves from sin? See **Isaiah 64:6.**

_____

5. Satan certainly will not help us—even if he could. Only God can restore us to life. But in order to do so, He must remove our sin—the cause of spiritual

and temporal death. In **Genesis 3:15** He gave the first indication of His plan for accomplishing this. You've read about the shedding of the blood of sacrificial animals by Abel, Noah, Abraham, and others. During the 10th plague in Egypt at the time of Moses, what was required to prevent the death of the firstborn?

6. What blood was shed to make atonement for Israel's priest **(Exodus 29:3, 12, 15-16, 19-21)?**

7. What sacrifice made atonement for the altar **(Exodus 29:36)?**

8. **Leviticus 16** describes the most holy day in the Jewish year. What is it called?

ATONEMENT IN THE NEW TESTAMENT

1. Are people still born sinful? (See 1 **John 1:8.**)

2. Yet we do not sacrifice animals for our sins. Why not? Read **Hebrews 9:19-28.** The Old Testament sacrifices were "copies" or "pictures" of the actual, universal atonement. According to **verse 26**, how has our sin been put away?

3. What does John say about Jesus' blood in **1 John 1:7?**

Do you see that, according to God's plan for our salvation, the blood that Jesus shed on the cross is our "ticket" to heaven?

JUSTIFICATION

Justification. What do we mean by this word? People use the word in two ways:

Objective justification. When Jesus suffered and died for us, He saved the whole world **(John 3:16).** In an objective sense, every person in the world has been justified.

Subjective justification, or personal justification. To personally receive the benefits of Christ's atonement, we must "accept" it—that is, we must not reject it. As Martin Luther points out in his explanation to the

Third Article, we cannot accept Christ's atonement on our own; we receive faith and are thus made holy only through the power of the Holy Spirit working through the Gospel.

Subjective justification can be compared to accepting and using the ticket provided to you. Just as a valid ticket, if unused, does not benefit its owner, so each individual—by the power of the Holy Spirit—must recognize Christ's mighty work of atonement (objective justification) for what it is and claim its promises in order to obtain its benefits (subjective justification). "Counterfeit" atonements are not acceptable to God for our entrance into heaven.

1. What does **Romans 3:20** say about the "counterfeit ticket" of good works when it comes to justification?

2. What is the valid "ticket" **(Romans 3:28)?**

3. Does **Galatians 2:16** agree?

4. What purpose do rules (the Law) serve according to **Galatians 3:24?**

5. When, by the power of the Holy Spirit, we receive and rely on the "ticket" of atonement, we are justified or "allowed to come in" to the presence of God. What do we experience there (**Romans 5:1** and **9**)?

6. How complete is our cleansing from sin? (See **Isaiah 1:18b.**)

Whenever Satan tries to make you doubt your salvation, read **Romans 8:31-39** aloud and know that you are more than a conqueror *through Him who loves us* **(verse 37).**

Christ did not enter a man-made sanctuary that was only a copy of the true one; He entered heaven itself, now to appear for us in God's presence. Nor did He enter heaven to offer Himself again and again, the way the high priest enters the Most Holy Place every year. . . . Christ was sacrificed once to take away the sins of many people.
Hebrews 9:24, 25, and 28

Session 33

Firstfruits—Grateful Response to God's Grace

FIRSTFRUITS AND TITHES FROM ISRAEL

You may have noticed that the people of Israel brought several kinds of offerings to God. We read about the burnt offering in **Leviticus 1**, the grain offering in **chapter 2,** the fellowship offering in **chapter 3,** the sin offering in **4:1—5:13,** and the guilt offering in **5:14—6:7.** Then, in **6:8—7:38,** God gave further instructions about these offerings.

Why did God ask the people to bring these offerings? Through some of them (such as the sin and guilt offerings) the people confessed their sins and received assurance that God forgave them. (Recall what we said about the atonement in the last session.) Other offerings (such as the grain offering) reminded the people how God provided them with food.

1. Read **Leviticus 7:12** and **16.** Why did the people bring the fellowship offering?

_____

_____

2. God told the people to bring the firstfruits of their crops when they celebrated the Feast of the Harvest **(Exodus 23:16** and **19),** the firstfruits of the wheat harvest when they celebrated the Feast of Weeks **(34:22),** and the firstfruits of grain for the grain offering **(Leviticus 2:12).** God also told the people to bring Him a tithe of everything from the land **(Leviticus 27:30).** This means that He asked them to give Him one tenth of their crops. The priests and Levites received these firstfruit offerings and tithes. Why? (See **Numbers 18:20-24.)**

_____

_____

Some of the tithes and firstfruits were used for festival celebrations and for the poor **(Deuteronomy 14:22-29).**

3. Summarize the directions God gave the people in **Deuteronomy 14:22-29.** Notice especially the attitude of the people as they brought these gifts **(verse 26).**

_____

_____

_____

4. Now find **Deuteronomy 26:1-15.** Notice the words the people were to use when they brought their firstfruits and tithes to God. What did the words in the following verses show about God or about the people's relationship with God?

verse 3 _____

verse 8 _____

verse 9 _____

verse 15 _____

5. To summarize, list four reasons why the people of Israel brought special offerings to God, especially offerings of firstfruits and tithes.

_____

_____

_____

_____

6. Do you recall what happened when Moses asked the people to bring offerings for building the tabernacle? Why did Moses have to finally tell the people to stop bringing offerings **(Exodus 36:2-7)?**

_____

_____

OFFERINGS TODAY

In the last section we saw how the people of Israel recognized God's love for them. They responded to that love in many ways, including offerings of their firstfruits and tithes.

Read **2 Corinthians 5:15.** This passage summarizes God's love for us and the way God moves us to respond to that love.

1. How did Jesus show His love for us?

_____

_____

2. How does the love of Jesus move His followers to respond?

_____

_____

_____

Such a response requires that we manage everything God has given us in ways that are pleasing to Him. The Bible has a word for this response of managing all the resources placed into our hands—*stewardship*. The following is a definition of Biblical, or Christian, stewardship.

Christian stewardship is the free and joyous activity by the child of God and God's family, the church,

   a. as a response to God's love in Christ

   b. in managing all of life and life's resources

   c. in a God-pleasing manner and in partnership with Him

   d. towards the ultimate purpose of glorifying Him

   e. by making disciples of all nations

3. This definition includes bringing offerings of money to God, but it suggests that we show our love to God in *many* ways. What are some other parts of life and life's resources that *you* manage?

_____

_____

_____

4. Choose two of those parts of life and life's resources. How can you manage them in a God-pleasing manner and in partnership with Him?

_____

_____

_____

5. How can you glorify God by making disciples of all nations as you manage life and life's resources? Use an example from your own life as you answer this question.

_____

_____

_____

_____

6. Money. Perhaps the management of other re-

sources we have received from God is more important, but we usually get more emotionally involved when we talk about stewardship of money.

Read **Mark 12:41-44.** Why did Jesus praise the widow?

_____

_____

7. Paul wrote about an offering in his letters to the Corinthians. What two guidelines did he give for their offerings in **1 Corinthians 16:2?**

_____

_____

_____

8. We find extensive remarks about offerings in **2 Corinthians 8** and **9.** First of all, Paul provided an example of generosity from the Macedonian Christians **(8:1-5).** What led them to give?

_____

9. How much did they give **(v. 3)?**

_____

10. With what attitude did they give **(vv. 3-4)?**

_____

11. What does each of the following verses say about giving?

9:6 _____

9:7 _____

9:8 _____

9:10 _____

9:11 _____

9:13-14 _____

9:15 _____

12. Make your own stewardship commitment. Write it on a separate sheet of paper. Share it with God but not with anyone else. Include a commitment of financial offerings to God, but also make commitments about how you will manage other parts of your life and life's resources.

He died for all, that those who live should no longer live for themselves but for Him who died for them and was raised again.

2 Corinthians 5:15

Session 34

Roots: Final Instructions at Sinai

Baby Margaret became one of God's children through Baptism when she was only one week old. At age three, when she started going to Sunday school, she began to memorize **Psalm 23**—one small phrase at a time—and she learned to sing a number of songs, such as "Jesus Loves Me, This I Know." Later, in her congregation's elementary school, she became familiar with stories from the Old and New Testaments, memorized hymn stanzas, and studied Luther's Small Catechism.

Step by step Margaret became aware of all the things God had done for her. Day by day she grew in her understanding and appreciation of what God had done for her to make her His child. Margaret's roots in God's family grew deeper and deeper. When she was older, she repeated many of these hymns, Bible verses and stories, and parts of the Catechism. Whenever she did this, she thought about her roots—she remembered what God had done for her. And as she remembered, her faith continued to grow.

ISRAEL'S ROOTS

Israel's experiences that are recorded in the first ten chapters of **Numbers** reminded them again of their roots. Again and again the people saw evidences of God's mercy and power. Again and again God told them to do something that would remind them and their children of all He had done for them. Now there would be a climaxing program of taking stock, rededicating, and remembering before they entered the next stage of their life with God. These final events at Sinai helped them remember their roots.

1. God instructed Moses to take a census (this explains the use of the term *Numbers*) of the Israelite community. What was the purpose of this census **(1:45)?**

_____

_____

_____

2. How many men were there over the age of 20?

_____

3. Which son of Jacob is father of two tribes as listed in the census **(verse 32)?** _____

4. Which son of Jacob is omitted from the census?

_____

5. Why?

_____

_____

6. In what way did the census help the people remember their roots?

_____

_____

7. Compare this incident with **Luke 2:1.** In what way can we think of the **Numbers** census as a shadow of this one? Who was about to begin a "journey" in each instance?

_____

_____

ORDERLINESS

1. Part of Israel's "taking stock" included planning ahead. Can you imagine the confusion that would result if the people in a city of more than a million inhabitants were told one day to "camp here" (even without the thousands of animals the Israelites had)? God organized the Israelites in a way that helped them move and set up camp in an orderly fashion. How would this help them?

_____

2. Using **Numbers 2** as your resource, enter the names of the 12 tribes in the boxes in the sketch on page 77.

3. Place the names of the sons of Levi in the proper ovals, according to **Numbers 3:21-37.** Who was assigned to camp directly in front of the tabernacle **(verse 38)?** _____

REDEDICATION AND REMEMBRANCE

The offerings of dedication brought by each tribe to the newly erected house of worship gave public testimony to Israel's covenant relationship with Yahweh. It was one year since they left Egypt, and each day for 12 days one of the 12 tribes, in turn, brought offerings and sacrifices to the tabernacle. Immediately after this, it was time to observe the first Passover festival. By constantly reminding themselves of their former slavery the people remembered their roots. They remembered to worship regularly and to gratefully serve Yahweh, who miraculously freed them, provided for them, and promised them great blessings.

1. Through worship, especially through the Lord's Supper, we recall being free from bondage. What bondage was this?

_____

2. When were we freed from it?

_____

3. How does worship help us remember that we're free?

_____

_____

TIME TO MOVE ON

1. God had now prepared the Israelites to function as His chosen people. It was time to move on. In order to visualize how this was accomplished, read **Numbers 10:14-33** and then place the proper sequence number next to each group named in the drawing of the camp plan. Place No. 1 by Moses and Aaron **(verse 33)**, No. 2 by Judah **(verse 14)**, and continue. What a sight this grand march must have been!

2. The pillar of cloud by day, the pillar of fire by night, and the ark of the covenant all reminded the Israelites of their roots—of their covenant relationship with God. As His chosen people, they had nothing to fear: God was present in their midst.

As members of the body of Christ we, too, have nothing to fear. What has God given us to remind us of our roots—of our covenant relationship with Him?

_____

3. We are truly blessed to have Bibles so readily available to us. We can read God's precious promises for ourselves. Why do we no longer need to depend on priests **(1 Peter 2:9)?**

_____

4. We no longer need an ark of the covenant to provide a place for us to meet with God. Why not **(Matthew 18:20)?**

_____

_____

A BLESSING FROM GOD

1. About the time the people finished the tabernacle, God gave Moses the words Aaron was to use when he blessed the people **(Numbers 6:22-27).** How did this blessing show that God loved the people?

_____

2. This is a three-part blessing. We can find special meaning in this. We can find a shadow of a truth that God revealed more clearly about Himself in the New Testament. What do you think this is?

_____

3. Tell about a time when you felt especially happy because you could be sure of God's blessing.

This is how you are to bless the Israelites. Say to them: "The Lord bless you and keep you; the Lord make His face shine upon you and be gracious to you; the Lord turn His face toward you and give you peace."

Numbers 6:23-26

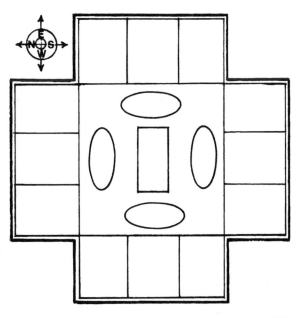

Session 35

Concluding Activities for Unit 5

Answer the following questions to help you review unit 5.

TERMS

On a separate sheet of paper write definitions of the following terms:

1. theocracy
2. atonement
3. tabernacle
4. tithes
5. firstfruits
6. census
7. ceremonial laws
8. objective justification
9. subjective justification
10. Levites
11. priests
12. ark of the covenant
13. mercy seat
14. most holy place
15. manna
16. foreshadow

SHORT ANSWER

Write a short answer to each of the following questions:

1. What were some ways God acted to increase the people's trust in Him?

_____

_____

_____

_____

2. Describe the relationship between work and worry.

_____

_____

_____

_____

3. How did the people know that God was responsible for the victory over the Amalekites?

_____

_____

_____

4. Why did the people ask Aaron to make a golden calf?

_____

_____

_____

5. Describe how this large nation was able to travel and camp in an orderly way.

_____

_____

_____

_____

6. How did the ceremonial laws help the people remember God and what He had done for them?

_____

_____

_____

7. How did the various people assist with the building of the tabernacle?

_____

_____

_____

Unit 6

The Covenant Nation Begins to Function

Do you remember the promises that God made to Abraham? Which ones had already been fulfilled by the time the Israelites left Mount Sinai?

Certainly Abraham already had descendants; they were becoming a mighty nation; they were prospering. Now they were ready for the next step—to occupy a land of their own! They were not to depend on their own military abilities. In **Exodus 34:10-11** God had promised, **Before all your people I will do wonders never before done in any nation in all the world. The people you live among will see how awesome is the work that I, the Lord, will do for you. Obey what I command you today. I will drive out before you the Amorites, Canaanites, Hittites, Perizzites,** Hivites and Jebusites.

God had controlled the 10 plagues, parted the Red Sea, and miraculously provided food and water for these millions of people. This same God would drive out the people now occupying the Promised Land. The time was ripe. The Israelites had been freed, nurtured, taught, and organized. They were ready to function as a nation, to serve as a channel for God's blessings to all people. How could they possibly fail? Only if they turned their backs on God.

Session 36

Equipped for Action (Israel Moves North)

G od hath not promised skies always blue,
Flower-strewn pathways, all our lives through;
God hath not promised sun without rain,
Joy without sorrow, peace without pain.
But God hath promised strength for the day,
Rest for the laborer, light for the way,
Grace for the trials, help from above,
Unfailing sympathy, undying love.

Anne Johnson Flint

1. Some people think of Christianity as a sort of insurance policy. If you faithfully "pay your premiums" in the form of church attendance, financial gifts, and good deeds, then God "owes" you a trouble-free life. According to **Genesis 3**, why will we never have a trouble-free life here on earth?

_____

2. How did Jesus teach His disciples to respond after they had done everything they were told to do **(Luke 17:7-10)?**

_____

3. On another occasion, Jesus' words affected His disciples so deeply that we find the words recorded in three of the four gospels: **Matthew 16:24-25; Mark 8:34-35;** and **Luke 9:23-24.** Copy one of these selections here. _____

_____

The second verse in each of these passages reminds us that things that seem like a loss may actually result in gain for those who give their lives to God.

ISRAEL GRUMBLES

1. The Israelites apparently hadn't learned to take hardships as stepping stones to success. Read **Numbers 11:1-3.** How did God react to the people's complaints? _____

_____

2. What did the people complain about in **verse 4?** _____

_____

3. At their complaints, Moses reached the end of his patience. Read what he said to God in **Numbers 11:10-15.** Notice that when God answered Moses, He didn't even mention the problem of food at first. What did He recognize as the greatest need of the people **(verse 17)?** _____

4. What did He tell Moses to promise the people **(verses 18-20)?**

_____

5. Paraphrase the reaction of Moses **(verse 21).**

_____

6. Paraphrase God's reply **(verse 23).**

_____

GOD DELIVERS

1. First God provided more Spirit-empowered leaders. Read **Numbers 11:24-30**. For some reason two of the leaders, Eldad and Medad, had not gone to the tabernacle, but remained in camp. Their prophecy in the camp caused some furor. Who brought the message to Moses **(v. 28)?** _____

2. Moses recognized the reason for his objection. What was it **(v. 29)?** _____

3. Here, in the second part of **verse 29**, we find another illustration of the exceptional character God had given Moses. How did *Moses* feel about others getting the Lord's Spirit?

_____

4. Next, **11:31-34**, God delivered the meat He promised. How many quail did each person gather?

_____

5. What happened because of their greed **(v. 33)?**

_____

RACIAL PREJUDICE AND PRIDE

1. Read **Numbers 12**. Why were Aaron and Miriam finding fault with Moses?

_____

We do not know what happened to Zipporah, the Midianite woman Moses married during his exile there. She may have died. This reference seems to be to a second wife of Moses.

2. Cush was in Africa, perhaps where Ethiopia lies today. Therefore some people speculate that the Cushite whom Moses named was black. At any rate, she was not a Israelite, and that hurt the pride of Aaron and Miriam. They were the recognized leaders of Israel. What titles did they hold **(Leviticus 21:10; Exodus 15:20; 29:1,5-7)?**

_____

3. But they were not satisfied. Even if Moses knew about their gossiping, he did not act in his own behalf. Why not **(Numbers 12:3)?**

_____

4. So God acted. What happened to Miriam?

_____

5. How did Aaron show that he had learned his lesson **(v. 11)?** _____

_____

6. Some would say that "it's only human nature" to find fault. But if we are new creatures in Christ, we no longer are slaves to our human natures. Rather, we will, through the indwelling of the Holy Spirit, begin to encourage and build each other up.

Read St. Paul's advice in **Galatians 5:24-26** and copy the last two verses here.

_____

_____

7. Summarize what **Romans 12:17-21** teaches about getting revenge.

8. While God wants us to obey His leaders and not gossip about them, He certainly does not want us to follow false prophets. Read **1 John 4:1-6**. How can we recognize them?

_____

9. What does Jesus tell us in **Matthew 7:15-20?**

_____

10. Jesus is our example. Let's look at how He dealt with unacceptable religious leaders. Read **Matthew 23**. Did Jesus tell the people that it's okay to be disrespectful? _____

11. Should the leaders be obeyed? _____

12. Beginning at **verse 13**, to whom was Jesus speaking? _____

13. Did He pretend to agree with them? _____

14. Did He state His objections clearly? _____

15. When will these leaders have to give account, according to **Matthew 12:33-37?**

_____

16. Meanwhile, what are we to do about them **(Romans 16:17-18; 2 Timothy 2:14; Hebrews 13:17)?**

_____

_____

Moses said, "Here I am among six hundred thousand men on foot, and You say, 'I will give them meat to eat for a whole month!' . . . Would they have enough if all the fish in the sea were caught for them?"

The Lord answered Moses, "Is the Lord's arm too short? You will now see whether or not what I say will come true for you."

Numbers 11:21-23

Session 37

God's Plan and Israel's Rebellion

When Joni Eareckson graduated from Wood-lawn Senior High School, she had just about everything a young woman could ask for: a loving, prosperous family, popularity, prize-winning athletic skills, an alert mind, acceptance at a fine college, a lovely home in the Baltimore suburbs, and a ranch where she could stable her horses. On July 30—just weeks after her graduation—a dive into the cool waters of Chesapeake Bay changed her entire life. She became paralyzed from the neck down!

Think for a moment how you would react in that situation. Would you give up on life?on God? Joni (pronounced Johnny) nearly did, but her family and friends encouraged her to believe that **in all things God works for the good of those who love Him (Romans 8:28).** Joni not only survived—she became a fine artist, married a loving husband, and helped others face their own doubts and crises with her books and personal testimony before large audiences. Her life is even the subject of a movie in which she stars. She remains almost entirely paralyzed, but God has made her a successful and caring individual.

Maybe you know someone who has suffered tragedy but who manages to function well and spreads cheer to others. And you probably also know people who, even though they have been abundantly blessed, always manage to find something to complain about and find excuses for failure. Be ready to tell about them.

ISRAEL'S GREAT OPPORTUNITY

1. The Israelites, poised on the border of the Promised Land, had about everything a nation could ask for. Strong, prosperous, and well organized, they were about to be given a beautiful homeland. Read **Numbers 13.** Notice the exact words God used when He addressed Moses in **verse 2.** *How* would the Israelites get the land?

_____

God told the Israelites to send one leader from each tribe to explore the land. Can you imagine how eager God was for the people to see this beautiful land that He had promised them—**a land flowing with milk and honey?** It had rugged mountains, rolling hills, broad plains, a seacoast, lakes, rivers, and natural resources. And it was to be His special gift to them!

Notice that Joshua, Moses' aide, was one of the 12 chosen leaders **(verse 16).** Moses told them, in effect, "Take a good look around!" Examine the maps in your Bible or in the library. Note the spot where they were camped **(verse 26)** and try to locate some of the places they visited.

2. How long were these 12 scouts gone **(verse 25)?** _____

3. Considering the fact that the area involved was about 300 miles long and 50 to 100 miles wide, they must have covered it pretty thoroughly. What indicates that the single cluster of grapes they found was exceptionally large **(verse 23)?**

_____

4. How eager the Israelites must have been to hear about their new homeland! How the "evidence" must have awed them when they saw it with their own eyes. How did the 12 leaders describe the land **(v. 27)?**

_____

5. In spite of all the positives, what single negative aspect did their report focus on **(verse 28-29)?**

_____

6. To whom did most of the spies look for victory in battle **(verse 31)?** _____

7. Caleb and Joshua had the same facts on which to base their decision as did the other 10 scouts. Why were they ready to go up and take possession of the land **(13:30; 14:7-9)?**

_____

_____

ISRAEL'S TRAGIC MISTAKE

Recognizing our limitations can be either a help or

a hindrance. It helped Joshua and Caleb see that they needed God to experience victory. Unfortunately, Satan keeps most people so busy thinking about their problems that they fail to turn to God for the solutions He has ready for them.

1. Use one word to describe the attitude of the 10 scouts (13:31-33). _____

2. What conclusion did the people of the community draw (14:1-4)?

_____

3. What was their attitude toward Moses, Aaron, Joshua, and Caleb (14:5-6, 10)?

_____

4. Against whom were the people actually rebelling? _____

MOSES INTERCEDES AGAIN

1. What offer did God repeat to Moses (14:12)?

_____

2. What reason did Moses give for not accepting God's offer (14:13-16)? _____

3. What did the nations already know about the Israelites?

a. _____

b. _____

c. _____

4. Whose words does Moses quote to give his prayer authority (Numbers 14:17-18)? _____

We read those words earlier, in Exodus 34:6-7.

5. What reasons did Moses give here for God to forgive these people (Numbers 14:19)?

_____

6. Did he say that the people *deserved* forgiveness? _____

7. In what way was this prayer of Moses a type of Christ? (See, for example, Luke 23:34.)

_____

8. How did God answer Moses' prayer (Numbers 14:20)?

_____

DO GOD'S WILL—IN HIS TIME

God had given the Israelites a task; He told them that the time was right; He promised to drive their ene-mies out before them. But the people listened to the lies of men rather than to the truths of God. They said, "We won't do it!"

Then, when they faced the consequences, they said, in effect, "Well, if *that's* the way you feel about it, we'll go!" But God does not want obedience in response to force. He wants obedience born of love.

1. What does Jesus ask us to do in each of the following passages in **Matthew?** When does He want us to do it?

What	When
4:17	
5:16	
5:24	
5:34	
6:19-20	
7:1	
7:24	
25:13	
25:31-44	

2. What major task does Jesus give us in **Matthew 28:19?**

_____

3. When is the right time to do this (Hebrews 3:7-15)? _____

4. Read **Hebrews 3:16—4:16.** Summarize our "marching orders" for today.

_____

_____

_____

_____

[Joshua and Caleb said,] *"The land we passed through and explored is exceedingly good. If the Lord is pleased with us, He will lead us into that land, a land flowing with milk and honey, and will give it to us. . . . Do not be afraid of the people of the land. . . . Their protection is gone, but the Lord is with us."*

Numbers 14:7-9

Session 38

Follow the Leaders God Gives You

It seemed that the entire school was buzzing with the news. Chuck Dolby, captain of the football team and a top candidate for all-conference quarterback, had been suspended from the team. He would not play in the last game of the season—the game that would determine the conference championship!

Chuck's coach called all the plays for the team, and for most of the season Chuck had been happy with this arrangement. But two weeks ago, in a game the team was winning easily, the coach decided to go completely with a running attack in order to keep the score down. After two series of plays in which they had failed to gain a first down, Chuck decided to disobey the coach. With three consecutive passes, he led the team to another touchdown. Then, when he came to the sidelines, the coach told him, "I told you to call running plays. You're benched for the rest of the game!"

Practices were tense the following week, and the team played poorly in the next game, losing by a missed extra point. In the locker room after the game Chuck angrily told the coach, in front of the whole team, "If you would have let me pass more often, we would have won!" Then Chuck left with some of his friends and went to a party where they all drank beer—and the coach found out about it.

After the coach suspended him from the team, Chuck went to him and apologized. He volunteered to apologize in front of the whole team if he could be reinstated for the last game. But the coach said, "I'm glad you apologized. I'd like to bring you back onto the team, but I can't. Twice you openly challenged the way I ran the team. And now you committed an offense that not only broke training rules; you also broke a state law."

Was the coach fair to Chuck? Be ready to talk about this story in class.

LEADERSHIP IN ISRAEL

God's covenant people had rebelled. For 40 years they would have to wander in the wilderness. Then a new generation of Israelites would enter the Promised Land. It was a bitter pill to swallow!

1. Whom had God appointed to lead the Israelites to the Promised Land **(Exodus 3:4-10)?** _____

2. Whom did God choose to be his assistant **(4:14-16)?** _____

3. Who appointed officials to help judge the people **(18:24-26)?** _____

4. Later, when Moses needed help teaching, warning, encouraging, and strengthening the people, how many new leaders were given God's Spirit of prophecy **(Numbers 11:24-25)?** _____

Gradually, God was developing the leadership skills of His people.

Power often goes to people's heads, and the Israelites were no exception. The Bible doesn't tell us what prompted the action (perhaps it was the refusal of Moses and Aaron to disobey God and go to battle with the people against the Amalekites and Canaanites—**Numbers 14:41-45**), but a large number of Israelite leaders decided to challenge Moses and Aaron.

5. What were the names of the three "ringleaders" **(Numbers 16:1)?** _____

6. How many other people joined in the rebellion **(16:2)?** _____

7. Who were they? _____

8. Of what do they accuse Moses and Aaron **(16:3)?** _____

_____

9. Was this a justifiable charge? _____

10. What was the end result of the challenge **(16:23-35)?** _____

_____

11. What shows that the people were still not convinced that Moses and Aaron were God's appointed leaders **(verse 41)?** _____

_____

12. So God provided still another object lesson. How many more people died before the lesson was over **(verse 49)?** _____

A LASTING REMINDER

The Israelites seemed to forget the spectacular evidences of God's providence that He had shown in the plagues, the passage through the Red Sea, the quails, etc. Again and again the people had challenged their leadership. Finally God provided a lasting, visible reminder that He is the one who chooses and appoints leaders.

1. Read **Numbers 17**. What did God say that the leader of each of the 12 ancestral tribes should bring to the tent of meeting? _____

2. These represented their leadership positions—like a king's scepter—only they were probably more crude. Perhaps they were shepherd's crooks, carefully chosen and treasured branches of trees. Where was Moses to place them? _____

3. How would God indicate who His chosen leader was?

_____

4. What happened?

_____

_____

5. The evidence was indisputable. No one questioned it. In order to maintain this attitude, where was Aaron's staff to be kept?

_____

WATER FROM A ROCK—AGAIN!

Do you recall how God provided water from a rock shortly after Israel crossed the Red Sea **(Exodus 17:1-7)**? Notice that God had told Moses to strike the rock with his staff.

1. Some time later (perhaps 20 to 38 years later) the people again faced a water shortage **(Numbers 20:1-13)**. What did God tell Moses to do this time?

_____

2. Notice Moses' words in **verse 10** and his actions in **verse 11**. Why would God later say **(verse 12)**, **"You did not trust in Me enough to honor Me as holy in the sight of the Israelites"**?

_____

_____

3. In spite of Moses' attitude and actions, what did God do for the people **(verse 11)**?

_____

4. But what consequences did Moses suffer?

_____

_____

"GOD OF GRACE AND GOD OF GLORY"

In one of our hymns (*Lutheran Worship* 398) we address God as "God of Grace and God of Glory." As God of glory, He has all authority, including the authority to establish leaders whom He expects us to follow. He demands complete obedience to His leadership, as we have seen in connection with the rebellion of Korah, Dathan, and Abiram; the budding of Aaron's staff; and Moses' disobedience at Marah. Note the judgment from God in **Numbers 16:31-33, 35, 46-49; 20:12**.

The incidents in today's session also show God's grace. Because of their rebellion, His people deserved to be cut off from God. What evidence of God's grace do you find in the following verses from **Numbers**?

16:20-27 _____

16:46-48 _____

20:11 _____

The worst thing that could possibly happen to us would be for God to desert us **(Matthew 27:46)**. Look for evidence of God's presence in **Numbers 16:19, 42; 17:8-9; 20:6**.

[Korah, Dathan, and Abiram said to Moses and Aaron,] "The whole community is holy, every one of them, and the Lord is with them. Why then do you set yourselves above the Lord's assembly?" [Moses said to Korah,] "It is against the Lord that you and all your followers have banded together."
Numbers 16:3 and 11

Session 39

Marking Time (Trials, Temptations, and Types)

More than anything else, Sharon wanted to be a lovable, successful, poised homemaker like her mother. Her mom occasionally worked part time, but her home was her castle and her family's happiness her dearest desire.

Probably the joy that radiated from her mom's face caused Sharon to want that same beautiful life for herself. She easily earned good grades and excelled in several sports, but would she be able to achieve her goals as a woman, wife, and mother? She sometimes wondered.

Sharon's grandma had no doubts. She had watched Sharon as a little girl gently cradling her baby dolls and serving "tea" to her teddy bears. Sharon's skills had progressed from helping set the table to preparing full-fledged meals.

Later, Sharon's own clothing allowance taught her the value of comparative shopping and led her to decide to learn to sew some simple tops and shorts when a costly choice of designer jeans left her short of money at the beginning of summer.

Since early childhood Sharon had been preparing for her chosen career! The consumer education course that the school offered to sophomores was just one more step toward her goal.

Do you ever feel you're just "marking time"? What's one of your goals in life? As you read on, you'll discover how God led the Israelites to their goal—the Promised Land.

ISRAEL'S GOAL: OCCUPATION OF THE PROMISED LAND

Since all the able-bodied men were going to die in the wilderness, a whole new generation had to be trained to carry out God's purposes and reap the blessings promised in God's covenant. Meanwhile, they were forced to wander in foreign lands. Sometimes they met with resistance from the inhabitants and had to go around territories when they could not get permission to travel through them.

1. Which nation refused passage in **Numbers 20:14-21?** _____

2. What did Moses call Israel in his request to the king? _____

3. Whose descendants settled in the land of Edom **(Genesis 36:8)?** _____

We can conclude from Moses' message that the news of the Israelites' slavery and miraculous delivery had spread through the whole Middle East. Small wonder that the nations feared them!

The passing of 40 years and the death of everyone over 60 at the end of that time had to take place before another opportunity to occupy the Promised Land could occur.

4. As Israel skirted the borders of Edom, who died **(Numbers 20:22-29)?** _____

5. Who became high priest in his place?

_____

Thus, the priestly office and tradition was preserved, and the prescribed sacrifices and religious festivals could continue without interruption, as the covenant required.

By now the Israelites were experiencing their 40th year in the wilderness **(20:28** and **33:38).** Thus, the activities from now on provided valuable training for their future leaders.

6. In some cases, the Lord allowed Israel to conquer the hostile nations. Which nation was destroyed in **Numbers 21:1-3?** _____

Notice that these people were part of a larger nationality called Canaanites. This was an encouraging foretaste of the victories that lay ahead as Israel acted to achieve its goal.

IMPATIENCE IN THE DESERT

1. Have you ever become impatient with God? Have you wanted Him to answer your prayers more rapidly? Have you ever watched a little child have a

temper tantrum? What are we actually saying when we try to specify all the hows and whys of our lives? Be ready to talk about this in class.

2. Read **Numbers 21:4-9.** Describe the sin of the people, the consequences of their sin, and the way God rescued them.

_____

_____

_____

3. Read **John 3:14-15.** The bronze snake was a type of Christ. When the Israelites obediently looked at it, God kept them alive. Compare that with the way God delivers us from eternal death through faith in Jesus.

_____

_____

_____

PROTECTED FROM WITHOUT; INFECTED FROM WITHIN

1. When the Amorites refused passage to the Israelites, Moses led a campaign against the Amorites that resulted in their defeat. Israel then occupied all the land between the Arnon and Jabbok rivers except for a part that was occupied by the Ammonites. Find these rivers on the map.

When Og, the king of Bashan, attacked, he met the same fate, and the Israelite occupation extended north to the Sea of Chinnereth. No wonder that the Moabites were terrified and tried to bribe a spiritist by the name of Balaam to cast an evil spell on Israel. But Moab's plan backfired, and God used Balaam to bless Israel instead—not just once but four different times!

2. Read **Numbers 25.** What caused the death of 24,000 Israelites?

_____

3. In spite of God's fierce anger, a brazen Israelite flaunted his disrespect by bringing a prostitute into the center of the camp. Who courageously acted to rid Israel of this blasphemy? _____

COUNTING OFF AND GETTING SET

The time had come for another census. It accomplished three things: it measured military strength; it determined how much land each tribe should receive; and it verified the death of the whole rebellious generation except for Joshua and Caleb.

1. Read **Numbers 27:12-23.** When Moses was told that he would soon die, what was his main concern? _____

_____

2. Who selected Moses' replacement? _____

3. God had carefully prepared Joshua for this task. Look up the following passages and (on another sheet of paper) tell what situations he has been placed in or how God has acted in his life. **Exodus 17:13; 17:14-16; 24:13; 33:11; Numbers 13:8; 14:6-9; 14:30; 14:38; 27:18; 27:19; 27:20; 27:21a; 27:21b**

4. Who was similarly commissioned in **Acts 13:2-3?** _____

5. What do we learn about today's leaders from **Ephesians 2:10?**

_____

From **2 Timothy 3:12-17?**

_____

_____

_____

How farsighted and gracious our God is! Rejoice in the knowledge that He is daily preparing you for your special tasks in the building up of His kingdom and is continually delivering you from deadly spiritual poison through Jesus' death on the cross.

Moses said to the Lord, "May the Lord, the God of the spirits of all mankind, appoint a man over this community to go out and come in before them, one who will lead them out and bring them in, so the Lord's people will not be like sheep without a shepherd."

Numbers 27:15-17

Session 40

Final Words from Moses (Part 1)

How do you get ready for a test? By rereading the text? By studying your notes? By writing down definitions of new words? By reviewing names of people and processes involved? By studying with a friend?

The Israelites were about to experience a major test—the occupation of the Promised Land. Moses, their leader for more than 40 years, was eager to make good use of their final "preparation time." The setting was the desert east of the Jordan River. The Reubenites, Gadites, and the half-tribe of Manasseh had been given the land the Israelites already occupied, on the condition that they would accompany their fellow Israelites into the Promised Land and stand by them until they also had land of their own **(Numbers 32:20-22).** Joshua had been commissioned as the new leader. So Moses' words recorded in **Deuteronomy** (which means "second giving of the Law") were a farewell that pre-

pared them for their test. He began with a thorough review.

REMEMBER GOD'S MIGHTY WORKS

1. All those under 40 had only *heard* about the terrible plagues, the awesome happenings at the Red Sea, and the Mount Sinai experience. How old were the oldest Israelites (other than Moses, Joshua, and Caleb) at this time **(Numbers 14:29-33; 26:64-65)**?

_____

2. How old were they during the **Exodus?**

_____

To refresh the memories of those who saw all of God's mighty works, and to be sure the younger ones heard of them, Moses carefully reviewed all that had happened during his leadership. Read **Deuteronomy 11:2-7.**

3. Complete the following activity on a separate sheet of paper. Divide your sheet into three columns. In **column 1** copy the Bible verses listed below. In **column 2** briefly tell what happened. In **column 3** tell what that incident was to mean to the people as they entered the Promised Land. (For example, **Deuteronomy 1:9-18** tells that judges were appointed. The people should not expect Joshua to answer every question or mediate every dispute that arose.)

Deuteronomy 1:9-18; 1:19-25; 1:26; 1:41-44; 2:7; 2:14; 2:5,9, and **19; 2:31** and **3:2; 3:5-6; 3:11; 3:12-13; 3:18-20; 4:3-4; 4:10-12; 4:34; 4:37**

REMEMBER TO OBEY

Next Moses turned his attention from *God's* covenant activities to *Israel's* responsibilities under the covenant.

1. Read **Deuteronomy 5:1-3.** With whom had God made the covenant at Horeb?_____

2. What do we call that part of the Law recorded in **Deuteronomy 5:6-21?** _____

3. How had God "delivered" this law originally **(5:22)?**

_____

4. What had the Israelites promised to do **(5:27)?**

_____

5. What purpose for the Law did Moses give in **5:29?** _____

6. God promised Israel specific blessings if they would obey Him. List the blessings He promised in the following verses from **Deuteronomy:**

4:6 _____

4:40 _____

6:3 _____

6:18-19 _____

7:12-13 _____

7:14 _____

7:15 _____

11:8 _____

11:13-14 _____

11:22-24 _____

11:25 _____

15:4-5 _____

ABOUT FALSE PROPHETS, IDOLATERS, ETC.

Moses had been the beneficiary of 120 years of life, the finest Egyptian schooling, extensive travel, well-honed administrative skills, and a direct "hot line" to God. God now led him to prepare the people for some of the problems they would face after they entered the Promised Land. What does he advise about the following? (Find your answers in the passages from **Deuteronomy** in parentheses.)

1. False prophets **(13:5)?** _____

2. Those who urge others to join them in idolatry **(13:6-9)?** _____

3. A rebellious town **(13:12-15)?** _____

4. Self-mutilation, as practiced by Canaanites **(14:1)** _____

5. Eating meat **(14:3-20)?** _____

6. Offerings **(14:23)?** _____

7. Finances **(15:1-3)?** _____

8. Hebrews slaves **(15:12)?** _____

9. The poor **(15:7-11)?** _____

10. Settling disputes **(16:18)?** _____

11. Difficult disputes **(17:8-9)?** _____

12. Choosing a king **(17:14-15)?** _____

13. Sorcery, witchcraft, etc. **(18:9-14)?** _____

CITIES OF REFUGE

1. Read **Deuteronomy 19:1-13.** In other nations at that time the next of kin would avenge the death of a family member. But God did not want His people to be ruled by vengeance. So, to protect the innocent and give the guilty a chance for a fair trial, He established cities of refuge. (See also **Numbers 35** and **Deuteronomy 4:41-43.**) Describe how God used the cities of refuge in the justice system He established.

_____

_____

_____

_____

_____

2. Jesus is our spiritual "City of refuge." What does Jesus say about those who come to Him **(John 6:37)?** _____

3. Why **(John 6:40)?** _____

_____

4. Once we flee to Jesus, what kind of people do we become **(Titus 2:14)?** _____

_____

How true are the words of the hymn writer:
> Wash me and take away each stain;
> Let nothing of my sin remain.
> For cleansing, though it be through pain,
> Christ Crucified, I come.
>
> Then all that you would have me do
> Shall such glad service be for you
> That angels wish to do it too.
> Christ Crucified, I come.
> *Lutheran Worship* 356

Hear now, O Israel, the decrees and laws I am about to teach you. Follow them so that you may live and may go in and take possession of the land that the Lord, the God of your fathers, is giving you.
Deuteronomy 4:1

Session 41

Final Words from Moses (Part 2)

Have you ever been involved in a stage production—either in the cast or backstage as a prompter, makeup artist, props person, wardrobe assistant, or stagehand? If you have, you know the excitement and anticipation that fill the air on opening night. Shortly before curtain time, the director calls everyone together for a final pep talk—words like, "Everyone do exactly what we practiced. No one's job is unimportant. We all need to be alert and cooperative, or we won't succeed."

You hear terse reminders about weak areas, carefully worded announcements of any last-minute changes, admonitions to "be on your toes," encouraging words of praise and commendation for all the hard work that everyone has already invested and, finally, the assurance that if everyone does his or her part, it will be a memorable performance.

MOSES FEELS THE TENSION

Surely no one in Israel was more aware of all that was at stake than Moses. He had dreamed of this moment from his earliest childhood, when at Jochebed's knee he heard of God's wonderful promises to their forefather Abraham. Moses' education as a prince of Egypt was undoubtedly absorbed into the framework of this covenant vision. His aborted leadership attempt at age 40 and his 40 years of maturing, shepherding, and traveling in the Sinai Peninsula were all part of the mosaic that made up the dynamic leader who approached Pharaoh with the demand, "Let my people go!" Moses' entire life—120 years—had as its goal the leading of Israel out of slavery and into the Promised Land. The moment of truth was at hand.

Small wonder that, after reviewing God's mighty acts in their behalf, Moses was increasingly frank in pointing out Israel's weaknesses. On another sheet of paper paraphrase Moses' warnings in the following passages: **Deuteronomy 4:23-28; 8:17-18; 8:19-20; 9:5-6; 9:13-19.**

MOSES IS SURE OF GOD'S MERCY

In spite of his misgivings about Israel's faithfulness, Moses was certain of God's faithfulness. Briefly paraphrase (again, on another sheet of paper) his words of encouragement to those who will remain faithful: **Deuteronomy 6:10-11; 7:9; 7:13; 7:20-24; 8:7-9; 9:2-3; 10:14-15; 11:24-25.**

DIVINE STRATEGY

1. Today the press would call Moses a "lame duck," since Joshua had already been appointed to lead the upcoming military campaign. But Moses was highly respected and still spoke with prophetic authority. Read what Moses advised about war in **Deuteronomy 20.** What "secret weapon" did Israel have to combat horses, chariots, and superior armies **(verse 1)?** _____

2. Who was to encourage the army just before battle **(verses 2-4)?**

_____

3. What attitude were the officers to have toward any unwilling soldiers **(verses 5-8)?**

_____

4. What were they to do before they attacked **(verse 10)?** _____

5. What was to be their strategy for all cities and nations within the boundary of the Promised Land **(verses 16-20)?**_____

_____

6. Read the texts listed below and summarize the reasons for such a purge:

Deuteronomy 20:18 _____

_____

Exodus 34:15-16 _____

_____

Deuteronomy 18:9-12 _____

_____

PREDICTIONS OF THINGS TO COME

Occasionally God gives His people a glimpse of the future through one of His prophets. **Deuteronomy** includes several such glimpses. Summarize each of them:

7:22 _____

_____

4:25-31 _____

_____

_____

God confirmed Moses' suspicions (to both Moses and Joshua) in **Deuteronomy 31:16-18.** He also told Moses and Joshua to write down the song He would give them and teach it to the Israelites. The song **(32:1-43)** would remind them in evil times what caused their misery.

FINAL FAREWELL

In **Deuteronomy 28**, Moses listed all the marvelous blessings in store for Israel if they would keep the covenant, and he reminded them of all the terrible curses they would bring upon themselves if they would disobey. This set the stage for the renewal of the covenant **(Deuteronomy 29:9-15).** It was a solemn moment. The conditions of the covenant had been taught and retaught. Now Moses had called everyone to-gether—even the aliens—to witness the renewal of the covenant.

The heart and core of the covenant are summarized in a single verse, **29:13.** They were to renew the covenant again after they crossed the Jordan.

Then, in the presence of all Israel, Moses encouraged Joshua to lead Israel faithfully and fearlessly in the conquest of the Promised Land. He then reminded the priests and Levites of their solemn responsibilities and blessed each tribe individually and the nation as a whole.

After reciting the "Song of Moses," Moses climbed Mount Nebo for a special God-directed viewing of the Promised Land. His labors completed, he died and was buried by the Lord Himself in a secret place. An appropriate eulogy concludes both the book of **Deuteronomy** and the entire section of the Bible known as the Torah.

Perhaps the most poignant plea Moses ever made is in **Deuteronomy 30:11-20.** Read this passage carefully. Now read **2 Timothy 3:16-17.** God tells us (through Paul) that *all* Scripture is useful to us. God never changes. The words in **Deuteronomy 30:11-20** are for *us!* God is pleading with *us* just as He did with the Israelites. Will we, through the Holy Spirit's power, consistently "choose life"?

[Moses said,] "I have set before you life and death, blessings and curses. Now choose life, so that you and your children may live and that you may love the Lord your God, listen to His voice, and hold fast to Him. For the Lord is your life, and He will give you many years in the land He swore to give to your fathers, Abraham, Isaac and Jacob."

Deuteronomy 30:19-20

Session 42

Israel Enters the Promised Land

How long has your pastor served your congregation? What would happen if he would leave? Would you and your family confidently trust God to send you another, equally capable spiritual leader? Or would you be suspicious of and uncooperative with a new minister? How do you think your attitude would affect the new pastor's effectiveness in your church and community? Perhaps you or someone you know has experienced a change of pastors recently. Be ready to share some of your insights on this matter with the class.

GOD'S LEADER IS DEAD! LONG LIVE GOD'S LEADER!

Moses, shepherd of Israel for more than 40 years, was dead. His aide, Joshua, had been well trained, but can you imagine how inadequate he must have felt as he got ready to step into the shoes of the great Moses? God, who knows even our hidden thoughts and feelings, mercifully came to Joshua to reassure him. Read **Joshua 1:1-9.** The human leadership may have changed, but God had not (and never will!) and His marvelous plans were waiting to be carried out.

1. What did God promise in **verse 3?**

_____

2. But "setting your foot" on someone else's turf can require a lot of courage! Three times God told Joshua to be _____ .

3. Briefly summarize God's instructions in **verses 7-8.** _____

4. Why could Joshua be sure of success **(verse 9)?** _____

5. To learn how Joshua responded, read **1:10-15.** It seems that he acted immediately. To whom did he speak? _____

6. What did he ask them to do?

_____

_____

7. What important announcement did he tell them to make to the people?

_____

_____

8. How thrilled the people must have been! To whom had the land been promised in **Genesis 13:14-15?**

_____

Genesis 26:2-3?

_____

Genesis 28:10-13?

_____

Exodus 6:6-8?

_____

9. Summarize the officers' response on behalf of all the people **(Joshua 1:16-18).**

_____

_____

When people under covenant with God agree to work together under His appointed leader, success is just around the corner!

A RECONNAISSANCE MISSION

1. Joshua, perhaps recalling his own experience as a spy 40 years earlier, secretly sent two spies to look over the land, especially Jericho. Read the story of their brush with death in **Joshua 2.** What is the name of the woman who saved the spies' lives? _____

2. What confession of faith did she make **(v. 11)?**

_____

3. How does God eventually remember her **(Matthew 1:1** and **5)?** _____

4. What agreement did she make with the spies?

_____

92

5. How did they escape?

_____

6. What was to be the sign to ensure her family's safety? _____

7. Paraphrase the report the spies give to Joshua.

_____

_____

GOD'S POWER AND PRESENCE REAFFIRMED

1. What would lead the way into the Promised Land **(Joshua 3:3-4)**? _____

2. What was the one major barrier between the Israelites and Canaan? _____

3. Just north of the Dead Sea, opposite Jericho, the Jordan is about 80 feet wide. Read **Joshua 3:14-17**. How did this miraculous crossing differ from the crossing of the Red Sea?

_____

_____

Examine a map to find where the water "piled up in a heap."

4. What was each tribe to carry out of the river **(4:1-3)**? _____

5. When did the water begin to flow again **(4:18)**?

_____

6. What fact made this miracle especially impressive **(3:15** and **4:18**)? _____

7. How did all this affect Joshua's reputation **(4:14)**? _____

8. What was the purpose of carrying the 12 stones out of the riverbed **(4:20-23)**? _____

9. What was God's purpose in performing this miracle **(4:24)**? _____

10. How did it affect all the kings west of the Jordan **(5:1)**? _____

SACRED RITES RESUMED

1. What religious rite did God institute at the time of Abraham as a "sign of the covenant" **(Genesis 17:11-13)**? _____

2. For how long had the practice of circumcision been suspended **(Joshua 5:5-6)**?

_____

3. What feast did the people celebrate at Gilgal **(5:10)**?

_____

4. Read **5:11-12**. What happened the day after the Passover? _____

5. The people had stopped complaining about their "monotonous" diet of manna, but eating bread and roasted grain from the Promised Land must have been cause for a truly joyous celebration! On the following day, a 40-year-long miracle came to an end. What was it? _____

OUR BREAD FROM HEAVEN

Manna was gone but not forgotten. Free food is always an attention getter. In the New Testament, especially after He fed the 5,000, people followed Jesus everywhere.

1. Read **John 6:25-35**. What did Jesus say was the reason the people were looking for him?

_____

2. He used this as another opportunity to teach them what is really important in life. What Old Testament miracle did the people refer to **(verse 31)**?

_____

3. What other name did they give it?

_____

4. Jesus went on to tell them that a new bread from heaven was now available, but He gave it still another name. What was it **(verse 35)**?

_____

5. How do we receive Jesus today?

_____

6. At what festival was the sacrament of Communion instituted **(Matthew 26:17-30)**?

_____

7. Read **1 Corinthians 11:23-32**. What familiar term does Jesus use in reference to the Lord's Supper **(verse 25**)? _____

This passage indicates that, just as the Israelites' physical and spiritual health would have suffered if they had failed to eat manna regularly, so our spiritual and physical health suffers if we fail to eat of the Living Bread regularly and thoughtfully. How precious the Lord's Supper is to us! How costly it was for Jesus to provide it for us! May the miracle of it all never cease to thrill our hearts!

Have I not commanded you? Be strong and courageous. Do not be terrified; do not be discouraged, for the Lord your God will be with you wherever you go.

Joshua 1:9

Session 43

Conquest: No Contest!

ISRAEL'S NOT-SO-SECRET WEAPON

Read **Joshua 5:13-15.** Joshua was undoubtedly also "trying his best to look brave and strong" when he confronted the man with a drawn sword! Even though Joshua knew that God had promised to "give" Israel the land, he did not know just how that would take place. How relieved he must have been to meet the commander of the army of the Lord!

1. To whose rescue did the army of the Lord come in **2 Kings 6:15-17?** _____

2. Who referred to its existence in **Matthew 26:53?** _____

3. According to **Revelation 19:13-14**, who leads this army? _____

4. What does **Matthew 24:30-31** say about this army? _____

What an awesome sight that will be!

JERICHO—A "PUSHOVER"

The "battle" of Jericho, described in **Joshua 6**, has been a favorite topic of Bible teaching and songs for generations. The military strategy is perhaps the most unorthodox imaginable. The involvement of a divine commander is evident to all. **Verses 21-24** indicate that the Israelites obeyed God's directive to utterly destroy both the inhabitants and their livestock (except for Rahab and her family, who continued to live with the Israelites, **verse 25**).

1. Joshua is known more for his military prowess than his prophecies, but in **Joshua 6:26** he warned a future "land developer" of family tragedies. Who was that person? _____

2. Nearly 500 years later an entry is made in **1 Kings 16:34.** Who are the three people through whom this prophecy was fulfilled?

_____

THE IMPORTANCE OF COMMUNITY RIGHTEOUSNESS

1. Read the specific warning Joshua gave to the Israelites in **Joshua 6:18-19.** What was to be done with the precious metals found in Jericho?

_____

2. Who would suffer if this order would be disobeyed? _____

3. Read **Joshua 7.** Who secretly ignored the warning about taking some of the "devoted things?"

_____

4. In the flush of success, Joshua planned another attack. Against which city? _____

5. The account does not mention any consultation with God before the attack. What happened?

_____

6. Where did Joshua and the elders turn?

_____

7. What was Joshua's main concern (**verses 8-9)?**

_____

8. God's description of the problem is very clear (**verses 10-13).** Paraphrase it.

_____

9. What had happened (**verse 15b)?**

_____

10. Can you picture the tension mounting as 11 tribes were found innocent; then all but one clan of the guilty tribe was cleared; then the search was narrowed to a single family and finally Achan stood alone? Note how kindly Joshua spoke to Achan. What did he call him? _____

11. Joshua encouraged Achan to recognize God's almighty power and omniscience and to confess his sin. Did Achan confess? _____

12. Nevertheless God ordered Achan and his whole family to be killed (**7:15).** Do you feel that Achan and his family all went to hell? Be ready to talk about this.

After the next attack on Ai, which was directed and blessed by God, Joshua took time carefully to obey the instructions Moses had given Israel in **Deuteronomy 11:29** and **chapter 27.**

COVENANT REVIEWED AND RENEWED

1. Read **Joshua 8:30-35.** Who was present?

_____

_____

2. Can you picture yourself in this situation: Two mountain slopes facing each other like a giant amphitheater, each covered with tens of thousands of people? Which tribes were on Mount Gerizim **(Deuteronomy 27:12)?**

_____

3. Which tribes were on Mount Ebal **(Deuteronomy 27:13)?**

_____

4. What was the purpose of the gathering?

_____

Thus, under Joshua's leadership, the covenant was reviewed and renewed. From this point on, all of Joshua's battle plans met with success. Whenever Joshua remembered to consult and rely upon the Lord, things went well for Israel. Occasionally, when he forgot, serious problems resulted.

Read **Joshua 9:1-21.** Locate Gibeon on the map. Reread **verse 14** for the secret of the Gibeonites' successful deception. Notice, in **verse 19,** how seriously Israel took an oath, even though it was the result of a deception.

JOSHUA'S MILITARY STRATEGY

1. With Gibeon subdued, Joshua has succeeded in occupying the heart of Canaan—the first step in the "best military strategy: divide and conquer." In **Joshua 10** we learn that God used the Gibeonite treaty to draw five Amorite kings from the south into battle with Israel. Did Israel have God's blessing for the battle **(10:8)?**

_____

2. What assistance did Joshua ask from God **(10:12)?**

_____

3. What was the three fold result **(10:13-14)?**

_____

_____

After "mopping up" activities completed the conquest of the south, Joshua and his troops returned to Gilgal.

Read **Joshua 11:1-15** for a concise description of the defeat of the northern kings. Use a map to locate the Waters of Merom, where the major battle took place. Archaeologists believe Hazor **(verse 10)** had a population of about 40,000 people at the time of the Israelite conquest.

CONQUEST COMPLETED

1. **Joshua 12** summarizes all the conquests of the Israelites. According to **Joshua 11:18-20,** how many treaties did Israel make?

_____

2. What were God's instructions (through Moses) about treaties **(Deuteronomy 7:2)?**

_____

3. Why was God so against these Canaanite nations? _____

_____

Compare the names of the descendants of Noah's grandson, Canaan **(Genesis 10:15-16),** with the occupants of the land promised to Abraham **(Genesis 15:18-21)** and the lands conquered by Joshua **(Joshua 12:8).** God knew way back then what sort of people they would be.

Does that mean that the Canaanites were forced by "fate" to be doomed everlastingly as idolators? Certainly Rahab is a clear example of the freedom that each Canaanite could have received if he or she would have rejected the wicked environment and turned to the true God.

Examine what God says in **1 Corinthians 10:13** about God's protection of His people. Then, on another sheet of paper, write a "mini-psalm" of praise to God for His universal love. If you prefer, write it from Rahab's point of view.

The Lord said to Joshua, "See, I have delivered Jericho into your hands. . . . I have delivered into your hands the king of Ai." . . . So Joshua took the entire land. . . . Then the land had rest from war.

Joshua 6:2; 8:1; 11:23

Session 44
Every Promise Fulfilled

Chuck had always thought of himself as a family man. His hard work in college and in his profession paid off and now, at 30, he had everything he had ever hoped for: an attractive, supportive wife, two healthy children, a responsible position with a growing company, and a fine home with a big yard and a two-car garage. With his major conquest behind him, the little daily hurdles became monotonous. But life at the office did bring one new challenge—competition with the other executives for the attention of the gorgeous new receptionist.

Suddenly Chuck realized that the "harmless" banter was making its way into his thoughts in an increasingly unhealthy way. What would be the end result if he "followed the crowd" at the office and continued to "play the game" by the world's standards? He remembered the words of **1 Peter 5:8-9, "The devil prowls around like a roaring lion looking for someone to devour. Resist him, standing firm in the faith."**

ISRAEL'S CONQUEST IS COMPLETED

Israel's dream of a land of their own was now a reality. The entire country was now under their control **(Joshua 18:1).**

1. Read **Joshua 13:1-8.** Even though large areas of Canaan had not been taken over **(verse 1)**, what command did God give Joshua **(verse 7)?**

_____

2. What would happen to the foreigners who remained **(verse 6)?**

_____

3. To which tribes had Moses already assigned land east of the Jordan?

_____

_____

4. When Moses had sent the spies 45 years earlier, apparently each spy had scouted certain areas on his own, and Moses had promised Caleb that he and his tribe would occupy the land he had scouted. Who lived in the land he had chosen for his own clan **(14:12)?** _____

5. What kind of people were they **(Numbers 13:28 and 33; Deuteronomy 9:2)?** _____

6. How can we tell that Caleb still had a strong faith in God **(Joshua 14:12)?**

_____

So Caleb and the rest of the tribe of Judah **(Joshua 15)** received the land promised to them by Moses—and any "mopping up" activities required to completely occupy it! Moses, aware of the dangers, had prayed for them in **Deuteronomy 33:7.**

7. Joshua was the other member of the original spy group who was still alive. He was from the tribe of Ephraim. Whose sons were Ephraim and Manasseh **(Genesis 48:1)?** _____

This may explain why they were the next to be given land **(Joshua 16)**, including the land chosen by Joshua for his clan **(19:49-50).**

8. Read **Joshua 17:16-18.** What complaints did the "people of Joseph" have?

_____

_____

9. What was Joshua's reply?

_____

_____

MISSION ACCOMPLISHED

1. Read **Joshua 21:43-45.** How do these words comfort you today?

_____

2 Read **22:1-9.** As Joshua released the three trans-Jordan tribes to return to their land, how did he summarize the law Moses gave them?

_____

_____

_____

3. These trans-Jordan tribes built an altar on the border of their territory that nearly caused a civil war. What did the other Israelites think it meant **(22:16)?**

_____

_____

4. What sacrifice were they willing to make to prevent this **(22:19)?**

_____

5. What did they fear **(verses 18-20)?**

_____

6. What was the real purpose of the altar **(22:27)?**

_____

_____

7. Did that explanation satisfy the Israelites **(22:31-33)?**

_____

Has someone ever misunderstood something you did? Have you ever judged a friend's motives hastily and regretted it later? Clear and open communication is vital to maintaining all good relationships—friends, families, congregations, and nations!

JOSHUA'S FAREWELL

1. If someday you feel that you are near death, what messages will you want to give to your loved ones? _____

_____

2. Read **Joshua 23.** This was Joshua's farewell. How did he encourage the Israelites **(verses 3-5)?**

_____

_____

3. What did he urge them to do **(vv. 6-8)?**

_____

4. What warning did he give the people **(verses 12-13)?**

_____

5. Of what did he remind them **(verses 14-15)?**

_____

6. What would result if they would worship other gods **(verse 16)?** _____

7. Joshua then briefly reviewed Israel's history before reaching the climax of his farewell address, in which he offered the people a choice. Read **24:14-26.** What was the choice?

_____

8. What choice does Joshua make for himself and his family? _____

9. How did the people answer Joshua's challenge **(24:16-18)?**

_____

10. What point did Joshua make in **verses 19-20?**

_____

_____

11. What problem does **verse 23** suggest?

_____

_____

Notice that in **verse 24** the people recommitted themselves (for the third time) to uphold the covenant.

Joshua's task was now complete. The people no longer needed a single leader. Each tribe, as a member of the loose confederacy of Israel, was responsible for its own government under God. Their continuing loyalty would be expressed by their participation in worship and the observance of the great festivals in Shiloh, the current location of the tabernacle.

What a marvelous future God had planned for His chosen people!

So the Lord gave Israel all the land He had sworn to give their forefathers, and they took possession of it and settled there. . . . Not one of all the Lord's good promises to the house of Israel ever failed; every one was fulfilled.

Joshua 21:43 and 45

Session 45

Concluding Activities for Unit 6

Answer the following questions to help you review unit 6.

TERMS

On a separate sheet of paper write definitions of the following terms:

1. false prophets
2. cities of refuge
3. trans-Jordan tribes
4. Joshua
5. Caleb
6. Jericho
7. Ai
8. Eleazar
9. Phinehas
10. Korah
11. fatalism
12. Shiloh

SHORT ANSWER

Write a short answer to each of the following questions:

1. What were the two different reports given by the 12 scouts after they returned from the Promised Land?

2. Compare the bronze snake on the pole with Jesus.

3. What were some of Moses' concerns before he died?

4. Which tribe did not receive an allotment of land in Canaan?

5. What did Moses do when God threatened to kill all the Israelites?

6. Explain why Israel was successful in some battles but unsuccessful in others.

7. What was the significance of the sprouting staff?

8. Why didn't Moses get to enter the Promised Land?

9. Compare manna and the Lord's Supper.

10. Compare the crossing of the Red Sea with the crossing of the Jordan River.

11. Compare Israel's travels in this unit with our travel through life.

12. Describe the orderly way God provided for Israel to travel and camp.

Unit 7
The Period of the Judges

During this unit, you'll read about three representatives of the judges—Deborah, Gideon, and Samson—leaders God appointed to lead the people in war against their enemies. You'll discover Israel's constant disobedience and God's constant love and help for His people. And—most important—you will remember that God keeps on loving you as He deals with your own sin!

Session 46

Introducing the Judges

READING THE SCRIPTURES
(Judges 1:1—3:6)

The **Book of Judges** picks up the story of God's covenant people, Israel, after the conquest of Canaan under Joshua. Often during this time, the people of Israel worshiped false gods and disobeyed the Lord God. God continued to love His people, but He would not allow them to destroy themselves and their relationship with Him. Therefore, He allowed the very people whose false gods Israel worshiped to become their oppressors. When Israel could no longer endure the oppression, they would cry out to the Lord God. He would then provide a judge to deliver them. Usually there would be a brief period of peace, after which the Israelites would again slip back into idolatry and disobedience.

As you read **Judges** you will encounter some graphic descriptions of the behavior of the people of that time. Do not allow yourself to be distracted by the gory details of the stories. Instead, look for God's purpose and activity with His people.

GOD HELPED TROUBLED ISRAEL

1. How did God react to the failure of Israel to subdue the many tribes living in Canaan?

_____

2. What conditions may have led to the ignorance of God described in **Judges 2:10?**

_____

3. What could be some consequences of not knowing God?

_____

4. Read **Deuteronomy 4:1-10.** What did God tell Israel to teach their children and grandchildren?

_____

5. What had Israel apparently failed to teach their children and grandchildren? **(Judges 2:10)**

_____

_____

_____

GOD HELPS ME, TOO

After reading **Judges,** do you get the impression that God deliberately brings difficulty to those who disobey Him—that this is how God punishes them for their sins? That would be a false impression! Jesus Christ has already borne that punishment for *all* our sins. The difficulties we encounter in life are *not* due to God's anger over our sins but *are* due to the problems we cause ourselves when we sin.

1. Think of a time when you were uncomfortable or embarrassed after doing something wrong. How did you behave? And what were some difficulties you experienced later?

_____

_____

_____

_____

2. The Israelites cried to the Lord when the needed help. A saying goes, "There are no atheists i foxholes" (which means that soldiers in combat ar likely to turn to God in times of danger). Describe briefl an experience that brought you or a friend closer t God.

_____

_____

_____

3. God wants to live in a close, loving relationship with us. Sometimes He allows us to experience difficulty so we may learn to depend on Him. Read **Hebrews 12:4-11.** The writer describes the purpose of God's disciplinary actions. Why do you think God allows those He loves to experience difficult times?

_____

_____

_____

_____

4. Read **Romans 5:8.** Describe your confidence in God's love for you in spite of your rebellion against God.

_____

_____

_____

I KNOW I CAN DEPEND ON GOD

Someone once said that the one thing we learn from history is that we never learn anything from history! We may laugh at the foolishness of the Israelites, who never seemed to learn from their mistakes. Yet their story is ours, too. We sin repeatedly, but God continues to love us. He sent us a deliverer, Jesus Christ, who died for our sins and set us free from the power of sin and death **(Romans 8:1-2).**

1. When tempted, Israel chose idols rather than God. What are some temptations that face you and other teenagers today? What things can easily become your "gods"?

_____

_____

2. Temptation does not have to result in sin. God promises to support us when we are tempted **(1 Corinthians 10:13).** What is that support?

_____

_____

How can _you_ depend on God when you are faced with temptation?

_____

_____

3. The Boy Scout motto is "Be Prepared." Using this advice, write a short, meaningful prayer that you might pray the next time you are tempted.

_____

_____

_____

The angel of the Lord . . . said, "I will never break My covenant with you."   _Judges 2:1_

Session 47

Who's in Charge? (Deborah and Barak)

READING THE SCRIPTURES
(Judges 4—5)

Have you ever been left "in charge" of anyone or anything? Maybe you've been responsible for collecting the props for a class play or for organizing a classmate's student-government campaign. Think about one time you've been "in charge." Was it fun? Was it easy or hard? Did you have any help from anyone? Do you enjoy being a leader? And did you ever have to be rescued?

The Book of Judges is filled with stories of God's compassion for Israel. It's an incredible love story. Rarely will you find examples of love, forgiveness, and rescue as they are portrayed in the **Book of Judges**, except perhaps in your own life, for God is as eager to forgive *you* as He was His people in **Judges.**

Several episodes have been selected to show what God did for Israel during the time of the judges. The first of these is the story of Deborah and Barak. Deborah was the only female judge in Israel. She was "in charge" of settling the Israelites' fights in the court. She generously praised others for their service to the Lord. As you read this account, you'll find out how God used Deborah and Jael, another important courageous woman, to accomplish His plan. Neither woman hesitated to do what was necessary to serve God.

As you read the story of Deborah, try to identify with one of the three main characters: Deborah, Barak, or Jael. Then answer these questions: With whom did you identify the easiest? And, in your opinion, who was the real hero or heroine in this Bible story?

GOD HELPS DYNAMIC DEBORAH

1. What was the situation for Israel when this account begins?

_____

_____

_____

2. What are the qualities of a good leader?

_____

_____

What leadership qualities did Deborah have? Give references from the story to support your answer.

_____

_____

3. Why do you think Barak asked Deborah to accompany him when he led Israel against Sisera's army?

_____

_____

4. God always intervened with His loving care and power to assure victory for Israel when they went into battle under the judges. Read **Judges 4:14-15; 5:4-5;** and **5:20-21.** How did God intervene against Sisera?

_____

_____

_____

GOD HELPS ME DAILY

1. What are some of the challenges you face each day of your life that require God's help? _____

_____

Do you ask God for help? _____

_____

Why or why not? _____

_____

2. When it comes to obeying God's Word, are you more like Deborah (energetic and courageous) or like Barak (hesitant and needing a supportive leader)? Give examples and reasons for your answer.

_____

_____

3. When you need encouragement or when you would like to give encouraging words to a friend, what word of the Lord could you share? (You might begin with **Psalm 37:5** in this Scripture search.) _____

_____

_____

4. Why is it important to remember to turn to God's Word when we feel depressed, tired, and unimportant?

_____

_____

_____

AM I A GOOD LEADER? AM I A GOOD FOLLOWER?

An Old Testament account of God helping His people may seem entertaining—but without meaning—for us living *now*. We look at the temptations we have today—immorality, drug abuse, alcohol abuse, murder, and more—and we have to admit that our society is oppressed by sin. Jesus Christ, our Savior, is the only hope and release from the control of sinful oppressions. The apostle Paul realized this as he struggled with the conflicts in his own life **(Romans 7).**

Just as God provided leaders for His people Israel then, He gives us good leaders to build up the body of Christ today **(Ephesians 4:11-13).** God desires that we, too, might overcome the sinful tyranny affecting our lives.

1. What are your goals for your life? How do your goals relate to God's Word? _____

_____

_____

2. People follow leaders who will help them achieve a desired goal. Who are some people you consider to be Christian examples for you to follow? List their names (adults and classmates) and note what you like about them. _____

_____

_____

_____

3. How can the people you listed help you achieve your own goals? How can you help them work toward their goals?

_____

4. Many times we choose our friends on the basis of what they look like, which group of people they belong to, and what they like to do. God selects His helpers with different criteria. He is more likely to choose His leaders on the basis of who is willing to be equipped and to serve Him.

What criteria did you use to select the leaders you selected for question 2? _____

_____

5. The apostle Paul gives us a formula for service in **Romans 12:1.** Read that formula. Do you think God could use you as a leader? How?

_____

_____

_____

I will make music to the Lord, the God of Israel.
Judges 5:3

The Lord made me have dominion over the mighty.
Judges 5:13 KJV

Session 48

MISSION: IMPOSSIBLE?
(The Story of Gideon)

READING THE SCRIPTURES
(Judges 6—8)

It's time for you to imagine . . .
"5—4—3—2—1—rockets fired—we have lift-off!" the space-shuttle controller announces. You've joined Space Shuttle Flight 201. Your mission includes taking 25 young men and women to Planet Zoto. Once there, you're instructed to build a space fortress, defend yourselves against the enemy Zotoans, and, in time, tell them about God's love for them, following the Lord's command to go, teach, and baptize all nations. Your resources are limited! Space Shuttle Control allows you to take along only what you can wear or carry in your backpack. You're halfway to Planet Zoto just since you've begun reading this!

How do you feel about being asked to complete this mission? Nervous? Excited? Alone? Thankful it's a hypothetical situation?

The story of Gideon is exciting! God asked Gideon to do the impossible and at the same time kept cutting back his resources. God assured Gideon that He would help him with the battles against the enemy. But, imagine how you would feel taking 300 troops into battle against a force of 120,000! No wonder Gideon asked God for signs that He would be with him!

GOD CALLS GIDEON AND HELPS ISRAEL

1. What had Israel done that God allowed the Midianites and the Amalekites to oppress them?

_____

_____

2. What thoughts might have gone through Gideon's mind when God told him to tear down his father's altar to Baal **(Judges 6:25-27)?**

_____

_____

3. In **Judges 6:36-40** Gideon asked the Lord to prove He would be with him in the battle against the Midianites. Why, if the Lord had actually spoken to him, did Gideon need further proof? _____

_____

_____

4. Gideon asked God not to be angry over his requests for signs. Why did Gideon fear God's anger? Was God angry with Gideon? Why or why not?

_____

_____

5. List several passages from the Gideon story that show God's love for Israel, either in statement or action by God.

_____

_____

_____

_____

_____

_____

GOD HELPS ME AND CALLS ME TO HELP OTHERS

1. What if —
Your disabled mother asks you to care for your brothers and sisters after school while she receives physical therapy. You have just been chosen a first-string basketball guard for your school team. Practices are after school. _____

_____

_____

A wealthy, disabled, elderly aunt and uncle offer you a year's expense-paid travel to accompany them around the world. They ask you to come along and would expect you to help them get on and off airplanes, meet scheduled tour buses, and run errands if they needed something. You would have to make up the whole school year of work and graduate after your own class. _____

_____

_____

2. Tell about a recent problem and how you faced it. If you asked God for help, how did He show His love to you?

_____

_____

_____

3. How can confessing a specific sin help you feel better? See **Romans 6:6-7.**

_____

_____

_____

4. We look for God's directions today just as Gideon did in the time of the judges. How do you look for God's direction for your life? What part does the Word of God play in directing you? Does Scripture encourage or discourage you to set a "fleece" before the Lord? Give reasons for your answers. _____

_____

_____

_____

_____

_____

5. You are God's representative wherever you go. How does what you say and do reflect God's love and forgiveness as well as His judgment? What would you say to a friend who coaxes you to share alcoholic beverages with her? to a parent who imposes too strict rules governing your curfews and free time? to a grandparent who doesn't accept your friends?

_____

_____

_____

_____

_____

6. If God asked you to speak for Him to those around you, what would you say to the classmate who cheats on a test? to your brother who likes to be part of "the gang"? How would you use the story of Gideon as an example of God's willingness to love, forgive, and direct our lives?

_____

_____

_____

_____

_____

_____

_____

WITH GOD ALL THINGS ARE POSSIBLE

The writer of the letter to the **Hebrews** quotes **Deuteronomy 31:6** and the Lord's words: **"Never will I leave you; never will I forsake you" (Hebrews 13:5).**

God's promise is the same for you today! Rejoice in His presence! Write a short paragraph telling how you feel after you read **Hebrews 13:5.** What do those special words mean for you?

_____

_____

_____

_____

_____

_____

I can pray: Dear Lord God, thank You for Your love and presence in Jesus Christ, my Lord and Savior. Amen.

I said to you, "I am the Lord, your God."

Judges 6:10

"The Lord will rule over you."

Judges 8:23

Session 49

Going God's Way?
(The Story of Samson)

READING THE SCRIPTURES
(Judges 13 —16)

Travel posters in the airline terminal caught Greg's attention. Go Eastern—Fly to the Warm Sunny South—Meet Me in Jamaica—Holiday Far Away in Mexico—Hawaii Welcomes You, Aloha!

Fluorescent lights and bright colors everywhere kept Greg's eyes jumping from one advertisement to another. "I've fought with Dad for the last time," Greg thought, "and I'm going my *own* way from now on. He won't have to worry about me using his car and getting home on time anymore!"

Which way would he go? After waiting his turn at the ticket counter, Greg finally decided to board a cheap flight to Kansas City. "Just a start," he thought. But when he opened his wallet to pay for the ticket, he found he had only $11—not enough even to take a cab home!

"Going my way?" asked Greg's dad as he tapped his son's shoulder from behind.

How do you think Greg answered his dad?

What do you predict Greg will do?

The story of Samson reads like a modern novel. Meet Samson—a headstrong, interesting, bold man born and raised under a vow chosen for him by God.

Nazirite Samson does not always take seriously the vow God uses to set him apart as His chosen leader for Israel.

Worldly acting Samson disregards his vow and suffers the consequences repeatedly before he finally asks God to help him. Yet God uses Samson in a unique way to punish the Philistines. And as He did through the previous judges, God works through Samson to show His love to His people.

GOD GIVES HIS SPIRIT AND POWER TO SAMSON

1. Describe the person (his physical appearance, attitudes, and mannerisms) you would choose to act the role of Samson if you were creating a movie account of **Judges.**

_____

_____

2. How was Samson different from Gideon? from Deborah?

_____

_____

_____

_____

3. Would you—or would you not—like to have Samson for a classmate? Why or why not?

_____

_____

_____

GOD GIVES HIS SPIRIT AND POWER TO ME

1. Samson possessed a rather "free spirit" and did as he pleased. Tell briefly what God's Holy Spirit will add to your life **(Galatians 5:22-23).**

_____

_____

_____

2. You realize you need God's help. You haven't been serious about your life. Write a short personal prayer. Ask God that, as you read and study His Word, He will send His Spirit and power into your life.

_____

_____

_____

_____

_____

3. When God gives you His Spirit, how will your life change? How will your changed life affect your friends and family?

_____

_____

_____

_____

_____

4. In a special notebook, keep a private "journal" for at least one week. Write in it some of the ways you want to do "your own thing." Tell how it feels to be serious—or not so serious—about things you're doing, about things that interest you, about people you like to be with. Write about times when your life changes, when something special or something not so good happens to you, and when you feel differently about something. List some of the ways you feel you could really use God's help. Use your journal entries for your personal prayer starters.

I DEDICATE MYSELF TO SERVE GOD

Sing or say these stanzas of "Take My Life, O Lord, Renew" (*LW* 404).

> Take my life, O Lord, renew,
> Consecrate my heart to you;
> Take my moments and my days;
> Let them sing your ceaseless praise.
>
> Take my hands and let them do
> Works that show my love for you;
> Take my feet and lead their way,
> Never let them go astray.
>
> Take my voice and let me sing
> Praises to my Savior King;
> Take my lips and keep them true,
> Filled with messages from you.
>
> Take my silver and my gold,
> All is yours a thousand fold;
> Take my intellect, and use
> Ev'ry pow'r as you shall choose.
>
> Make my will your holy shrine,
> It shall be no longer mine.
> Take my heart, it is your own;
> It shall be your royal throne.
>
> Take my love; my Lord, I pour
> At your feet its treasure store;
> Take my self, Lord, let me be
> Yours alone eternally.

How do you feel, knowing that God accepts you as a volunteer to serve Him in ways He will show you?

Write a prayer especially asking God to use you in serving Him. You might include a sentence or two for each of these acrostic headings in your prayer:

Adoration (I praise you, God, for . . .)
Confession (I'm sorry, Jesus, for . . .)
Thanksgiving (I thank you, Lord, for . . .)
Supplication (I ask you, Lord, for . . .)

_____

_____

_____

_____

It is for freedom that Christ has set us free. . . .The only thing that counts is faith expressing itself through love.

Galatians 5:1a and 6b

Session 50

Reviewing the Judges

The following exercises will help you review the judges.

1. On a separate sheet of paper list each major character in the stories of Deborah, Gideon, and Samson. Tell who each character was and the role he or she played in the story.

2. Write a brief definition of a judge in Israel.

_____

_____

3. Why were the Israelites so often oppressed by the heathen people who surrounded them?

_____

_____

_____

4. How does the period of the judges fit into the history of the nation of Israel as you know it so far?

_____

_____

5. Why was the idolatry of the surrounding nations potentially harmful to Israel?

_____

_____

6. Why did God want Israel to eliminate the heathen people completely from Canaan (see **Deuteronomy 13**)?

_____

_____

7. Why would the presence of heathen nations be a test of the faithfulness of Israel to God?

_____

_____

8. Read **Deuteronomy 4:1-10; Joshua 1:6-9;** and **Judges 2:10.** What had Israel failed to do after the death of Joshua?

_____

_____

9. Write a description of the nature of God's love based on His behavior toward Israel during the period of the judges.

_____

_____

10. What lessons have you learned from the **Book of Judges** that could be applied to your own life?

_____

_____

God demonstrates His own love for us in this: While we were still sinners, Christ died for us.

Romans 5:8

Unit 8

The Monarchy— a United Kingdom

God continued to love and care for His people in Israel through their troublesome times. During this unit, you'll read how God chooses special leaders for His people and how He directs them as they rule over a united kingdom.

God wants us to trust Him to guide our lives, too, as He guided the Israelites. He blesses us and strengthens us when we trust in His will for us.

Session 51

Israel's Tribes Unite—the Monarchy Begins

READING THE SCRIPTURES (1 Samuel 4 —7)

You have just finished studying the period of the judges and have seen how God periodically raised up leaders to get the nation back on track when they strayed into idolatry. This session's Scripture reading illustrates the discord and lack of leadership common in Israel at this time.

The incidents recorded in **1 Samuel 4:1-10** show that Israel was still plagued by enemies like the Philistines and suffered defeats in battle.

God chose the last great judge, Samuel, whose leadership prepared the way for a king in Israel.

GOD ALLOWS BATTLES BETWEEN ENEMIES

1. What was the reaction of the soldiers of Israel to their defeat by the Philistines in **1 Samuel 4:3?**

_____

_____

_____

_____

2. How did the Israelites plan to bring success to their army **(1 Samuel 4:3-4)?**

_____

_____

_____

_____

3. Look at the Philistine response in **verses 6-8.** How might their statement have affected the next battle had it not been for the statement in **verse 9?**

_____

_____

_____

_____

GOD HELPS ME FIGHT MY ENEMIES

1. The Israelites experienced demoralizing defeats. As a result they groped for anything that might

help them defeat the Philistines. Think of a time when you felt defeated. What did you "battle"? Where did you look for help? _____

_____

_____

2. Some people look to pills, alcohol, or other chemicals for help when they feel defeated or alone. What could you tell someone who is desperately looking for help. Read **2 Corinthians 4:6-11.** What is the "treasure" that God gives us to remember and to share with others? _____

_____

_____

3. Israel turned to the ark of the covenant, the symbol of God's presence in Israel. Having the ark did not make up for their poor relationship with God—just as carrying a Bible does not take the place of having a proper relationship with God today! What should Israel have done? _____

_____

_____

What would God have me do? _____

_____

_____

_____

4. What are the most serious problems our country faces? What solutions do you suggest to these problems?

_____

_____

_____

_____

_____

5. How might God be preparing you to be a leader—part of the solution to the problems of our country? _____

_____

_____

_____

6. How do you feel, knowing that God will bless you in His service when you respond eagerly to His call? _____

_____

_____

_____

Here I am! I stand at the door and knock. If anyone hears My voice and opens the door, I will go in and eat with him, and he with Me.

Revelation 3:20

Session 52

Samuel: God's Spokesman

READING THE SCRIPTURES
(1 Samuel 1—7)

Don played goalie for his high-school soccer team. He and his teammates had just won the state championship soccer tourney. Three colleges in the state wanted Don to accept their scholarships and play for their teams for the next school year. What a decision he had to make! Until then, Don had dreamed that someday he would be a marine biologist and work with oceanographers Jacques Cousteau and his crew. But only after the last soccer game did Don realize what he really wanted to do with his life. He had started talking to the losing soccer team players in the locker room. They told Don they were on their way to an evening Bible class and invited him and his friends to come along. Don and some of his teammates joined

them for burgers and shakes and the Bible class that followed. Don had never known guys so committed to God! They shared their faith and prayed together—they showed Don how alive God's love can be in people! Not long after that, Don decided to go to college to become a director of Christian education, to help young students share their joy and enthusiasm for the Lord. Don still plays soccer, he continues to read about life in the oceans, and he dedicates himself to sharing his best Friend, Jesus, with his young friends around him.

Read the Scripture passages for this session. Do you think Samuel and Don are in any way alike? Though Samuel didn't choose his career and Don did, what important job did God have for each of them? Is Samuel a unique person compared to the Old Testament leaders you have studied so far? Dedicated to the Lord even before he was born, Samuel remained so consistently faithful to the Lord that he seems almost too good to be true! How did God show His continuing love for Israel and the new leader, Samuel?

GOD CHOOSES SAMUEL TO LEAD ISRAEL

1. Read **1 Samuel 1:1—2:10.** Briefly describe Samuel's mother, Hannah. What do you like about her?

_____

_____

_____

_____

2. Describe Hannah's attitude toward God. List some ways Hannah probably influenced Samuel at home and helped form His attitude toward God.

_____

_____

_____

3. Look in a Bible dictionary to find the meaning of the word *Belial*, a word used in **1 Samuel 2:12 (KJV)**

to describe Eli's sons. What does *Belial* mean and how does it fit Eli's sons? _____

_____

_____

4. Write a brief description of Samuel's character and attitude based on **1 Samuel 2:18** and **chapter 3**. How would Samuel fit into your own group of friends?

_____

_____

_____

_____

GOD CHOOSES ME FOR SPECIAL JOBS

1. According to **1 Samuel 7:15**, Samuel was a judge in Israel. Based on your knowledge of his character (and the description you wrote above), what kind of a political leader would Samuel be today? Would you vote for Samuel if he were running for a political office today? Why or why not? _____

_____

_____

2. From **1 Samuel 3:1-9** we can assume that Samuel was a very obedient youngster, eager to serve Eli and the Lord. How would you compare your own willingness to obey those in authority over you? Does a willingness to obey have anything to do with your commitment to the Lord? Give reasons for your answer.

_____

_____

_____

_____

3. **The Lord was with Samuel as he grew up (1 Samuel 3:19).** Do you believe that the Lord is with you as you are growing up? Why or why not? Find Scripture verses that assure you that God *is* with you.

_____

_____

_____

_____

AM I WILLING TO WORK FOR GOD?

We sometimes erringly think of Bible events as just stories. (Who would believe that God would bring such great blessings to His people through a child who was given to the Lord's service through a promise made even before the child was born?) We thank God for His Holy Word and the Biblical truths and blessings He gives us. Our loving God is waiting to bring many blessings to us through people who are willing to serve Him. Is it possible that you are one of those persons?

1. Samuel did not have a career choice, but you do. Assume that God has an important assignment for you. List what you might do to discover His will for your life.

_____

_____

_____

_____

_____

2. Though Samuel did not choose his career, he certainly was influenced by others. List people who positively influenced Samuel as he grew up. Then list those people who could help you as you prepare for the future.

They influenced Samuel: *They influenced me:*

_____

_____

_____

_____

3. Write a prayer asking God to help you *trust* Him for your future and to help you *offer* your services to Him willingly for whatever job He gives you.

_____

_____

_____

_____

4. Choose one person from whom you could ask career advice. Then meet with that person. Ask how to begin planning for your career. List the suggestions you receive on a separate paper.

The Lord will guide you always.

Isaiah 58:11.

Session 53

Saul: Israel's First King

READING THE SCRIPTURES
(1 Samuel 8 —14)

Do you ever feel like you're totally out of it? That you can't quite get it all together? You know you've got the brains, but your body is still waiting to be built—it's lacking in all the right places. Or you feel good about your school's *group* activities, but your social life with the *one* date you want for your own is the pits. You look in the mirror and ask, "Who's this?" You wonder what you're gonna do with yourself. And you wonder *when* you're gonna feel good about *all* of you. Well—if it makes you feel better—you'll find when you read today's Scripture account that people in Bible times had their flaws, too!

God chose for Israel a young man remarkable in physical stature but unremarkable in personality. One of his servants appeared to have much better prospects for leadership than Saul **(1 Samuel 9:6-7).**

By now you realize that God is never limited by human weaknesses. When God came upon Saul with

His Holy Spirit, Saul's life was changed **(1 Samuel 10:6 and 10).** As you read this section, inventory your own resources. Has it occurred to you that God may be just as eager to be involved in your life as He was to be involved in Saul's?

Regardless of what we have to offer God, everything we have is a gift from God. He asks us to be in His service. And remember—God works miracles in our lives!

GOD'S INVOLVEMENT IN SAUL'S LIFE

1. God chose Saul as Israel's first king. What did God do to prepare Saul for leadership **(1 Samuel 10:10)?**

_____

_____

2. If Saul were running for political office today and you were his campaign manager, you would have to capitalize on his strengths and help him overcome his weaknesses. Make a list of Saul's strengths and weaknesses to help you get a picture of his qualifications for leadership.
Saul's strengths:

_____

_____

Saul's weaknesses:

_____

_____

3. Describe what you think were Saul's greatest challenges.

_____

_____

GOD'S INVOLVEMENT IN MY LIFE

1. Saul was reluctant to lead. Yet God was looking to him to be a leader in Israel. God has some leadership expectations for all of us—He expects us to be ex-

amples for others. What kinds of expectations do you find in

1 Samuel 12:24?

_____

Romans 12:1?

_____

1 Peter 1:14-16?

_____

2. Read **Romans 8:2.** God frees us from limiting ourselves and from worrying if "we're good enough." List some of your talents, abilities, attributes and resources that would help you fulfill God's expectations (as you outlined them in question 1).

_____

_____

_____

_____

3. God encourages us to be realistic about ourselves and to recognize His unlimited love and resources for us. On what resources can you depend to help you live up to God's expectations? (See **Galatians 2:20; 5:22-25**; and **Romans 12:2**.)

_____

_____

_____

_____

I STEP INTO FAITHFUL SERVICE

1. Read **1 Peter 5:5-9.** What does Peter say to:
a. the proud? _____

_____

_____

_____

b. the timid? _____

_____

_____

_____

2. Saul had to analyze and attack difficulties in manageable steps, especially when he had no weapons with which to fight. We can do this, too. Write about one problem you face. Then begin by asking God to help you solve this problem. Follow by listing steps to help you solve the problem. Make your steps small enough for you to manage. Don't forget to ask other people for help! Be prepared to share your problem-management list with your class.

I'll ask God to help me with my problem. And I'll list and use these steps to help solve my problem:

a. _____

b. _____

c. _____

d. _____

Pray this prayer, or write one of your own, when you're needing help with your problems.

Jesus, I believe in You. I trust You to take care of me and help me with my problems.

Jesus, I have faith in You. I know You'll use Your power in my life to use me in miraculous ways.

Jesus, I trust in You. I believe You're my Friend and I can rely on You to be there when I need You.

Jesus, I thank You. You give me freedom to be me, freedom from being tangled in sin, through your suffering, death, and resurrection. I count on Your forgiveness when I ask for it.

Jesus, I love You. I need You beside me in everything I say and do. Amen, Jesus, Amen.

_____

_____

_____

_____

_____

_____

_____

_____

Be sure to fear the Lord and serve Him faithfully with all your heart; consider what great things He has done for you.

1 Samuel 12:24

Session 54

Saul: The Failing King

READING THE SCRIPTURES
(1 Samuel 15 —31)

Tony couldn't seem to do anything right. His grandma complained that he hadn't taken out the trash. His mom declared war—he had put clean jeans into the laundry *again*! "Why can't you wear a pair of jeans more than one time?" she begrudgingly asked, overloaded with work. "Take out this trash and get your room cleaned before supper!" she shouted at Tony. Tony couldn't take any more yelling and hassling from anybody. Not after a day of school and work at the market. So he split.

Lately, the only time Tony felt good was when he joined the three-wheeler group of guys at the gas station. He had saved his after-school working money two whole years to buy a used three-wheeler. Now he was out to have fun and forget all the griping at home. Six riders on their three-wheelers screeched out of the station and raced through alleys and parking lots leaving rubber and smoke behind. Tony felt exhilarated! "This beats taking orders!" he thought just before he came face to face at high speed with a huge dumpster.

Tony remembers waking up in the hospital. How do you think this story ends? Would you tell Tony, "I told you so!"? Was his accident the consequence of his deliberate disobedience? Have you ever had anything happen to you when you disobeyed someone? Did you have to suffer the consequences?

As you read this session's Scripture account, you'll learn that Saul experienced some early military success as Israel's first king. His deliberate disobedience, though, soon spoiled his reign. It cost him his position as king and prevented any of his descendants from becoming king.

Saul's deliberate acts of disobedience included:

1. Offering a sacrifice, a privilege reserved for the priests **(1 Samuel 13:7-14)**.

2. Sparing Agag and the best of the sheep and cattle of the Amalekites **(1 Samuel 15:3, 9-23)**.

3. Consulting the witch at Endor **(1 Samuel 28:7-25)**.

Do you feel sorry for Saul? People frequently do. Perhaps they see themselves in a person like Saul. While it is regrettable that Saul experienced so much trouble, we must realize that it was his own fault. De-

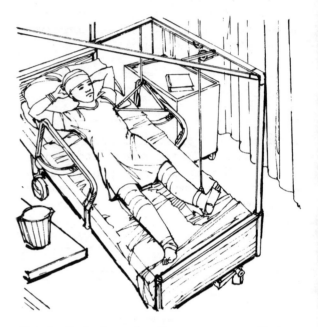

liberate disobedience has its consequences. God rescinded Saul's right to be king, but lovingly allowed him to live. Unfortunately, Saul did not learn from his mistakes.

SAUL—THE DISOBEDIENT KING

Assume that you are either the prosecuting attorney or the defense counsel in a trial to determine Saul's guilt or innocence. Identify which role you are playing. Then write a single paragraph either accusing or defending Saul.

Be sure to use Scripture references to defend your statement.

_____

_____

_____

_____

_____

_____

I AM DEAD TO SIN AND ALIVE TO GOD THROUGH CHRIST

Just as Saul deliberately sinned against God, we, too, are capable of disobeying God on purpose.

1. What are some human motives that lead us to disobey? (One example is the human ego, which lusts for power.) List several. _____

_____

_____

_____

_____

2. What, in your opinion, was the motive behind Saul's disobedience? _____

_____

_____

_____

3. Saul was given God's Holy Spirit to lead and empower him. Those who believe in Jesus and are baptized also receive God's Holy Spirit. What role does the Holy Spirit play in your life today? (You may wish to read **John 16:5-11; Romans 8:1-17; 1 Corinthians 12:1-13; Galatians 5:16-25; Ephesians 1:13-14;** and **1 John 4:13** before answering.)

_____

_____

_____

_____

4. Silently confess a time when you disobeyed God. Then ask God to forgive you and to give you His power to help you feel forgiven and happy.

I PRAISE THE LORD!

Fear of being caught in disobedience can take away the joy of being a child of God. While we should respect God, He does not want us to live in fear. Through Jesus Christ we are now friends of God. God is a God of love. The apostle **John wrote a great deal** about God's love for us in **1 John 4:7-21.** John says that perfect love casts out fear.

1. What do the following verses tell you about God's love? **1 John 4:7; 1 John 4:9; 1 John 4:10; 1 John 4:13; 1 John 4:17; 1 John 4:18; 1 John 4:21; 1 John 1:9.**

2. How do you feel about God's love for you?

_____

_____

_____

_____

3. What can you do to help others experience God's love?

_____

_____

_____

This might be a good time to count your blessings. Sometimes it's hard when things seem so messed up, as they were in Tony's case and in Saul's situation. Sometimes it's hard when your life seems to have little order. But counting your blessings really can help. Think about different areas of your life. Write down some of the neat things that have happened to you

in your family life: _____

_____

_____

_____

in your school life: _____

_____

_____

in your social life: _____

_____

_____

_____

in your spiritual life: _____

_____

_____

You can count your blessings! And thank and praise God for giving you a reason to be happy each day of your life! Thank Him for His forgiveness and His power for you to live! Be alive in Christ!

We should fear, love, and trust in God above all things.

(Meaning of the First Commandment)

Session 55

David: Preparation for Leadership

READING THE SCRIPTURES (1 Samuel 16—30)

David grew to be a young man whose life was filled with adventure. Through his experiences while protecting his father's flocks, God gave him the confidence he needed to fight Goliath. His greatest asset was his faith in God **(1 Samuel 17:37.** God's presence in David's life sustained him during some very trying times in the court of Saul, while he lived like a fugitive, and when his own children caused hirn grief.

Rather than being overwhelmed by his circumstances, David grew from them. God helped him become the mightiest warrior Israel had ever known.

Imagine yourself in David's position. How would you have reacted to the challenges he faced?

GOD HELPS DAVID LEAD HIS PEOPLE

The Israelites were intimidated by the giant, Goliath. Yet David was calm, confident, and ready on the offensive.

1. What was the source of David's confidence according to **1 Samuel 17:45?** _____
_____
_____
_____

2. When David was faced with Saul's repeated attacks he responded differently to Saul than he had to Goliath. Why did David react the way he did toward Saul? (Consider **1 Samuel 24** before answering.)
_____
_____
_____
_____

3. Saul's jealousy prevented him from enjoying

David's services as a soldier. Write a brief description comparing the personalities of Saul and David.
_____
_____
_____
_____
_____
_____
_____
_____

GOD GIVES CONFIDENCE TO ME

1. Does David's confidence and success against Goliath give you any encouragement for your own life? If so, how? If not, why not? (Read **Ephesians 1:18-21**).
_____
_____
_____
_____
_____
_____

2. Who are the Lord's anointed ones today? How do you react to those who are the Lord's servants?
_____
_____
_____
_____
_____

3. Do you have David's positive attitude when you have to deal with people who appear to be your ene-

mies? Why or why not? What would help you have more confidence?

_____

_____

_____

_____

_____

O LORD, RENEW MY HEART TO YOU

1. David seemed to enjoy what he was doing whether it was herding sheep, facing the enemies of Israel, or playing his harp for the king. Since his self-confidence came from God, do you think his contentment and patience did also? Give reasons for your answer.

_____

_____

_____

_____

2. Are there any changes God must make in your life to help you be the person you desire to be? What are they?

_____

_____

_____

_____

Now you can "clean up your act" and make a new commitment to God. You can proclaim Him as Lord of your life.

Look up each of these Bible references and match each reference with the phrase it describes. Draw a star symbol beside those that describe an area of your life you'd like to change or improve. Pray about these changes you'd like to see happen for you.

1 Thessalonians 5:17	Change in knowing Bible truths
2 Timothy 2:15	Change in my personal attitude
Ephesians 4:32	Change in how I treat others
Proverbs 15:13	Change in serving God
2 Peter 3:11	Change in family relationships
Colossians 3:20	Change in my facial expressions
Galatians 6:9	Change in my prayer life

3. It has been suggested that the first step toward change is to begin acting as though you already are the person you wish to become. Step out in faith. After asking God to give you confidence and the ability to be the person He desires you to be, list two things you will do differently tomorrow.

_____

_____

_____

_____

Be strong in the Lord and in His mighty power.
Ephesians 6:10

Session 56

David: The Warrior King

READING THE SCRIPTURES
(2 Samuel 2—10 and
1 Chronicles 11—20)

Not everyone agreed that David would be king of Israel after Saul's death. But after many years, God made David successful. David, the warrior, became king, and through him God fulfilled a promise made long before Abraham **(Genesis 15:18).** What was that promise? _____

_____

_____

God also promised that David's kingdom would endure forever **(2 Samuel 7:16)**, meaning that the Messiah would come from David's descendants. We know that the Messiah is our Savior and King, Jesus Christ.

As you read these portions of Scripture, briefly list the events that happened before David became Israel's king:

1. _____

2. _____

3. _____

4. _____

5. _____

GOD UNFOLDS HIS PLAN FOR ISRAEL

1. In the previous lesson, you learned that David respected Saul as the Lord's anointed. According to **2 Samuel 4:9-12,** what was the extent of his respect?

_____

_____

_____

2. David cared about his people **(2 Samuel 8:15)** and continued to respect the family of Saul **(2 Samuel 9).** David showed mercy to his enemies and at the same time was ruthless to the enemies of God **(2 Samuel 8:2).** How would you explain David's behavior?

_____

_____

_____

3. Read **2 Samuel 3:1** and **5:10.** What was the source of David's leadership ability, his compassion, and his success?

_____

_____

_____

_____

4. God's ultimate purpose in making David a successful king over Israel (apart from His love for David) is revealed in **2 Samuel 7:1-17.** What had God accomplished through David?

_____

_____

_____

_____

GOD KEPT HIS PROMISE TO DAVID

1. Read **2 Samuel 7:16.** How did God keep His promise to David?

_____

_____

_____

Then read **Psalm 89:1-4** and **35-37.** What do these verses tell us about God's promises kept to David?

_____

_____

_____

_____

2. Read **Luke 1:32-33.** Write how God kept His promise to David as told in these verses.

_____

_____

_____

_____

_____

GOD KEEPS HIS PROMISES TO ME

1. Read and think about **John 3:16.** What has God done to keep His promise and show His love to you?

_____

_____

_____

_____

2. In what other ways has God kept promises to you personally? _____

_____

_____

_____

_____

I THANK AND PRAISE GOD

1. David frequently wrote poems or psalms, describing how he felt about God's presence in His life. See **Psalm 30, 33,** and **21.** He even danced enthusiastically before the Lord **(2 Samuel 6:14).** Write a short praise-poem thanking God for helping you.

_____

_____

_____

_____

_____

2. List other ways you can express your praise to God. Check the ways you can praise God publicly.

_____

_____

_____

_____

_____

The plans of the Lord stand firm forever . . . blessed is the nation whose God is the Lord.
Psalm 33:11-12

Session 57

David: The Man

READING THE SCRIPTURES
(2 Samuel 11—19)

The Bible doesn't hide any facts about God's people that would prevent us from seeing them as they really were. In this way, God shows us the undeserved love He had for them—and has for us. This section of **2 Samuel** shows a side of David that is the exact opposite of the courageous, God-fearing man who grew from shepherd boy to king. David sinned with Bathsheba and then compounded the problem with further sins of murder and deceit. Try to identify with David's fears and his repentant spirit as you read the account.

If what you knew about David was based only on the information you read from **2 Samuel 11:1—12:25**, what would you think of him? _____

_____

_____

_____

_____

3. Nathan courageously confronted King David **(2 Samuel 12:1-12).** What technique did Nathan use to show David his sin? And what do you think about this technique? _____

_____

_____

_____

_____

_____

4. Read **Leviticus 20:10.** Compare this verse with the actual punishment David suffered. Which punishment do you think was more severe and why?

_____

_____

_____

_____

_____

_____

DAVID'S MISERY FROM SIN

1. David was sensitive about his wrongdoing and feared the consequences. In fear, he made several unsuccessful attempts to cover up his sins. Describe some of the feelings David might have had.

_____

_____

_____

2. The account of David's sins was written for our benefit, not for our entertainment. The consequences of his sins were staggering. Do you think he would have behaved otherwise had he known in advance the extent of misery that would result from his actions? Describe the extent of the misery unleashed by David's sins.

_____

_____

_____

_____

MY MISERY FROM SIN

1. Is my conscience working for me? Can I understand David's fear of being discovered? Think of a time you sinned. Did you panic at the thought of being caught? Tell some of your thoughts and emotions you experienced when you sinned and felt such panic:

_____

_____

_____

_____

_____

_____

_____

2. Our sins make us feel miserable. And we feel even more miserable when our sins multiply. The sins we commit again and again eventually lead to new sins.

We experience a "sin build-up." Write one important thing you have learned from David's experience:

_____

_____

_____

_____

GOD RESCUES ME WITH HIS LOVE AND FORGIVENESS

1. David's response to Nathan serves as a good example for us. What is implied in David's words, "**I have sinned against the Lord**" (2 Samuel 12:13)?

_____

_____

_____

2. Read **Psalm 51.** David wrote this in repentance over his sin. List several verses that are meaningful to you and tell why. _____

_____

_____

_____

_____

_____

_____

3. Use **Psalm 38:18, 21-22** as a beginning of your own confession to God. Ask God to forgive you for specific sins. Thank Him for correcting you as your loving heavenly Father. Accept His forgiveness and this renewal in your life. Then go joyfully about your work today.

4. Read **1 John 1:8-9.** What is God's promise to us sinners? _____

_____

_____

Read **Romans 8:2.** How do you feel after reading this verse?

_____

_____

_____

_____

The wages of sin is death, but the gift of God is eternal life in Christ Jesus our Lord.

Romans 6:23

Session 58

Solomon: Judge, Poet, Teacher

READING THE SCRIPTURES
(1 Kings 1:28—4:34)

As David grew too old to handle the government affairs in Israel, one of his sons tried to get himself declared king. When the prophet Nathan discovered the plot, he quickly arranged with Bathsheba to have David declare Solomon the next king over Israel. Solomon secured his position as king by disposing of those who might threaten him.

You will note that the Bible gives us no information about experiences Solomon might have had to prepare him for the throne. If anyone doubted his leadership ability, that doubt might have been dispelled quickly when Solomon demonstrated his God-given wisdom in judging the case between the two women, each of whom claimed to be the mother of the same child.

This section of Scripture assures us that all was going well in Israel. The people were content and Solomon ruled wisely. Israel appears to have been the most prosperous nation in the world at that time. The reason for their prosperity was quite simple—the Lord had established His people and intended to shower His blessings on them as He had promised Abraham.

Read **1 Kings 3:3-15.** Then read **Matthew 6:33.** Write the lessons these two passages teach us.

_____

_____

_____

_____

_____

_____

GOD'S BLESSINGS FOR SOLOMON AND HIS PEOPLE

1. Have you dreamed of having unlimited wealth (winning the lottery) or unlimited power (being president of your own company) at one time or another? Solomon had the opportunity to request anything from God that he wanted **(1 Kings 3:5).** What do you think of Solomon's choice **(1 Kings 3:7-9)?**

_____

_____

_____

_____

2. Solomon's request seems motivated by his sincere desire to serve the Lord and His people. How did God react to Solomon's request?

_____

_____

_____

3. According to **1 Kings 3:16-28; 4:1-19;** and **4:29-34,** Solomon was a capable administrator, judge, poet, and teacher. How did the people benefit from God's blessings on Solomon's various activities **(1 Kings 4:20)?** _____

_____

_____

_____

4. Solomon needed more than wisdom to be a good ruler. He also needed courage to act according to his convictions. List at least two examples from the first four chapters of **1 Kings** that show Solomon's courage. _____

_____

_____

_____

_____

_____

_____

5. What was the source of Solomon's courage? (Read **1 Kings 3:3** for help.) _____

_____

GOD'S BLESSINGS FOR ME

1. If you had been in Solomon's position and received an offer from the Lord as he did, how would you have responded? Why? _____

_____

_____

_____

2. God *has* given you the privilege of asking Him for anything you want! Read **Matthew 7:7-8** and **Matthew 18:19-20.** What would you ask from God?

_____

_____

_____

_____

3. Do you believe that God will grant your request? Why?

_____

_____

_____

4. Describe what might be accomplished if and when God does grant your request.

_____

_____

_____

5. What is the value of knowing God's will and having the confidence that He is present in your life?

_____

_____

_____

6. List some responsibilities that accompany God's gifts to us: _____

_____

_____

_____

_____

THE LORD IS ACTIVE IN MY LIFE

1. Read **Galatians 5:22-23.** Paul lists the fruit of the Spirit in these verses. Choose words from these verses that describe your own life and list them:

_____

_____

_____

_____

2. Write a short prayer confessing your sins and asking God to bless you with specific fruits of the Spirit. Pray then, expecting God to hear you and help you live in His ways.

_____

_____

_____

_____

_____

_____

Seek first His kingdom and His righteousness, and all these things will be given to you as well.
Matthew 6:33

Session 59

Solomon: The Builder

READING THE SCRIPTURES
(1 Kings 5—9 and 1 Chronicles
22; 28—29)

Your first impression of this section of Scripture may be that you are reading material intended for a building contractor or an architect. Some of the units of measure might be hard to understand, but you can decipher them with the help of a Bible dictionary.

The building of the temple was an exciting event in Israel. To some, the project might have appeared overwhelming, its cost beyond comprehension, and its significance hard to grasp. It took seven years to complete the magnificent structure, which Solomon then dedicated to the Lord in a two-week-long ceremony.

The people of Israel probably showed high interest in the progress of the temple construction since it would be the place where their God would dwell. How would you feel if you were an Israelite helping to build the temple? Remember, the temple had significance not only for the people in Israel, but also for the nations around them who saw how they honored their God.

THE TEMPLE IN ISRAEL

1. From your reading this section of Scripture, what kinds of events and projects do you think occupied Solomon's time while he was involved in building the temple? Did he focus on domestic affairs, war, or politics? Give examples to support your answer.

_____

_____

_____

_____

_____

_____

2. Solomon's temple proper was about 90 feet long, 30 feet wide, and 45 feet high. Walk around the outside of your own church building and estimate its

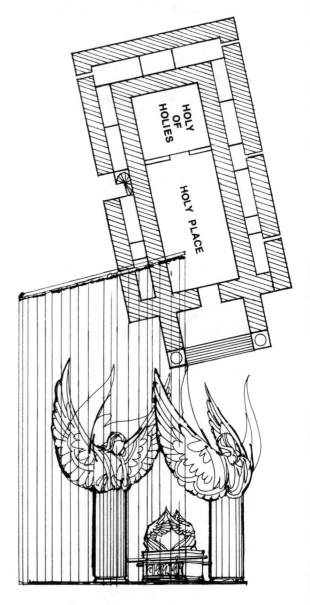

dimensions. How does your church compare in size to Solomon's temple? _____

_____

_____

_____

3. Describe the interior decorations of the temple sanctuary according to **1 Kings 6:20-22.**

_____

_____

_____

_____

_____

_____

Imagine you are walking into the temple sanctuary. Tell how you might react.

_____

_____

4. Read again **1 Samuel 8:10-18** and then **1 Kings 5:13-18.** If any of those who heard Samuel's warning were still alive when Solomon reigned, what might their reaction have been?

_____

_____

_____

5. David gathered about 3,750 tons of gold to be used for the temple **(1 Chronicles 22:14).** Call a bank to ask how much one ounce of gold is worth today. Then compute the approximate value today of David's gold. _____

_____

TEMPLES TODAY

1. Do you think Solomon's temple was worth all the money spent on it? Why or why not?

_____

_____

_____

2. Write briefly how you feel about worshiping in your home church. How do the surroundings, the decor, and the atmosphere affect your worship attitude?

_____

_____

_____

AM I A TEMPLE FOR THE LORD?

1. Note that the stone blocks for the temple were prepared at the quarry so no "**hammer, chisel, or any other iron tool was heard at the temple site while it was being built**" **(1 Kings 6:7).** Read the suggestion from **1 Peter 2:1-12** that God is even now shaping His people into a permanent temple. **1 Corinthians 3:16** tells you that _you_ are God's temple and that His Spirit lives in _you._ Do you believe what God says? In what ways has He shaped _your_ life so you are a suitable temple for Him?

_____

_____

_____

(If you find it hard to see God at work in your life, talk to your pastor or one of your teachers about this concept.)

2. The temple in Israel cost an enormous amount in materials, time, and energy. Yet everything involved was God's own property, for He had created all of it. God delights in giving enormous gifts back to us. He blessed Solomon with a palace larger and costlier than the temple itself. Have you discovered the joy of giving all that you are and all that you have to the Lord? Tell how you feel knowing that God accepts and uses you and blesses you as His "temple."

_____

_____

_____

3. Now read **Romans 12:1.** What is the significance of St. Paul's encouragement to present your entire being to God as a "living sacrifice?"

_____

_____

_____

What implications does it have for your life?

_____

_____

_____

_____

We have not received the spirit of the world but the Spirit who is from God, that we may understand what God has freely given us.

1 Corinthians 2:12

Session 60

Solomon: The Fool

READING THE SCRIPTURES (1 Kings 11)

In this section of Scripture, we meet a different Solomon. Suddenly he is no longer wise, wealthy, and sought after. He is a fool. Solomon's love of women and his desire to make political alliances by marrying foreign women resulted in a harem of 700 wives and 300 concubines (inferior wives).

Eventually Solomon's wives led him to commit other sins. In spite of repeated warnings to follow the Lord God faithfully, Solomon actually built places of worship for the false gods of his wives. Idolatry returned to Israel. What had been accomplished by David was undone by David's son.

Did Solomon have it so easy with all of his wealth, power, and fame that he became irresponsible? How would you have reacted in Solomon's position? In what ways did God keep His promises to Solomon?

_____

_____

_____

_____

SOLOMON ABUSES GOD'S BLESSINGS

1. God's gifts to Solomon of wealth, wisdom, and fame were all good and given in love. Why did they become a problem for Solomon?

_____

_____

_____

2. Compare the dramatic confrontation you read about between David and Nathan (2 Samuel 12:1-14) with the account of Solomon's reprimand by God in 1

Kings 11:1-13. What similarities and differences do you find? _____

_____

_____

_____

_____

_____

Read 1 Kings 11:9, 11-12. Then write a few statements describing the intense feelings God might have had over Solomon's disobedience.

_____

_____

_____

_____

3. In a Bible dictionary (Unger's Concise Bible Dictionary, for example), look up Chemosh, the god of Moab, and Molech, the god of the Ammonites. Describe these false gods and the rituals that were part of their worship.

_____

_____

_____

4. God waited until after Solomon's death to punish Israel for Solomon's sin. What would you have done? Why? _____

_____

_____

Who turns out to be more loving toward Solomon, you or God?

_____

_____

_____

_____

AM I USING OR ABUSING GOD'S BLESSINGS TO ME?

1. You should have discovered that the worship of *Chemosh* and *Molech* included some horrible practices involving children. Read **Luke 17:2.** God still cares about children today. List some ways children and their faith can be harmed today:

_____

_____

_____

How do parents "sacrifice" their children to idols today?

_____

_____

What can be done to stop harmful behavior toward children today?

_____

_____

2. List examples of idolatry today:

_____

What can you do, as a child of God, to overcome idolatry?

_____

_____

_____

What do you think will happen if idolatry continues in our country?

_____

_____

_____

Does God care anymore if we worship false gods? Defend your answer.

_____

_____

_____

3. What gifts and blessings has God given you? Tell how you are using what He has given you.

_____

_____

_____

_____

4. While God's gifts to us are good, left to our natural inclinations we have a tendency to misuse or ruin them. Tell ways that we can be sure to use God's gifts properly. Cite Scripture passages to support your answer.

_____

_____

_____

_____

GOD'S PROMISES FOR ME TO REMEMBER

1. Read **Romans 15:8; Hebrews 9:14-15;** and **1 John 2:25.** What important promise does God make and keep for you?

_____

_____

2. Tell in your own words (or paraphrase the words of the hymn "Take My Life, O Lord, Renew" [*LW* 404]) how you respond to God's love and great promises for you. _____

_____

_____

_____

_____

May the God of hope fill you with all joy and peace as you trust in Him, so that you may overflow with hope by the power of the Holy Spirit.
Romans 15:13

Session 61

Reviewing "The Monarchy— a United Kingdom" 1 Samuel; 1 Kings 1-11

The questions that follow will help you review the material covered in this unit and will help you gain an overall picture of the way in which God established His people in their own land. It will be helpful for you to write the answers to each of the questions.

1. What were the unique circumstances that led up to the birth of Samuel?

_____

_____

_____

_____

2. For what sin was Eli punished?

_____

_____

_____

3. Describe Samuel's role in Israel as prophet, priest, and judge, using references from Scripture to support your answers.

_____

_____

_____

_____

_____

4. What were Saul's qualifications for being king of Israel? How did God help Saul become an effective leader?

_____

_____

_____

_____

5. Give examples of the unique problems Saul faced as Israel's first king.

_____

_____

_____

_____

6. What were two of Saul's deliberate acts of disobedience, and how did God react to each of them?

_____

_____

_____

_____

7. Why did David accept Goliath's challenge, and why did he feel he could be successful against Goliath?

_____

_____

_____

_____

8. How did David demonstrate his respect for Saul as the Lord's anointed? _____

_____

_____

9. Describe the relationship between David and Jonathan. Tell how David showed respect for Jonathan's son. _____

_____

_____

_____

10. Describe David's attitude toward the Lord God.

_____

_____

11. What family problems did David face, and what was their cause? _____

_____

_____

_____

12. Summarize David's accomplishments as king of Israel.

_____

_____

_____

_____

_____

13. What gift did Solomon request from God?

_____

_____

14. List three of Solomon's accomplishments.

_____

_____

_____

15. How did Solomon offend God?

_____

_____

_____

16. Think about the lives of Samuel, Saul, David, and Solomon. Write down one lesson you learned from each of them.

a. Samuel _____

_____

_____

b. Saul _____

_____

_____

c. David _____

_____

_____

d. Solomon _____

_____

_____

17. How did God show His love to each of them?

_____

_____

_____

_____

_____

_____

_____

_____

18. How did God use Samuel, Saul, David, and Solomon to bless Israel?

_____

_____

_____

_____

_____

19. Whom do you consider to be the greatest king and why?

_____

_____

_____

20. What effect did the idolatry of Solomon's many wives have on Solomon and the rest of Israel?

_____

_____

_____

_____

_____

Unit 9

Worship in the Old Testament

What do we do when we "worship" God? We acknowledge Him as our God and give Him worth—our praise, thanks, honor, and trust. We tell Him how much we value Him and His role in our lives.

Worship actively involves our intellect, our emotions, our senses, and our spirit. We can worship deliberately or spontaneously. The people in the Old Testament worshiped God in a way He set for them. In this unit, you will learn about worship activities in the tabernacle and in Solomon's temple, discuss the subject of "giving," and learn more about the types and prophecies of Christ. You'll also discover some ways worship can be more meaningful for you!

Session 62

Worship in the Wilderness

READING THE SCRIPTURES
(Exodus 25—27; 33:4—40:38)

You are leaving the period of the monarchy in Israel to review the history of the worship activities of the people of Israel. Today you will review the construction of the tabernacle—God's wilderness home and the place where His people worshiped Him. As you read, look for the simplicity of the design and the dignity and function of the furnishings.

Think of a time when you may have worshiped in an outdoor setting or in a makeshift chapel. Was your worship especially meaningful? Imagine yourself in Israel having to go through the rituals and sacrifices that God demanded. What do you think the typical Israelite thought of God? What feelings did the Israelites have during their worship services?

GOD'S TENT

1. What is a tabernacle?

_____

_____

_____

_____

2. What resources did the Israelites have for building the tabernacle? Where did they get them?

_____

_____

_____

_____

3. The furnishings for the tabernacle were simple. What were they, and where were they located?

_____

_____

_____

_____

4. Why was it important that the tabernacle could be moved easily? _____

_____

_____

_____

GOD'S GLORY

1. According to **Exodus 40:34-38**, how did God make His presence known in the tabernacle?

_____

_____

_____

_____

2. How is God present with us today?

_____

_____

_____

_____

3. List some ways God reveals His glory today.

_____

_____

_____

_____

4. How do you know God is present when you worship Him today? Give some references from Scripture to support your answer.

_____

_____

_____

_____

_____

WHAT DOES IT ALL MEAN?

The tabernacle was important to the Israelites not only because it represented God's presence, but also because of the worship that took place there regularly. The worship of the Israelites was much different from ours. Do you know why?

1. What was the reason for the repetition of the sacrifices year after year **(Hebrews 10:1-4, 11)?**

_____

_____

_____

_____

2. How did the death of Christ serve as the sacrifice that satisfied God for all time **(Hebrews 10:5-10, 12-18)?**

_____

_____

_____

3. What does your worship of God mean to you? What has influenced your opinion?

_____

_____

_____

_____

_____

_____

4. Write a description of God as you think of Him.

_____

_____

_____

_____

Ascribe to the Lord the glory due His name. Bring an offering and come before Him; worship the Lord in the splendor of His holiness.

1 Chronicles 16:29

Session 63

Worship in Solomon's Temple

READING THE SCRIPTURES
(1 Chronicles 22—26; 2 Chronicles 3—7; Numbers 18; Hebrews 9:1—10:18)

Wow! That's a lot of reading! True, but there is a reason for it. There was nothing haphazard about the way the people of Israel worshiped God. Everything done by the large staff of priests and their helpers had meaning and purpose. And worship was an important part of the daily life of the Israelites, especially those who lived in Jerusalem, where the temple was. As you read, be on the lookout for the people and procedures that God required for worship. How do the arrangements compare with your worship experiences today? You will discover that you have more freedom to express your love for God because of what Jesus Christ has done for you.

STAFFING A TEMPLE

You will discover as you read that a lot of people were involved in Israel's worship procedures.

1. Identify the group described in:

a. **1 Chronicles 23:13** and **24:1-19**

_____

_____

b. **1 Chronicles 23:28-32**

_____

_____

c. **1 Chronicles 25:1-8**

_____

_____

d. **1 Chronicles 26:19**

_____

_____

_____

e. **1 Chronicles 26:20**

_____

2. What responsibilities did each group have?

a. _____

_____

b. _____

_____

c. _____

_____

d. _____

_____

e. _____

_____

IMPERFECT SACRIFICES

Read **1 Chronicles 23:28-32** again. Much activity took place in the temple each day, and even more took place on the days when festivals were celebrated.

1. Why, do you suppose, did God require such frequent sacrifices?_____

_____

_____

_____

2. Why is there a difference between Christian worship and that of ancient Israel?

_____

_____

_____

_____

3. Ask your pastor, DCE, church secretary, or altar guild member to describe some of the special preparations that go into a worship service. (You may wish to coordinate this with classmates who may belong to your church. Visit these staff people as a group, so they are not bombarded with questions.) What are some of your findings?

_____

_____

_____

_____

4. Select one of the preparations that is new to you and explain its purpose.

_____

_____

_____

_____

_____

_____

_____

_____

_____

_____

DRAW NEAR TO GOD

In Session 59 you had a look at the splendor of Solomon's temple. Read **Hebrews 9:24** and **10:1.** Here you discover that the temple was only a glimpse of God's real dwelling place and the perfect sacrifice of Jesus Christ was foreshadowed by the sacrifices performed in the temple. Based on the above information:

1. What did Jesus Christ accomplish for you personally?

_____

_____

_____

_____

2. Express your feelings over the sacrifice of Jesus Christ in a prayer to God. Be prepared to read it in class.

_____

_____

_____

_____

_____

_____

3. Identify something that has made your worship experience more meaningful. It might be a part of the liturgy, a special liturgy, a hymn, song, poem, special reading, or art object. Be prepared to share this information with the class.

_____

_____

_____

4. Have you learned anything in recent sessions that makes your worship more meaningful? If so, what?

_____

_____

_____

_____

Christ was sacrificed once to take away the sins of many people; and He will appear a second time, not to bear sin, but to bring salvation to those who are waiting for Him.

Hebrews 9:28

We have been made holy through the sacrifice of the body of Jesus Christ once and for all.

Hebrews 10:10

By one sacrifice He has made perfect forever those who are being made holy.

Hebrews 10:14

Where these [sins] have been forgiven, there is no longer any sacrifice for sin.

Hebrews 10:18

Session 64

God Moves His People to Give

READING THE SCRIPTURES
(Exodus 25:1-8; 2 Samuel 24:18-25; 1 Chronicles 29:1-9)

The subject of this session is *giving*. Dad shared Saturday, his day off work, by helping construct a children's playground at the neighborhood park.

Uncle Ted surprised his two young nieces with two sleds that his own children had outgrown.

Each Wednesday, Grandma delivers hot, nutritious "Meals on Wheels" to elderly and physically handicapped shut-ins living in her small town.

Five-year-old Bethany drops the shiniest pennies, nickels, and dimes from her bank into her Sunday school class offering basket. "I picked the shiniest coins for Jesus!" she exclaims.

Each of these examples illustrates a loving, giving experience. One person willingly shared something of himself or herself with others. In what way did each person give?

Giving—sharing—means offering the use of your time, your abilities, and/or your money to serve others in a specific way.

Can you remember when someone gave something of himself or herself to you? And can you think of a time when you shared yourself with someone else?

As you read the Scripture selections listed above, find out what—and why—the people gave in the Old Testament times.

GIVE, GIVE, GIVE

These passages will help you understand the opportunities the people of the Old Testament had for giving.

1. Read each passage and explain what is happening.

a. **Genesis 14:20** _____

b. **Leviticus 27:30-34** _____

c. **Genesis 4:3-5** _____

d. **Genesis 8:20** _____

e. **Exodus 23:15** _____

f. **Exodus 25:2** and **36:5** _____

_____

2. Which of the above refer to gifts or sacrifices that were

a. required _____

b. spontaneous _____

GIVING—MY DUTY OR PRIVILEGE?

In *A Christmas Carol*, Charles Dickens pictures Ebenezer Scrooge first as a stingy old man and then as a generous loving person. Each of us probably experiences some of Ebenezer Scrooge's different feelings.

But let's see what God has to say about giving. Look up the passages listed below. On a separate sheet of paper summarize what you learn from each.

1. Reasons for my giving
   a. **John 3:16**
   b. **2 Corinthians 8:9**
   c. **1 John 3:17**
   d. **Acts 20:35**
   e. **Proverbs 3:9-10**
2. Attitudes about my giving
   a. **2 Corinthians 9:7**
   b. **Exodus 36:3-5**
   c. **2 Corinthians 8:13**
3. The extent of my giving
   a. **2 Corinthians 8:12**
   b. **Luke 21:1-3**
   c. **Genesis 14:20**
4. The nature of my giving
   a. **2 Corinthians 8:5**
   b. **Romans 12:3-8**
5. The purpose of my giving
   a. **1 Chronicles 29:7-8**
   b. **Proverbs 19:17; 28:27**
   c. **Galatians 6:6**
   d. **Philippians 4:15-16**

ATTITUDE CHECK

Your attitudes about giving have been influenced by various experiences. Sometimes we may even have a good attitude about giving and then have a bad experience when people take advantage of us. God only encourages us to give. He does not ask us to give only to those we think deserve our help. Remember, we never did anything to deserve Jesus Christ, whom God gave as our Savior.

1. Check the statements below that describe your attitude toward giving. Be honest with yourself, okay?
   _____ 1. I give like a stingy Scrooge.
   _____ 2. I give like a generous Scrooge.
   _____ 3. I use my talents for myself.
   _____ 4. I use my talents for others.
   _____ 5. I don't think about giving very often.
   _____ 6. I look for opportunities to give.
   _____ 7. I have no plan for giving regularly.
   _____ 8. I have a plan for regular giving.
   _____ 9. I seldom experience joy in giving.
   _____10. I often experience joy in giving.

2. Now tabulate your responses. Count the number of odd-numbered responses and the even-numbered responses and record them below.

   _____ odd-numbered responses

   _____ even-numbered responses

If you checked the even-numbered statements, you probably have a more positive attitude toward giving. If you checked more of the odd-numbered statements, you might like to reevaluate your giving attitudes.

3. Are you satisfied with what you have discovered about yourself? If not, perhaps the next activity will be of some help to you.

I GIVE MYSELF TO GOD AND TO OTHERS

We live at a time when we are encouraged to satisfy, gratify, and magnify ourselves, and here we are talking about giving to others. Doesn't it sound like we are trying to swim upstream against popular opinion? Actually we are focusing on things that have eternal value!

1. Read **2 Corinthians 8:1-15.** Which verses stand out for you? Why? _____

_____

_____

_____

2. What does **2 Corinthians 8:5** mean to you?

_____

_____

3. Think of someone who needs a gift from you— a listening ear, a loving touch, help with homework, lunch money, a hospital visit. Name that person and what you have to share with him or her.

_____

_____

_____

4. Speak to God in personal prayer about your giving attitudes. Ask Him to help you be responsibly loving and giving. Thank Him for the happiness that giving returns to you.

Be imitators of God . . . as dearly loved children and live a life of love, just as Christ loved us and gave Himself up for us as a fragrant offering and sacrifice to God.

Ephesians 5:1-2

Session 65

Types and Prophecies of Christ in the Old Testament

READING THE SCRIPTURES (Genesis 3:15; Exodus 29:38-42; Isaiah 53:7; Genesis 22:1-12; Leviticus 16:6-22; Isaiah 52:14)

This session will help you discover how God prepared His people to recognize and receive Jesus Christ. You will be reminded of how wonderful God's love is for you and what Jesus did for you. Remember, God's Holy Spirit is working in you through the Word, so expect a blessing.

You will encounter the word *type* periodically in reference to some event, object, or person that resembles Christ and was supposed to help people identify Christ when He came. How does a dictionary define the word *type* as we are using it?

_____

_____

_____

"THE SCRIPTURES . . . TESTIFY ABOUT ME" (John 5:39)

1. In the following passages you will find types (sacrifices or prophecies) of Christ. Identify each and comment on how it describes Him.

a. **Exodus 29:38-42**

_____

_____

b. **Leviticus 16:6-22**

_____

_____

c. **Genesis 22:1-12**

_____

_____

d. **Leviticus 22:17-20**

_____

_____

2. If you did not know Christ as you do, what would you discover about Him from the above passages?

_____

_____

_____

3. Find New Testament passages that describe Christ. (You may use a concordance.)

_____

_____

_____

_____

HINDSIGHT, FORESIGHT, AND INSIGHT

If we could look into the future we might make fewer mistakes. As it is, we must use our best judgment and act on the basis of the insights we gain from our knowledge and experiences. God generously gives us insights that help us prepare for the future. He did the same for Israel.

1. What insights do these prophecies give about Jesus?

a. **Isaiah 53:7**

_____

_____

b. **Isaiah 53:4-6**

_____

_____

c. **Isaiah 52:14**

_____

_____

2. We have the advantage of knowing the prophecies about Christ as well as their fulfillment. What advantage should we have?

_____

_____

3. Read **Deuteronomy 4:29** and **1 Timothy 2:3-6.** What do you learn about God from these passages?

_____

_____

4. Read **Isaiah 53:3** and **Romans 1:18-23.** In spite of God's interest in them what do some people do?

_____

_____

_____

WHY DID JESUS HAVE TO DIE?

In **Genesis 3:19** we learn that human beings will die because of the sin of Adam and Eve. Until Jesus came and died for us, we were doomed to eternal separation from God because of our sin. Now some dramatic things have happened. Read on to discover what they are.

1. Read **Exodus 12:13** and **Leviticus 16:15-16.** What was God looking for?

_____

_____

_____

2. How often were Passover and the Day of Atonement celebrated?

_____

_____

_____

3. Read **Hebrews 9:11-14** and **Revelation 5:6** and **9-10.** What did Jesus do that satisfied God? How often did He do it?

_____

_____

4. Read **Romans 6:4-6.** What else has Jesus done for you?

_____

_____

5. In the Old Testament, God's people brought sacrifices to God. In Jesus Christ, God brought the sacrifice Himself. Read **John 1:12.** How do we have the right to be children of God?

_____

_____

6. Write a prayer of thanks to God for what Jesus Christ has done for you based on what you have discovered in this session. Be prepared to share your prayer in class.

_____

_____

_____

_____

_____

_____

God did not send His Son into the world to condemn the world, but to save the world through Him.
John 3:17

Session 66

Making Worship Meaningful

How would you like to express your feelings about God to Him? This session provides an opportunity for you and your classmates to develop a meaningful worship service.

PLAN A MEANINGFUL WORSHIP SERVICE

1. Get together with one or more of your classmates to design a worship format that could be used in one of your school chapel services. After you come up with some ideas, share them with others in your class. Your whole class, finally, will decide on the format you will use.

2. Read **Acts 2:42-47** before proceeding. What were some of the things the disciples of Christ did when they got together?

_____

_____

_____

_____

_____

_____

_____

_____

3. Here are some questions to think about as you organize your suggestions for the worship service.
   a. What has God done for me?
   b. How can I show my love for God in worship?
   c. How can I share my love for God with others?
   d. What talents do I have for use in worship? ·
   e. How can I present a gift to God?
   f. Do I have a leadership gift to be used in worship?

4. Outline the specific worship activities, explain their purpose, and make assignments for each.

5. Your teacher may decide to base your grade for this unit on the worship format you design. That makes this assignment important, but not nearly as important as what you say to God through your worship. Make sure your primary goal is to offer a meaningful worship experience.

May God bless you and make you a blessing to others.

EVALUATE A WORSHIP SERVICE

Attend and evaluate a worship service. Use the following outline:
1. Your name; name of church; location; pastor; date; time
2. Outline of service activities
3. Central theme or focus of the service
4. Opportunities to praise God
5. Opportunities to share faith with others
6. Way that God's Word was presented (readings, sermon, etc.)
7. Sacraments, if any, that were celebrated
8. Something that made an impression on you
9. Something that was lacking
10. Your overall impression of the service

We proclaim to you what we have seen and heard, so that you also may have fellowship with us. And our fellowship is with the Father and with His Son, Jesus Christ.

John 1:3

Unit 10

A People Divided

Emily started working at "Fashion Fair" soon after she turned 16. Twice each month she spent a large part of her paycheck for new clothes and accessories and deposited the rest of her money in her savings account. She planned to use that money to go with friends to the beach the week of spring break. Emily's unemployed father and part-time working mother barely managed to pay the family's bills. But Emily wasn't about to put any of *her* money into *their* funds! She only wanted to buy what she liked and wanted. Emily thought she'd have it made if she could keep working, keep earning, and keep spending!

Think of three things that *you* value most in *your* life. Where do these three things rank compared to your relationship with God? Often, it's so easy to slide into a life-style where we want, want, and want some more. Then, it seems, the more we get, the more we want, and the cycle continues until we've made many "gods" out of material things in our lives. We tear ourselves away from the true God and suffer when we lose our loving relationship with Him.

Matthew 22:37-38 reminds us of an important command God gives us. Jesus says, **"Love the Lord your God with all your heart and with all your soul and with all your mind. This is the first and greatest commandment."** And because God made us, keeps us in His love, saves us from all our sins, and gives us His Word to hear and learn, we're able to say, "I know God, and I love Him. I want to put Him first in my life. And I know that everything else will fall into place for me!" By the power of the Holy Spirit, who lives and works in our hearts, we can fear, love, and trust in God above all things. We can know God and keep Him "number one" in our lives!

Throughout this unit, you'll be reading about how God's people suffered as a result of practicing idolatry and how God constantly loved and protected them. You'll learn more about His patience, His expectations, and His willingness to forgive those who repent of their sins.

Session 67
The Kingdom Torn Away

READING THE SCRIPTURES
(1 Kings 11—12)

Do you think history repeats itself? You might find that happening in this session. Winston Churchill has been credited with saying, "The one thing we learn from history is that we never learn anything from history." Do you agree with that statement?

In this session you'll discover that once again the kings of Israel practice idolatry and the Lord must intervene. A split in the kingdom of Israel is about to occur as a result of idolatry. Things *will* get worse before they get better. Read the Scripture accounts to find many events that have long-term effects on God's people.

AN OLD PROBLEM

How well do you remember Solomon's mistakes (Session 60)? Let's review.

1. Read **1 Kings 11:1-10.** Then identify Solomon's weaknesses.

a. **1 Kings 11:1** _____

_____

b. **1 Kings 11:2** _____

_____

c. **1 Kings 11:3-4** _____

_____

d. **1 Kings 11:5-8** _____

_____

2. Solomon's greatest sin was the sin of "apostasy." Look in a Bible dictionary and write the definition of "apostasy."

_____

_____

A DRAMATIC SOLUTION

God didn't tolerate Solomon's apostasy. He told Solomon that he would lose the kingdom to one of his subordinates **(1 Kings 11:11).**

1. Twice God appeared to Solomon and emphasized the importance of faithful obedience **(1 Kings 3:5** and **9:2).** What were the occasions?

_____

_____

_____

2. What did God say to Solomon during his appearances?

_____

_____

_____

3. What was to be the long-range solution to the problem of Solomon's sin **(1 Kings 11:11-13)?**

_____

_____

4. What was God's immediate response to Solomon's sin **(14-40)?**

_____

_____

_____

5. What do you think God was trying to do by punishing Solomon? (Think about what God did at the time of the judges, when He allowed Israel to be oppressed in an effort to wipe out idolatry and bring His people back to Himself.) _____

_____

_____

THE DIVISION BEGINS

Solomon was an impressive king. It's a shame that his foolishness led to the breakup of a great nation after his death. Read **1 Kings 12** to learn about the events and prime characters who were part of the breakup.

1. Who was Rehoboam **(1 Kings 11:43)?**

_____

_____

2. What mistake did he make **(1 Kings 12:1-14)?**

_____

_____

3. How did Rehoboam's decision fit into God's plan?

_____

_____

_____

4. What did the slogan "To your tents, O Israel" mean?

_____

_____

5. What promise had God made to Jeroboam **(1 Kings 11:34-39)?** _____

Was it necessary for Jeroboam to rebel against Rehoboam?

_____

_____

6. What did Jeroboam do to secure his position?

a. **1 Kings 12:25** _____

b. **12:26-30** _____

c. **12:31-33** _____

7. Even if you didn't know the eventual outcome, what would you predict would happen to Israel because of what Jeroboam did?

_____

_____

_____

_____

God says to His people, I will be an enemy to your enemies, and will oppose those who oppose you.
Exodus 23:22

Session 68
Blatant Apostasy

READING THE SCRIPTURES
(Jude 1-25)

During this session, you'll be studying apostasy—the primary case for the division of Israel. You'll take a look at a New Testament letter that describes apostasy in terms relating to our world today. Jude, the author of the letter, is believed to have been one of Jesus' brothers. He wrote about some perplexing problems that the early Christians faced. Read the verses from Jude. Do any of the things he described still exist today? What advice and encouragement does he give? How is it valuable today?

I WANT TO REMIND YOU

1. Jude wrote his letter to remind his readers that certain evil men had infiltrated the ranks of their church. What three characteristics did Jude say made them dangerous (v. 4)?

_____

_____

_____

2. Jude refers his readers to some important historical truths about God. Of what three things did Jude remind his readers (Jude 5, 6, and 7)?

_____

_____

_____

3. The deeds of the men in verse 4 had earned them God's wrath. God compares their deeds to three things in Jude 11. What are they? (You might use a Bible commentary to help answer this question.)

_____

_____

_____

_____

4. The infiltrators were also to be identified by other negative behaviors. What were they (Jude 16)?

_____

_____

_____

_____

DID YOU KNOW THIS?

If you look closely at some of the things that were a part of Solomon's apostasy, you'll find that they were both immoral and idolatrous. Let's face it—evil is in our world. The Israelites weren't the only ones who faced temptations and challenges.

1. Look at the world around you. What are some of the things that test your faith?

_____

_____

_____

_____

2. Look at the adult world—you'll be an important person in it soon! What spiritual challenges do you anticipate facing then? _____

_____

_____

_____

ABOUT THE SALVATION WE SHARE

According to 1 John 2:16, the things of this world are appealing. We all feel good about having things like a comfortable home, audiovisual equipment, fun vacations, money in the bank, a new car, and lots more. But because they sometimes lure us away from God, they're nothing but trouble. According to Jude 12-13, immoral and idolatrous behavior leads to emptiness. It has no value compared to knowing Christ (Philippians 3:8-11).

1. Read **Jude 24.** What is Jesus Christ able to do for us?

_____

_____

_____

_____

2. According to **Jude 25**, what does Jesus Christ deserve?

_____

_____

_____

_____

Who shall separate us from the love of Christ? . . . I am convinced that neither death nor life, neither angels nor demons, neither the present nor the future, nor any powers, neither height nor depth, nor anything else in all creation, will be able to separate us from the love of God that is in Christ Jesus our Lord.

Romans 8:35 and 38

I know whom I have believed, and am convinced that He [Jesus Christ] is able to guard what I have entrusted to Him for that day.

2 Timothy 1:12b

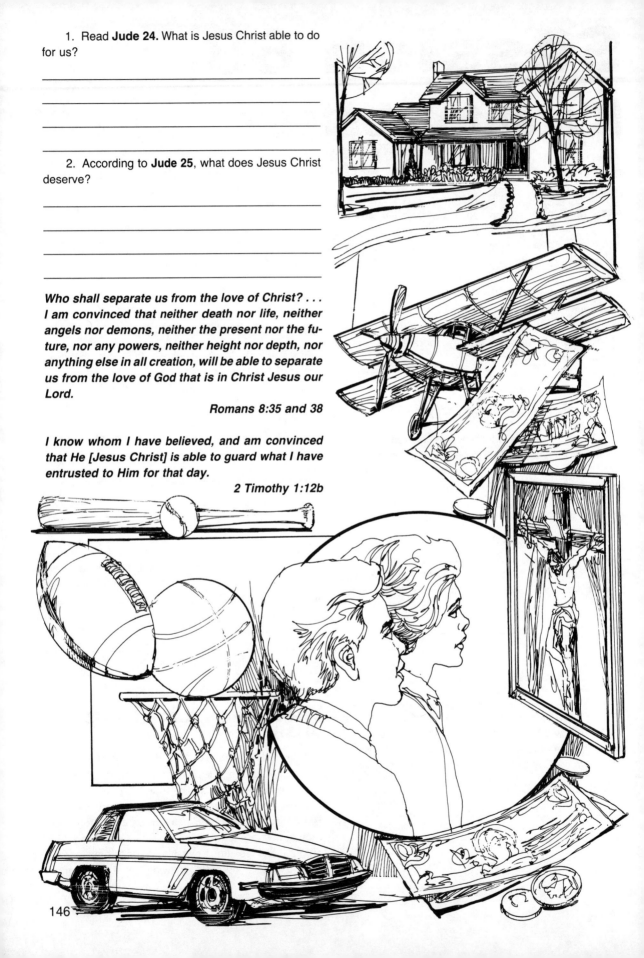

Session 69

Jeroboam—Setting a Course for Israel

READING THE SCRIPTURES
(1 Kings 12:20—14:20)

Have you ever hiked with Scouts or a "Y" group and followed a leader who was responsible for setting the course for the whole group? Did your leader chop hatchet marks into the trees along the path to make sure you'd get back safely along the same route? Or did your leader become one of the group and, while having fun hiking and talking, forget his responsibility to keep everyone else on the right course, causing everybody to get lost? Something like this happened a long time ago in Israel. You'll find out more about it in today's session.

Jeroboam was the first king of the 10 northern tribes (which were known as Israel). He reigned for only 22 years, but during that time he set a disastrous course for Israel. The Scripture account of Jeroboam's reign is brief but it gives you an accurate description of his behavior and attitude. The leaders of a nation have tremendous responsibility to both God and their people. But even a dictator can get away with only as much as the people will allow. Thus the whole nation of Israel shared Jeroboam's guilt. Read **1 Kings 12:20—14:20**. Look for things that show Jeroboam's attitude toward God. Also look for evidence of God's incredible love for His people.

REBELLION

1. Refer again to the whole Scripture reading for this session. How did Jeroboam rebel against God? List at least five examples of his wrongdoing.

_____

_____

_____

_____

_____

_____

2. God gave Jeroboam at least two warnings. Identify the passages that tell the warnings and explain them. _____

_____

_____

_____

RETRIBUTION

If someone gives you retribution, they have paid you back by either rewarding or punishing you. Can you think of a time when someone gave you retribution for something you did?

Someone has said that if God doesn't punish America for its immorality, He will have to apologize to Sodom and Gomorrah. How do you feel about that statement? It's both a warning and an expectation that God will be consistent in punishing sin. God will allow sin to continue unchecked only so long, and then He'll put an end to it. Jeroboam should have realized that God wouldn't tolerate what he was doing.

1. Read **1 Kings 13:33.** What was Jeroboam's attitude toward God? _____

_____

_____

2. Jeroboam had to pay for his sins. What did it cost him **(1 Kings 14:12-16)?** _____

_____

_____

3. What caused the Lord's anger **(1 Kings 14: 15b)?** _____

_____

4. How would you have reacted to God's warnings if you were Jeroboam? _____

_____

5. Pretend you are Jeroboam and you've just heard the Lord's warnings. Write a prayer confessing what you did wrong and ask for forgiveness.

_____

_____

_____

_____

_____

_____

_____

_____

REMNANT

A remnant is a small part of something that remains from the original. An example would be a "remnant of fabric"—a portion of a piece of cloth—that is left from the large bolt of fabric. "Remnant" also describes the people who remain faithful to God when those around them are unfaithful.

1. Read **2 Chronicles 11:13-17.** What do these verses tell you about the remnant in Israel during the time of Jeroboam?

_____

_____

_____

2. Describe God's remnant. Why was this remnant important? And how did the people feel toward God?

_____

_____

_____

3. Tell how you've seen God's love shown in the account of Jeroboam. _____

_____

_____

4. What have you learned from this session that helps you in your own daily living? _____

_____

_____

_____

_____

Your righteousness is like the mighty mountains, Your justice like the great deep. O Lord, You preserve both man and beast.

Psalm 36:6

All have sinned and fall short of the glory of God, and are justified freely by His grace through the redemption that came by Christ Jesus.

Romans 3:23-24

Session 70

Ahab and Elijah

READING THE SCRIPTURES (1 Kings 16:29—22:40)

Ahab's life was a life of extremes. He was incredibly wicked most of the time. But when God confronted him through the prophet Elijah, Ahab humbled himself before the Lord. When he didn't get his own way, Ahab pouted like a child. He also allowed his wife to influence him to do evil.

Read **1 Kings 16:29—22:40** to find out how God kept Ahab under control and to see how God used His prophet to influence Ahab.

FROM BAD TO WORSE

1. Read the summary of Ahab's behavior in **1 Kings 16:29-34.** Describe his attitudes and behavior using the following verses:

a. v. **31** _____

_____

_____

b. v. **32** _____

_____

_____

_____

c. v. **33** _____

_____

_____

d. v. **34** _____

_____

_____

2. Identify and describe Ahab's evils from these passages:

a. 1 Kings 20:42-43 _____

_____

_____

_____

b. **1 Kings 21:4 and 16** _____

_____

_____

3. Now that you know something about Ahab, write a short description of his character.

_____

_____

_____

_____

_____

GOD'S ENVOYS FOR ISRAEL

In the past session you learned that God had a remnant of believers in Israel. At the time of Ahab the most prominent believer was Elijah. You'll be taking a closer look at Elijah in the next session, but for now, let's see what some of his assignments were.

1. Read **1 Kings 18:1-15.** Who were the two men of God mentioned? _____

2. One was more prominent than the other as far as public service to God was concerned.

a. Who was the more prominent servant? _____ What did he do? _____

b. Who was the other servant and what great service did he do? _____

_____

3. Read **1 Kings 21:17-24.** Elijah had to deliver a stern message to King Ahab. Put yourself in Elijah's place. How do you think you might have felt if you were Elijah? _____

_____

_____

GOD'S ENVOYS FOR US

Sometimes God controls wickedness by placing His spokespersons in the right place at the right time. Elijah was a great man of God. And great men and women of God surround you right now, too!

149

1. Think of the people you know—young and old, men and women. Are any of them special representatives of God in your life? (They don't have to be like Elijah to be God's representatives. They may be your parents, your neighbors, or someone you know at church or school.) Name one or two people you thought of. _____

_____

2. God sends special envoys—representatives—to us to help us, to give us guidance, to support us when we're down, to comfort us when we're hurt, to encourage us to live our lives in Christ Jesus. They are special blessings from God.

Write a prayer naming one of the special persons you identified in question 1. Describe what that person has done and thank God for sending that special envoy into your life. Also pray for God's blessings on that person.

_____

_____

_____

_____

_____

_____

_____

_____

_____

There will be trouble and distress for every human being who does evil . . . God does not show favoritism.

Romans 2:9 and **11**

He gave some, apostles; and some, prophets; and some, evangelists; and some, pastors and teachers; for the perfecting of the saints, for the work of the ministry, for the edifying of the body of Christ. . .

Ephesians 4:11-12

Session 71

Elijah—God's Servant

READING THE SCRIPTURES
(1 Kings 18:16—19:21)

In this session you will discover important and practical truths about God. God cares for us. He shows that in the way He cared for Elijah, by His promises through Isaiah, and through the ministry of Jesus Christ.

Elijah had some very special needs. He worked hard for the Lord against some difficult odds. But the Lord was with him. You'll realize that God is with you, too.

Read **1 Kings 18:16—19:21.** What were some of Elijah's challenges? How did God help him through them?

ORDINARY MAN—
EXTRAORDINARY GOD

1. Read again **1 Kings 18:16-45.**

a. Elijah set up a contest with the prophets of Baal. What were the rules? _____

_____

_____

b. What did the prophets of Baal do to influence their god **(1 Kings 18:26-29)?** What was the result?

_____

_____

_____

c. What did Elijah do to influence the Lord God?

_____

_____

_____

d. How did God make it obvious that He is the only living and all-powerful God **(1 Kings 18:38)?**

_____

_____

_____

_____

2. Why do you think the prophets of Baal were

slaughtered after the contest? (See **Deuteronomy 13:1-11.**) _____

_____

_____

_____

3. Why do you think God made Elijah run before Ahab's chariot all the way to Jezreel, a distance of about 15 miles **(1 Kings 18:46)?**

_____

_____

_____

4. Read **1 Kings 19:1-4.** What do you discover about Elijah that shows he was an ordinary person?

_____

_____

_____

GOD SERVES HIS SERVANT

1. God had given Elijah another special assignment and helped him through it. But now Elijah needed God's help for problems of his own. What were Elijah's needs?

a. **1 Kings 19:5** _____

b. **1 Kings 19:6 and 8** _____

c. **1 Kings 19:9-13** _____

d. **1 Kings 19:14-18** _____

2. How did God care for Elijah in each of these instances? _____

_____

3. God gave Elijah the important gift of a friend. Who was he? _____

4. What do you think of God's service to His servant? _____

_____

_____

_____

HOPE IN THE LORD

1. Have you ever experienced any of Elijah's feelings or needs? What were they?

_____

_____

2. What caused those feelings or needs?

_____

_____

_____

3. Do you think God cares about your feelings or needs? Why? _____

_____

4. What does God say to you in each of the following passages?

a. **Matthew 20:25-28** _____

b. **2 Corinthians 1:3-5** _____

c. **1 Peter 5:7** _____

d. **Isaiah 40:27-31** _____

5. After reading the above passages, would you like to make any changes in your answer to question 3? Write your new answer.

_____

6. Have you ever reached the point where, like Elijah, you felt you had enough **(1 Kings 19:4)?** Remember, God loves *you*, and is eager to minister to *your* needs. Write a prayer asking Him to minister to your needs. _____

_____

_____

_____

_____

_____

[The Lord] gives strength to the weary and increases the power of the weak. . . . Those who hope in the Lord will renew their strength. They will soar on wings like eagles; they will run and not grow weary, they will walk and not be faint.

Isaiah 40:29 and 31

Session 72

Israel Taken Captive

READING THE SCRIPTURES (2 Kings 17)

Have you ever read a good book and felt that its ending was very disappointing?

After reading all the evil deeds Israel committed before the Lord, the account of the last days of Israel seems almost anticlimactic, like the ending of the book that disappointed you. You'd almost expect God to get so tired of the continual idolatry of the people that He would unleash some horrible destructive force against them. Instead, God brought Israel's enemies against them. Certainly the people suffered terribly, but God chose not to reveal most of that misery to us.

Samaria lay under siege for three years. That certainly was not a pleasant experience. (Sometime read the story of the siege of Stalingrad during World War II to learn about the misery of war.)

Read **2 Kings 17.** Try to imagine all that was happening in Israel.

THE END OF THE LINE

Have you ever seen a game in which a player made a mistake that resulted in the loss of the contest? Imagine the sinking feeling that comes with such a mistake! The last king of Israel made a mistake that lost the nation to its enemy. It took three years for Samaria to fall, but when it did, the nation of Israel ceased to exist. This exercise will help you understand how it all happened.

1. Read **2 Kings 15:30.** How did Hoshea become king?

_____

_____

2. What additional information do you get from **2 Kings 15:29** about the conditions in Israel when Hoshea took the throne?

_____

_____

_____

3. Why did the king of Assyria consider Hoshea a traitor **(2 Kings 17:4a)?**

_____

_____

4. What did Hoshea's decision cost him personally **(2 Kings 17:4b)?**

_____

_____

NO WAY BACK

During the war in Vietnam entire villages were relocated because homes were situated in a particularly volatile war zone. Those who were not involved can only speculate on the demoralizing effects such moves had on the Vietnamese people.

Though it wasn't to help the people, something similar happened as a result of Shalmaneser's invasion.

1. Read the following passages to learn how the Assyrians dealt with the people of Samaria. Write a brief description of each incident.

a. **2 Kings 17:5** _____

_____

b. **v. 6** _____

_____

c. **v. 24** _____

_____

2. According to **2 Kings 17:25-26,** a new problem developed in Samaria.

a. What was the problem?

_____

_____

b. How did the Assyrian king respond **(verses 27-28)?**

_____

_____

_____

c. Was the problem solved **(verses 29-40)?** Describe what happened.

_____

_____

_____

3. In your opinion, why did the Lord do what is described in **verse 25?**

_____

_____

_____

4. Read **2 Kings 17:41.** How does the passage compare with your previous definition of *apostasy?*

_____

_____

_____

5. According to **2 Kings 17:23,** how long did the effect of the Assyrian invasion last?

_____

6. Read **verses 7-23,** a description of what went wrong in Israel. Summarize these verses in your own words. _____

_____

_____

_____

7. What do you think of the way God dealt with Israel's disobedience? How did God demonstrate His love?

_____

_____

_____

_____

CONSISTENCY

You probably know some people who aren't consistent. You can never count on them. They change their minds frequently, often for no good reason. Inconsistent people don't always make good friends. God is different.

1. Jesus, who is the visible expression of the invisible God **(Colossians 1:15),** is proof of God's consistency. What does **Hebrews 13:8** say about Jesus?

_____

_____

2. **Hebrews 13:5b,** quoting **Deuteronomy 31:6,** tells us of another consistent promise of God. What is this promise? _____

_____

3. According to **Psalm 118:1,** in what other way is God consistent? _____

_____

4. What is the promise of **Psalm 118:6-7** (quoted by the writer of **Hebrews** in **13:6**)?

_____

_____

5. Explain how God can have such a strong hatred for sin and such a strong love for the sinner.

_____

_____

6. What meaning does God's consistency have for you personally? _____

_____

_____

No matter how many promises God has made, they are "Yes" in Christ.

2 Corinthians 1:20a

Session 73

Reviewing "A People Divided"

Unit 11 has focused on the division of Israel into two kingdoms and the activities of several kings of the Northern Kingdom. This review session will help you put everything into perspective.

1. What were the main causes for the division of the kingdom? _____

_____

2. Who were the principal characters at the time of the division? _____

_____

3. The following words or terms are used in reference to the two kingdoms. Write each one in a blank below the kingdom to which it refers.

Words: *south, Jeroboam, Jerusalem, 10 tribes, north, Rehoboam, Samaria, one tribe*

Judah	Israel
_____	_____
_____	_____
_____	_____
_____	_____

4. How did Jeroboam respond to God's promise to make him a successful king?

_____

_____

5. Name some things Jeroboam did to prevent his people from going to Jerusalem to worship.

_____

_____

6. What is a *remnant* and how has the term been used in this unit? _____

_____

7. How did Ahab differ from Jeroboam?

_____

_____

8. Describe the character of Ahab's wife, Jezebel.

_____

_____

9. Give details of the plan by which Jezebel acquired Naboth's vineyard for Ahab.

_____

_____

10. Describe the contest between Elijah and the prophets of Baal. _____

_____

_____

_____

_____

11. Under what conditions did Hoshea ascend to the throne in Israel? _____

_____

12. What decision by Hoshea resulted in the siege of Samaria? _____

_____

13. How was Israel prevented from ever becoming a significant nation again?

_____

_____

_____

14. Briefly describe the characteristics of the kingdom of Israel. _____

_____

_____

15. Describe the religious behavior of the inhabitants of Samaria after the invasion by Assyria **(2 Kings 17:29-33).** _____

_____

_____

Unit 11

Kings and Prophets of Judah

Judah, also known as the Southern Kingdom, experienced a few good times before ending in captivity. Through the lives of the kings and prophets of Judah, God continued to show His love to His people. He kept them from total destruction and guided them in spite of their sinful ways. Then God lovingly corrected His people and graciously forgave their sins for Jesus' sake. And even now, He assures us of that same love and forgiveness when we tell Him we're sorry for our sins.

Session 74

The Southern Kingdom— Asa

READING THE SCRIPTURES (1 Kings 15:9-24; 2 Chronicles 14—16)

Asa, a descendant of David, took the throne in Judah following Rehoboam and Abijah. Asa reformed Judah through his aggressive leadership. Unfortunately, during the last part of his reign, he didn't rely on God for direction in his personal or political affairs. Read the accounts of Asa's reign in **1 Kings** and **2 Chronicles**. Look for the things Asa did right and the things he did wrong. How did God show His love for Asa? and for the people of Judah?

ENTHUSIASTIC BEGINNINGS

The account of Asa's reign begins with encouraging words—he **"did what was good and right in the eyes of the Lord his God"** (2 Chronicles 14:2).

1. List the "good and right things" Asa did:

a. **2 Chronicles 14:3** _____

_____

_____

b. **v. 4** _____

_____

_____

c. **v. 5** _____

_____

_____

d. **v. 6** _____

_____

_____

2. The people of Judah enthusiastically promised to serve the Lord—they made an intense commitment to "seek the Lord" with all their hearts and souls.

a. How serious were they according to **2 Chronicles 15:13-14?**

_____

_____

b. How committed do *you* think these people really were? Why?

_____

_____

_____

c. According to **2 Chronicles 14:6, 7,** and **11,** why was Judah at peace?

_____

_____

WITH THE LORD

1. The reason for Asa's success is summarized in **2 Chronicles 15:15**. Compare the passage with **Deuteronomy 4:29**.

Then summarize the two passages in your own words.

_____

_____

_____

2. Asa didn't always make the right decisions. Describe what he did in the following situations.

a. **2 Chronicles 16:1-6** _____

_____

_____

b. **v. 10** _____

_____

_____

3. There were reasons for Asa's failures. Explain what was wrong with his actions according to:

a. **2 Chronicles 16:7** _____

_____

_____

b. **v. 12** _____

_____

_____

4. What lesson should Asa have learned from his experiences? _____

_____

_____

5. In **Deuteronomy 28** Moses described some of the blessings and curses that the people of Israel could expect for obedience and disobedience. Spend some time reading the chapter. When you obey God, how can you expect Him to bless you?

_____

_____

_____

_____

How will God show His displeasure when you disobey Him?

_____

_____

_____

God always acts for the good of His people. What does He promise in **verse 13**?

_____

_____

_____

EAGER FOR THE LORD

1. Have you heard of the Spanish Inquisition? (Ask a history teacher for information if you're not familiar with the term.) It may appear that the people went a little overboard with their method of enforcing their covenant **(2 Chronicles 15:10-16)**. They meant business. Who would be the kind of people who would not seek the Lord? _____

_____

_____

2. In **2 Chronicles 15:9** we learn that the faith of the people of Judah and the evidence of the presence of the Lord attracted many people from Israel. Read through **verse 15**. How did the people show they were "seeking the Lord"?

_____

_____

_____

3. The life of a Christian today can be attractive to others. Do you agree? What does St. Paul say in **2 Corinthians 2:14-16**?

_____

_____

_____

4. Now think about the role God (Jesus Christ) plays in your own life.

a. Do you look for Him with your whole heart?

b. Is God accomplishing things through you and with you?

c. Are you a fragrance—or "aroma"—of Jesus Christ to others?

5. Each of us feels inadequate in the areas described in question 4. But St. Peter encourages us in **2 Peter 1:3-11**. Summarize Peter's encouraging words.

_____

_____

_____

What does Peter say we should be eager to do each day?

_____

_____

How do Peter's words make you feel?

_____

_____

_____

_____

Praise be to the God and Father of our Lord Jesus Christ, who has blessed us in the heavenly realms with every spiritual blessing in Christ.

Ephesians 1:3

Session 75

Jehoshaphat—a Step Forward

READING THE SCRIPTURES
(1 Kings 22:41-50; 2 Chronicles 17:1—21:3)

Success in Ten Easy Steps, Successful Living, Achieving Success Before 30 . . . Many books on today's market claim to have the secret for success. Can you trust what they tell you?

In this session you will read about the successes and failures of one of the kings of Judah, a man named Jehoshaphat. Jehoshaphat learned that success was to be found in the Lord God. Perhaps you will discover the same!

WALKING IN DAVID'S WAY

We see God's love for David again when Jehoshaphat is praised for walking **"in the ways his father David had followed."** David remained faithful to God, and his faith became a standard against which the faith of others was measured.

1. What "faithful" things did Jehoshaphat do?

a. **2 Chronicles 17:3-6** _____

_____

_____

b. **vv. 7-9** _____

_____

_____

c. **2 Chronicles 19:4-11** _____

_____

_____

2. Jehoshaphat also showed other leadership ability. What did he do according to **2 Chronicles 17:12-19?** _____

_____

_____

3. What do you think Jehoshaphat was like?

_____

_____

159

ACHIEVING SUCCESS IN THE LORD

By now you should be forming an opinion about the successes and failures of Israel and Judah. Don't assume that God was nice to Israel when they were good and cruel to them when they were bad. Such a view is superficial.

1. Read **2 Chronicles 18** and describe briefly what happened in:

a. **vv. 1-7** _____

_____

_____

b. **vv. 8-27** _____

_____

_____

c. **vv. 28-34** _____

_____

_____

2. What was the significance of what Jehoshaphat did according to **2 Chronicles 19:1-3?**

_____

_____

3. Describe briefly what happened according to:

a. **2 Chronicles 20:1-12** _____

_____

_____

b. **vv. 13-17** _____

_____

_____

c. **vv. 18-30** _____

_____

_____

4. What are the significant differences between the events in **2 Chronicles 18** and **2 Chronicles 20:1-30?**_____

_____

_____

5. Write in your own words what you believe the reasons are for Jehoshaphat's successes or failures.

_____

_____

_____

GOD IS MY STRENGTH

Here is a fable:

Once there was a young man whose wealthy and powerful father was the king of a faraway country. The royal young man enjoyed a pleasant and prestigious royal life. When he needed anything, all the king's resources were his. He hadn't earned any of the benefits he enjoyed. They were his simply because he was the king's son. The king loved him and took care of him.

As the young man matured, he discovered some people who hated his father. He was shocked to find out the same people hated him too because he was the king's son! And as he looked around, he thought other people enjoyed life more because they didn't have to worry about being the king's son.

One day the young man decided he didn't want to live with the king anymore. He left home. He experienced a different world and determinedly set out to enjoy it. But—he found that no one cared about him anymore, no one told him the truth, and no one took care of his needs. He got into trouble by making friends with the wrong people.

The king, angry with his son's foolish behavior, tried constantly to convince him to come home. The young man stubbornly refused, believing he could straighten out his own life. Life for him was a disaster compared to earlier days when things had gone so well. He couldn't understand. Now everything was empty and meaningless.

The king persisted in loving his son and finally convinced him to return home. His son now knew that the good things he had once enjoyed were gifts from his loving father. He had no resources to provide those things for himself. Now he realized what his father meant to him and he was happy again!

You can see through this fable easily. Our relationship with God is a little like the fable of the king and his son.

1. Read **1 Peter 2:9** to learn about your royal relationship as a child of the King of kings.

2. How does God feel about you according to **Romans 5:8-11?**

_____

_____

Give thanks to the Lord, for His love endures forever.

2 Chronicles 20:21b

Session 76
Ahaz—a Step Back

READING THE SCRIPTURES
(2 Kings 16; 2 Chronicles 28)

Have you ever felt you've taken 10 giant steps forward and then fallen behind 11? Well, that's what happened in today's Bible account.

Things were going fine in Judah. It appeared that Asa knew the formula for success and so did his son, Jotham. Then Ahaz became king, and the nation went back to idolatry. The Lord punished Ahaz through Syria and Israel, but Ahaz stubbornly continued on his course of wrongdoing. It's bewildering to try to figure out why there were such dramatic differences from king to king. But differences occur in our families, too.

As you read the accounts in **2 Kings** and **2 Chronicles,** look for the devastating effects of Ahaz's idolatry as well as God's signs of love and mercy.

HEAVY CASUALTIES

Ahaz's sin cost the nation!
1. What did Ahaz do wrong?

a. **2 Chronicles 28:2** _____

_____

b. **2 Chronicles 28:3** _____

_____

_____

c. **2 Chronicles 28:4** _____

_____

_____

_____

2. What was the devastating effect of Ahaz's sin **(2 Chronicles 28:5-8)?**

_____

_____

_____

3. Study your own family tree to determine how faith in God has changed from generation to generation. Write your findings on a separate sheet of paper.

a. Ask your parents and grandparents, if possible, or other relatives close to you, to describe the faith of as many of your direct ancestors as they can remember.

b. Find similarities and differences. Then write a brief sketch of each relative.

c. Summarize your findings, noting any obvious patterns.

d. Comment on why you think people did or did not express their faith in God.

GOD'S MERCY FOR JUDAH

1. How would you describe *mercy?* You might look up its meaning in a good Bible dictionary.

_____

_____

_____

_____

God's love and mercy never fail. Ahaz's sin caused Judah to suffer. (Many shared in the practice of idolatry.)

2. Read **2 Chronicles 28:9-15.** How did God show mercy on Judah?

_____

_____

3. What had Israel done wrong according to **2 Chronicles 28:9-10?** _____

_____

4. How does this event in Scripture demonstrate:
a. God's love for His people?

_____

_____

_____

b. God's authority over the nations of the world?

_____

_____

_____

GOD'S MERCY FOR ME

1. How do you feel after you've learned about God's mercy for the people of Judah?

_____

_____

_____

_____

2. Read these references and write the words used that mean *mercy:*

a. **Psalm 52:8** _____

b. **Psalm 57:3** _____

c. **Psalm 106:1** _____

3. Think of something new you learned during this session and write about it here.

_____

_____

_____

_____

_____

_____

Praise be to God, who has not rejected my prayer or withheld His love from me!

Psalm 66:20

Session 77

Hezekiah

READING THE SCRIPTURES
(2 Kings 18—20; 2 Chronicles 29—31; Isaiah 36—39)

The spiritual life of the people of Israel and Judah had its ups and downs. In fact, their switch from idol worshiping to faithfully worshiping the Lord sometimes happened within the lifetime of one of their leaders. In this session you will study the life and times of such a leader—Hezekiah, the 12th king of Judah.

Hezekiah is important in Scripture. Read one of the Scripture references and see if you can find out why. What do the references tell you about Hezekiah? How would you describe him? If Hezekiah ran for president (or prime minister) of your country would you vote for him? campaign for him? contribute money to his campaign? Would you want Hezekiah for a friend? Why or why not?

A LEADER FOR GOD'S PEOPLE

Leaders sometimes do more than tell people what to do. Some leaders inspire others to do their best. Others set examples that encourage their followers to reach personal goals. Once in a while a leader may have to push, prod, or even nag a little to get things done.

The ability to lead is a gift from God. God makes leaders out of His people (1 Timothy 4:12). How about you? When have you had a chance to lead? You might discover how you can be a leader by studying the details of Hezekiah's life.

1. Good leaders know themselves. Read 2 Chronicles 29:1-2.

a. Based on Hezekiah's actions, what do you think he knew about himself?

_____

_____

b. Was Hezekiah decisive or uncertain in his actions? Explain your answer.

_____

_____

2. Good leaders associate with "winners"—those who can help them win. According to 2 Chronicles 29:4; Chronicles 32:6-8; and 2 Kings 19:2-7, who were Hezekiah's assistants and what were they like?

_____

_____

_____

3. Good leaders are not proud. They give credit where credit is due. Whom did Hezekiah credit for his success (2 Chronicles 29:36 and 31:11-12)?

_____

_____

4. Now it's your turn to describe one of Hezekiah's characteristics. Read 2 Chronicles 31:21 and 32:7-8 again. What other characteristic can you find? Describe it.

_____

_____

_____

5. Hezekiah had weaknesses, too (2 Chronicles 32:24-26 and 2 Kings 20:12-19). How did God respond to Hezekiah's sins?

_____

_____

_____

GOD LOVES HIS PEOPLE

The relationship between God and His people during Hezekiah's reign is remarkable.

1. Describe the feelings of the people of Judah as expressed in 2 Chronicles 29:36.

_____

_____

2. Do you remember the session on "giving"?

163

How did God's people demonstrate their love for Him according to **2 Chronicles 31:2-14?**

_____

_____

3. Read **Isaiah 38.** God showed mercy to Hezekiah. How did Hezekiah respond **(Isaiah 38:17)?** What does his response show about his attitude toward God?

_____

_____

_____

4. Notice that the previous three questions focused on the response of the people to God. Now describe what God was like to His people.

_____

_____

YOU—A LEADER

1. Have you ever wondered why you have been required to study God's Word? There is an important purpose in addition to the fact that God works through His Word to bring you to and keep you in a good relationship with Himself. Read **2 Timothy 3:14-17.** What does **verse 17** tell you? Suppose you were training to be a leader. What would you need?

_____

_____

_____

2. How does **Ephesians 2:8-10** help you understand God's plan for you?

_____

_____

_____

3. Read **Romans 12:4-8.** Where can you be a leader now? What unique opportunities has God given you to be a leader? (Don't overlook the obvious: you can be a leader for the Lord as captain of a team, president of a club, chairperson of a group, member of student government, etc.) _____

_____

_____

4. Life won't always be easy. When times get tough, remember how Hezekiah brought his needs to the Lord. Also remember that Hezekiah shared his *good times* with the Lord! Pray, sharing your good times and your needs with God. You might list some of each to organize your prayer thoughts.

MY NEEDS: _____

_____

_____

_____

MY GOOD TIMES: _____

_____

_____

_____

Because of His great love for us, God, who is rich in mercy, made us alive with Christ even when we were dead in transgressions—it is by grace you have been saved.

Ephesians 2:4

In Your love you kept me from the pit of destruction; You have put all my sins behind Your back.

Isaiah 38:17

Session 78

Manasseh—a Reversal

READING THE SCRIPTURES
(2 Kings 21:1-18; 2 Chronicles 33:1-20)

As you read the Scripture account of Manasseh's reign, you'll find two reversals in Israel's direction as a nation. The first happened when Manasseh assumed the throne at the age of 12 and brought back some of the most wicked practices the nation had ever witnessed. The second came when he repented of his sin and God forgave him and restored him to rule.

Read the accounts in both **2 Kings** and **2 Chronicles** and look for things that might be happening in your own life. What can you learn from Manasseh's experiences?

THE DEPTHS OF GOD'S LOVE

Read **Luke 7:36-50**—the story of the sinful woman who washed Jesus' feet with her tears and then anointed them with expensive perfume. Jesus pointed out to his critics that the woman had repented of her sins and that He then forgave her.

1. Manasseh repented of his many sins. You'll find the record of his repentance only in **2 Chronicles 33:10-13.** What were Manasseh's sins according to:

a. **2 Chronicles 33:2** _____

_____

_____

b. **2 Chronicles 33:3** _____

_____

_____

c. **2 Chronicles 33:4-5** _____

_____

d. **2 Chronicles 33:6** _____

_____

e. **2 Chronicles 33:7** _____

_____

2. What is your impression of Manasseh? Would he be someone you'd like for a friend? for a leader in your school? for a teacher? Why or why not?

_____

_____

_____

3. What are some of the same "Manasseh sins" people commit today (sins that you, too, may be doing)?

_____

_____

_____

4. What did God do to stop Manasseh's sinful behavior **(2 Chronicles 33:10-11)?**

_____

_____

5. How did Manasseh react to God's punishment **(2 Chronicles 33:12-13)?** How do you know he was sincere **(33:15-16)?**

_____

_____

_____

6. Manasseh didn't get to do everything he intended to do after his short captivity. What do you learn from **33:17** and **33:21-25?**

_____

_____

_____

7. How do you know that God loved Manasseh?

_____

_____

GOD'S LOVE FOR YOU REQUIRES NO WAITING!

"Fast Photos!" blinks the sign in the shopping mall. "Drive-thru Window" reads the bright-yellow arrow at the fast-food place. Lots of TV and radio commercials try to attract our attention to the quick services and express lanes that shopping places offer us.

Have you taken a number and waited to be helped lately at a Customer Service desk? at an optic center for new contact lenses or eyeglasses? at a bakery? at a Dairy Queen? The lines sometimes are unreal! And sometimes we're impatient customers—demanding to be helped immediately! But sometimes we're the opposite—procrastinators. We won't make important decisions or do our jobs until the last moment! Does any of this sound familiar? Well, Manasseh almost lost everything because he kept ignoring his responsibility to God.

1. Read **2 Chronicles 33:10.** What had God done that was special? How did Manasseh react?

_____

_____

_____

2. God loves you, too! Think of a time you've done something wrong and you felt *terrible*! Maybe you *still* feel bad. God loves you—no matter *what* you've done. You need only sincerely say, *"Lord, I'm sorry. Please forgive my sin of . . ."* Take time now to sincerely repent of sins that have been making you feel heavy and sad. How do you feel after repenting?

_____

_____

3. Just think—you've sinned and you've told God you're truly sorry. How happy and free you can feel now that you're free from all the guilt! God's capacity and desire to love you are enormous. Read the following passages. You'll discover more about God's great love for you!

a. The apostle Paul wrote descriptive reassuring words about God's love. Read **Ephesians 2:4-5** and write in your own words what God did for you.

_____

_____

b. Paul tells about the mystery of God's love for us in Christ, and then later (in **Ephesians 3:14-19**) he shares a prayer for us. What did Paul pray for?

_____

_____

c. In your own words, describe how much God loves you.

_____

_____

Something to do each day we live:

Let's humble ourselves before God. Let's repent and confess our sins. And let's claim God's forgiveness and power for the *new life* we have in Jesus Christ. He frees you from sin and guilt feelings. He gives you courage and power to live and love as His child. You can live in *joy. God loves you!*

If we confess our sins, He is faithful and just and will forgive us our sins and purify us from all unrighteousness.

1 John 1:9

Session 79

Josiah

READING THE SCRIPTURES
(2 Kings 22:1—23:30; 2 Chronicles 34—35; Jeremiah 3:6-13)

King Josiah loved the Lord and tried to turn the people back to God. Unfortunately, it was too late. Josiah knew that the nation of Judah was in trouble when he heard what the Book of the Law contained. His warnings and discipline didn't affect the people. Through the prophet Jeremiah God revealed that Judah had not learned a lesson from what God had done to Israel. Even now Judah only pretended to return to the Lord **(Jeremiah 3:6-10)**.

Josiah tried to restore worship in Judah. As you read the Scripture accounts of Josiah's reign, think about his youthfulness, his feelings when he found the Book of the Law, the changes Josiah made, and the disaster that followed his reign.

A PROPHECY FULFILLED

1. Nearly 300 years before Josiah became king, God told Jeroboam that one day a man named Josiah would destroy the altars in Bethel **(1 Kings 13:1-5)**.

Read **2 Kings 23:15-16.** How accurate was God's prediction? _____

2. Josiah led the people well. Tell what Josiah did according to **2 Kings 23:4-25.**

_____

_____

_____

3. Read **Jeremiah 3:6-10.** God compares idolatry with adultery and speaks of divorcing Israel because of her adulteries. Do you think the people of Judah felt as sincere toward God as Josiah felt?

_____

_____

How does Jeremiah describe Judah's attitude in this passage?

_____

_____

_____

4. **2 Chronicles 35** tells about the celebration of Passover and its special meaning for the people. Read **verses 1-19.** What one special thing did Josiah do for the people?

_____

_____

AN APPROACHING DISASTER

1. God had reached his limit. He couldn't put up with the wickedness of His people any longer. According to Huldah, the prophetess **(2 Chronicles 34:28)**, what did God intend to do?

_____

_____

2. Have you ever been involved in a traffic accident? in or close to a tornado-stricken area? in a fire at home or school?

How do you act when you believe that disaster is near?

_____

_____

Did the people of Judah behave as though they were facing disaster?

_____

_____

3. Tell how Josiah reacted to God's message in **2 Chronicles 34:29-33.** _____

_____

Tell what you think of King Josiah's reaction.

_____

_____

_____

_____

GOD GIVES US HOPE FOR THE FUTURE

Things looked dark in Judah. But you know from the Scripture account that hope was on their horizon. God sent His Son Jesus at just the right time to accomplish what no king of Israel or Judah could have ever accomplished.

1. Read **1 Peter 1:3-5.** Describe in your own words our real source of hope.

_____

_____

_____

2. How are you like the kings or the people of Judah?

_____

_____

_____

3. Remember—**Hope in Jesus Christ is a sure thing for us who belong to Christ.** Think about your relationship with Christ. Is it sincere? Or is it there for appearance's sake? Personally evaluate what you believe and how you feel about the Lord. Sometimes it helps us to reaffirm our beliefs when we talk about them with a friend. Only God knows what's in your heart. Tell Him of your love for Him. Praise and thank Him for Jesus Christ!

The anger of the Lord will not turn back until He fully accomplishes the purposes of His heart.
Jeremiah 23:20

My hope is built on nothing less than Jesus' blood and righteousness.
Lutheran Worship 368

Session 80
The Fall of Judah

READING THE SCRIPTURES
(2 Kings 23:31—25:30; 2 Chronicles 36; Jeremiah 2—39)

You'll need to read a lot of Scripture to understand what is happening in this session. At least read **2 Chronicles 36** and **Jeremiah 5—7.** You'll find that God presents His case against Judah in the **Book of Jeremiah.**

How do you suppose God felt after He constantly showed His people mercy and tried to draw them back to Himself? How do you act toward people you disagree with? toward people who don't do things your way? Are you patient with them? Was God patient with His people?

THE END

Read **2 Kings 23:31—25:30** and **2 Chronicles 36** to discover what led to the fall of Judah. Then answer these questions:

1. Who were the four kings who reigned after Josiah? How long did each king reign? What was each king like?

a. **2 Kings 23:31-35** and **2 Chronicles 36:1-4**

_____

_____

b. **2 Kings 23:34—24:7** and **2 Chronicles 36:4-8**

_____

_____

c. **2 Kings 24:8-16** and **2 Chronicles 36:9-10**

_____

_____

d. **2 Kings 24:17—25:7** and **2 Chronicles 36:10-14**

_____

_____

2. Read the following Scripture passages and tell what happened in each one—leading to the capture of the nation of Judah.

a. **2 Chronicles 36:5-7** and **2 Kings 24:1-2**

_____

_____

_____

b. **2 Chronicles 36:9-10** _____

_____

_____

c. **2 Chronicles 36:11-14** _____

_____

_____

3. The Scripture accounts in **2 Kings** and **2 Chronicles** tell us very little about the fall of Jerusalem. Read a Bible commentary for more information about the fall. List some of the ways the people suffered during the siege according to **2 Kings 25:1-21** and **2 Chronicles 36:15-20.**

_____

_____

_____

GOD IS JUST

Two girlfriends, Heather and Michele, shopped at the mall on Saturday and went into their favorite boutique—a jewelry shop. Seven minutes later, thinking they were alone, they sat on the bench in the middle of the mall and giggled.

"I got a triple-twisted gold chain!" whispered Michele to her friend. "I can't wait to wear it with my new dress!"

"Wait till you see the pretty earrings I took!" Heather confided to Michele.

Just then a well-dressed young woman interrupted their secret conversation. "Excuse me, young ladies, but I'd like you to follow me." She identified herself as a plainclothes security guard and took the girls to the mall's security office, where both Heather and Michele confessed to shoplifting small jewelry items.

How do you suppose Michele and Heather were punished? Would the boutique be "just" in punishing them for shoplifting? (Someone who is "just" is morally right, or righteous.)

In this session you will read a lot about God, who is "just" to the people of Judah. What do you think it means when you hear "God is a just and loving God"?

Jeremiah contains God's warnings to His people, and it lists the reasons for the punishment they are about to receive.

1. The following passages describe the people of Judah. Tell in your own words what each passage says.

   a. **Jeremiah 5:1-6** and **11-13** _____

_____

_____

   b. **Jeremiah 7:1-15** and **30-31** _____

_____

_____

2. Jeremiah knew that God was right in His decision to punish the people of Judah. What does Jeremiah say in **Jeremiah 10:23?** What does he mean when he says, **"A man's life is not his own . . . to direct his steps"?**

_____

_____

_____

3. Jeremiah also pleads for God's mercy but doesn't ask God to excuse the people from His punishment. What does he ask of God in **Jeremiah 10:24?**

_____

_____

What are some ways God lovingly reprimands you?

_____

_____

How does it feel to be corrected by your parents? by your teachers? by your friends? and by God?

_____

_____

Why should you feel happy to have those people who love you correct you?

_____

_____

GOD IS LOVE

The Concordia Self-Study Commentary tells us that God didn't let the ruins of Jerusalem and the captivity of His children become their grave. God kept His promise to bless all nations in Abraham's seed **(Genesis 12:3).** Through all of Judah's turmoil and downfall, God loved His people and continued to take care of them. How does God's ever-present love and care affect your life? _____

_____

_____

How does God's gift of His Son Jesus affect your life **(John 3:16)?** _____

_____

_____

There is no God apart from Me, a righteous God and a Savior; there is none but Me. Turn to Me and be saved . . . for I am God, and there is no other.
Isaiah 45:21b-22

Session 81

Reviewing "The Kings and Prophets of Judah"

The following activities will help you summarize and put into perspective the reigns of the various kings of Judah you've studied during this unit.

A. On a separate sheet of paper write an outline of the main characteristics of the reigns of the following kings:

Asa, Jehoshaphat, Ahaz, Hezekiah, Manasseh, Josiah, and **Zedekiah.** Follow this format:

1. King's name:
2. Principal characters during his reign:
3. Length of his reign:
4. Summary of his reign—main events:
5. Names of the king's predecessor and successor:
6. Description of the king's relationship with God:
7. Effect this king had on Judah:

B. Take a closer look at a few of the principal characters from this unit. Briefly tell something special you learned from studying each of these kings:

1. Hezekiah **(2 Chronicles 29—31)**

_____

_____

2. Josiah **(2 Chronicles 34—35)**

_____

_____

_____

3. Manasseh **(2 Chronicles 33:1-20)**

_____

_____

C. Tell how the accounts about Manasseh are different in **2 Chronicles** and **2 Kings.**

_____

_____

_____

D. List ways that God showed His love for His people during the reigns of the kings of Judah.

_____

_____

_____

_____

E. Describe some of the things you learned from this unit that will help you be a good leader in God's church.

_____

_____

_____

_____

_____

Unit 12

Overview
of the Prophets

God sent messages to His people through His helpers, the prophets. Each of these prophets—Isaiah, Jeremiah, Ezekiel, Daniel, and Jonah—shared God's messages. Though reluctant prophets at times, God chose and supported each one. He prepared each man for His service. God asks each of us to be watchpersons today, too, warning people of the danger of sin and alerting them to the coming of Jesus, their Savior.

Session 82

Isaiah

READING THE SCRIPTURES
(Isaiah 1—12 and 49—57)

As you read these selected chapters from Scripture, you'll read about Isaiah's call, God's message of judgment on the sins of Judah, and the assurance of God's presence, mercy, and deliverance through His Messiah, Jesus Christ.

You've recently found out why God had to punish His people. Now you'll discover more about His plan to redeem His people through His Son Jesus.

GOD'S CALL

God communicates through ordinary people, and Isaiah was one of these people.

1. Read **Isaiah 6.** In your own words describe what Isaiah saw according to **verse 1-4.**

_____

_____

_____

_____

2. How did the vision affect Isaiah **(6:5)?** Describe what it was like for him to stand in the presence of God. What would it be like for you?

_____

_____

_____

_____

3. What was Isaiah's problem, and how did God deal with it **(6:6-7)?** _____

_____

_____

4. Is it necessary for God to deal so dramatically with those who serve Him today? Why or why not?

_____

_____

_____

_____

5. The hymn "Hark, the Voice of Jesus Calling" (*LW* 318) includes Isaiah's response to God in **Isaiah 6:8, "Here am I. Send me!"** Why do you think Isaiah was so eager to serve God? Do you think God has anything special for you to do for Him? How do you know?

_____

_____

_____

_____

_____

GOD'S JUDGMENT

Would you agree, from studying the history of God's people, that they were a sinful and rebellious group? Apparently they thought they could fool God by offering sacrifices while they sinned freely and worshiped idols.

1. Read **Isaiah 1—5.** List the problems that Isaiah describes in:

a. **1:4-7** _____

_____

_____

b. **2:6-8** _____

_____

_____

c. **1:10-15** and **21-23** _____

_____

_____

2. God is no fool. He sees through the lies that people use to justify their wicked behavior. Tell how God responded to the lies and wickedness of Judah according to:

a. **Isaiah 1:24-25** _____

_____

_____

173

b. **2:12—4:1** _____

_____

_____

GOD'S PROMISE

God kept on loving His people in spite of their sin. One of the most exciting messages in **Isaiah** is the promise of _Immanuel._ Read **Isaiah 7** and **53.**

1. What is the Messianic promise recorded in **Isaiah 7:14?**

_____

_____

_____

2. What does the name _Immanuel_ mean? What reassuring message does this name give us? (Look in a Bible dictionary.)

_____

_____

3. The Jews weren't ready for the Messiah when He came. Maybe they expected a king like David or Solomon. What was Jesus like? Tell how Isaiah described Jesus in **Isaiah 53:2-3.**

_____

_____

_____

4. Isaiah's description of Jesus' work tells us that

He received a punishment that should have been ours. Describe what was done to Jesus **(Isaiah 53:4-9).**

_____

_____

_____

5. Read **53:9b** and tell how Jesus was different from us.

_____

_____

6. Think about everything God has done for you through Jesus Christ. Read in **Ephesians 3:11-12** how God has accomplished His eternal purpose in Jesus Christ. Paul says that "**In Him and through faith in Him we may approach God with freedom and confidence.**" How different this is from the way Isaiah saw God in **Isaiah 6:5!**

Write a prayer praising God for His assurance of _Immanuel_, His mercy, and deliverance from sin.

_____

_____

_____

_____

_____

_____

"Come now, let us reason together," says the Lord. "Though your sins are like scarlet, they shall be as white as snow; though they are red as crimson, they shall be like wool."

Isaiah 1:18

Session 83

Jeremiah

READING THE SCRIPTURES
(Jeremiah 1; 13:1-11; 16:2-9; 20:7-18; 23:5-8; 25:1-14; 26; 29:10-14)

In this session you'll learn about the man Jeremiah and the message the Lord gave through Jeremiah. You'll also discover that God knew you even before you were conceived—"from eternity"—and has had a good plan for your life!

Read the sections of **Jeremiah** listed above and look for God's messages, Jeremiah's personality traits, and evidence of God's personal interest in you.

A FIRED-UP PROPHET

1. Read **Jeremiah 1:1-2** and **6.** Jeremiah was reluctant to be God's prophet. Why did he hold back?And how was he different from Isaiah?

_____

_____

_____

_____

2. Tell how God reassured Jeremiah **(vv. 7-10).**

_____

_____

_____

_____

3. God placed some demanding restrictions on Jeremiah's life-style. Read these passages and explain what God expected of Jeremiah.

a. **Jeremiah 16:2-4** _____

_____

_____

b. **vv. 5-7** _____

_____

_____

c. **vv. 8-9** _____

_____

_____

4. The passages also explain *why* God placed such strict demands on Jeremiah's life-style. What was God's reason?

_____

_____

_____

5. In serving the Lord, Jeremiah became very unpopular with the people. Read **Jeremiah 20:8** and **26:8-9.** Tell how the people responded to what Jeremiah said. _____

_____

_____

6. Read **Jeremiah 20:14-18.** Describe how the people's response affected Jeremiah. How did he feel and what did he say?

_____

_____

_____

7. Although his job demanded so much from him, Jeremiah kept speaking for the Lord. Read how he describes what motivates him in **Jeremiah 20:9-13.** What is his motivation? _____

_____

_____

THE LORD SAYS . . .

Maybe you've heard yourself tell a brother, a sister, or a friend something that began like, "Dad says . . ." or "My grandmother says . . ." Were you trying to convince your listener that what you had to say was true?

Jeremiah usually began his messages with "This is what the Lord says." What did the Lord have to say to Judah? What does He have to say to you? Read and answer the following questions to understand the Lord's message through Jeremiah.

1. Read **Jeremiah 13:1-11.** Describe in your own words the "object lesson" God gave for Judah.

_____

_____

_____

2. On another occasion God predicted the Babylonian captivity. According to **Jeremiah 25:11-12** how long would the captivity last?

_____

3. According to **Jeremiah 29:10-14**, what would God do after the captivity was over?

_____

_____

4. Why do you think God gave His reassurances with His warnings? _____

_____

_____

I KNEW YOU

Perhaps the most reassuring words Jeremiah could have heard from the Lord are those of **Jeremiah 1:5,** where God assures him that He knew Jeremiah even before he was conceived.

1. What do God's words, "I knew you," mean to you personally? Do you think God knew you before you were conceived?

_____

_____

2. Read **Romans 8:28-39.** Tell what good news and encouragement Paul gives us about God's knowledge of us.

_____

_____

3. Those who belong to God and live according to His direction can anticipate facing ridicule and persecution. What does the apostle Peter tell you in **1 Peter 4:12-19?**

_____

_____

ON FIRE FOR THE LORD

1. When it comes to being a Christian, do you feel reluctant to tell others about Jesus? Are you sometimes afraid to be a Christian in public? You're not alone! Remember, Jeremiah had fears and misgivings, too. So do other Christians around you. What are you afraid of? List some things that make you hesitate to show you're a Christian. Then on a separate paper write a prayer asking God to help you deal with your fears and to help you show your Christian love for others.

_____

_____

2. Challenge yourself this week to be on fire for the Lord! Reach out to a neighbor or friend. Tell *one person* about the Lord and the peace and joy that come from knowing Him. Pray that at the right time your conversation will focus on Christ. Pray for the Holy Spirit to work in that friend so he or she may know our Savior personally.

A folk song stanza says:
"It only takes a spark to get a fire going
And soon all those around will warm up in its glowing.
That's how it is with God's love, once you've experienced it!
You spread His love to everyone; you want to pass it on!"

PASS IT ON by Kurt Kaiser
© Copyright 1969 by LEXICON MUSIC, INC. ASCAP
All rights reserved. International copyright secured. Used by special permission.

Before I formed you in the womb I knew you, before you were born I set you apart.

Jeremiah 1:5

Session 84

Ezekiel

READING THE SCRIPTURES
(Ezekiel 1—3)

Ezekiel was one of the people of Judah taken captive during the reign of Jehoiachin. While he was in Babylon, God called him to be a prophet. Ezekiel had some unique experiences compared to other prophets you've studied. As you read these Scripture passages you'll learn about the time when Ezekiel lived, his first vision, and his call from the Lord. Read the entire **Book of Ezekiel,** if you have time, to find out how the Lord was always with Ezekiel.

GOD IS WITH EXILED EZEKIEL

1. Let's find out about this prophet Ezekiel. Read **Ezekiel 1:1.**

a. How old is Ezekiel?

_____

b. Where is he?

_____

c. What did he experience?

_____

_____

_____

2. **Verses 2** and **3** give more information about Ezekiel.

a. What was the time in history?

_____

b. What was Ezekiel's profession?

_____

c. What was his father's name?

_____

d. What was his experience with the Lord?

_____

_____

3. Write one or two sentences describing Ezekiel as you know him now.

_____

_____

_____

_____

_____

_____

_____

GOD SHOWS HIS PRESENCE TO EZEKIEL

The exiled people of Judah felt depressed **(Psalm 137)** and probably wondered where God was. Many of them didn't understand why they were having so much trouble. Have you ever asked God why you've had certain challenges in your life? You've probably felt a lot like the people of Judah felt long ago. God dramatically showed Ezekiel through a vision that His presence and His power would help prepare Ezekiel for the big job ahead of him.

1. Read **Ezekiel 1:4** and list the first four parts of Ezekiel's vision.

a. _____

b. _____

c. _____

d. _____

2. Read **Ezekiel 1:5-14** and describe the living creatures that Ezekiel saw.

a. **v. 5**—their form: _____

b. **v. 6**—their appearance: _____

c. **v. 7**—their legs and feet: _____

_____

d. **v. 8**—their hands: _____

e. **v. 9**—their motion: _____

f. **v. 12**—their power: _____

Now read **Ezekiel 1:10-14** and add to the descriptions you've already written.

_____

_____

_____

_____

3. Tell how Ezekiel describes his vision of wheels **(1:15-21).** _____

_____

4. Ezekiel apparently had a hard time describing what he saw. He uses phrases such as "what looked like" and "the appearance of." How did he describe the noise the creatures made **(1:24)?**

_____

_____

5. Then Ezekiel heard a voice and saw another figure **(v. 25-28).** Who do you think was the figure? (Notice that Ezekiel fell face down when he saw it.)

_____

6. What do you think the vision meant?

_____

_____

_____

7. On a separate sheet of paper, draw a picture of what Ezekiel saw. Use the first chapter of **Ezekiel** to help you remember the details of his vision.

GOD CALLS EZEKIEL TO SERVE HIM

1. In the next two chapters you'll read God's call to Ezekiel. You'll notice that God usually spoke to him as "son of man." God did three basic things with this "son of man." Look in the following verses and write what God did with Ezekiel.

a. **2:2** _____

_____

b. **2:3** _____

_____

c. **3:17** _____

_____

2. According to **3:18-19** how important was Ezekiel's job?

_____

3. God gave Ezekiel special messages then and He gives us messages today to reveal Himself as King and Lord.

a. Read **Ezekiel 4.** What did the Lord tell Ezekiel to do? What message did the Lord give the exiles through him?

_____

_____

_____

b. Read **Matthew 28:19-20** and tell what you think God expects of you.

_____

_____

What message does God give you to tell other people? Read **1 John 5:1-12.** Use a concordance to help you find other Scripture passages to answer this question. _____

_____

_____

_____

_____

_____

4. What do you think about God's prophet Ezekiel and his exiled life, his majestic visions, and his messages from the Lord? Tell how you feel about his awesome responsibilities and his dramatic ministry. You might finish reading the **Book of Ezekiel** to discover more about God's plan for his work.

_____

_____

_____

_____

_____

I will save My people from your hands [false prophets]. And then you will know that I am the Lord.
Ezekiel 13:23

You My sheep, the sheep of My pasture, are people, and I am your God, declares the Sovereign Lord.
Ezekiel 34:31

Session 85

Daniel

READING THE SCRIPTURES (Daniel 1—6)

Do you ever wonder how some people seem to "have it all"? As you read about Daniel and how God worked in his life, you might think he'd easily win the contest for "God's All-Around Man." Think about the following questions while you read the Scripture passages:

Was Daniel a typical Israelite? Would he be considered a Christian today? Did he stay faithful to God? How did he obey authority? And why was he so successful? What can *you* learn from Daniel?

FAITHFUL TO GOD, BLESSED BY GOD

God's man Daniel lived the way God intended His people to live. Daniel loved God, depended on God, and obeyed God. His life wasn't a series of "lucky breaks"! God blessed Daniel with a faithful and successful life.

1. What do you learn about Daniel and his friends from **Daniel 1:3-4?** _____

_____

_____

2. Daniel wouldn't take special favors that would change his relationship with God. What was the temptation, and how did Daniel react to it (**1:5** and **11-16)?**

_____

_____

_____

3. How did God bless Daniel and his friends (**1:17**)?

_____

_____

_____

4. Daniel faithfully worshiped God. Tell what happened in **Daniel 6.** What was the plot against Daniel?

And what did he continue to do? What would you do in the same situation?

_____

_____

_____

_____

5. Daniel was a good manager, and the people respected him for using God's gifts wisely. (You could say he was a good "steward." Have you heard the word *stewardship* used frequently at church? Did you know that as a believer, you're a steward of God, of His gifts, and of His graces? That's what **1 Peter 4:10** (tells us.)

How did Daniel use his gifts from God? And to whom does Daniel give credit for all his abilities?

_____

_____

_____

How about you—how are you using your gifts from God? And to whom do you give credit for all your abilities?

_____

_____

_____

Do you think God did all the work and Daniel got all the benefits? It might seem that way! But you must realize that when God gives gifts to His people, He wants us to use those gifts. When we refuse, the body of Christ suffers and we miss the joy God offers us in His gifts.

OUR STRENGTH COMES FROM GOD

1. Where did Daniel get all his talent and success?

_____

_____

2. Read **2 Corinthians 13:4-5; Ephesians 1:13;**

1 Corinthians 2:12, 14-15; Matthew 18:19-20; 1 Corinthians 12:1-11; and **2 Corinthians 12:9.** List some of the things God has given you, according to these passages. _____

_____

_____

_____

3. Now comes the hard part! Think of all these gifts God gives you. Tell *one thing* you'd like to do with your blessings.

_____

_____

_____

You are God's young woman or young man, just as Daniel was God's man. You are "positively a possibility" for the Lord—and you will know what God has in mind for you when you use His gifts to you. Just trust Him to help you use those gifts, and He will keep you in His love and peace.

We say with confidence, The Lord is my helper. I will not be afraid.

Hebrews 13:6

Each one should use whatever gift he has received to serve others, faithfully administering God's grace in its various forms.

1 Peter 4:10

The Lord preserves the faithful.

Psalm 31:23

Now it is required that those who have been given a trust must prove faithful.

1 Corinthians 4:2

Session 86

Jonah—a Minor Prophet

READING THE SCRIPTURES
(Jonah 1— 4)

What a bummer!" muttered Janet to herself. "I'm gonna help decorate for the prom after school instead of going to Gramma's like she asked me. She'll just have to find someone else to help her rake all those leaves. I've got better things to do!"

We don't have God's capacity to love, do we? He asks us to share His Word and his love with others, but so often we don't. Sometimes we even shut people out of our lives because they're different, because we like doing other things better, and because we like "doing our own thing." Do you think Janet's attitude showed any willingness to share God's love and concern with her grandmother? As you read the chapters of **Jonah** ask yourself, "What is God telling *me* in these words? Is Jonah a bigot? Am I?" (Look up *bigot* in a dictionary if you don't know its meaning.)

SAYING NO TO GOD

Jonah kept calling God "Lord." He must have known He was almighty God. Does it seem incredible to you that Jonah could recognize the almighty God who created him and then become angry and refuse to obey Him? Or is this typical—even of us?

1. Tell about Jonah to someone who isn't in your class. Emphasize that God wanted to show mercy on Nineveh and wanted Jonah to be the one who took His Word there. Tell your friend how Jonah ran from God, how he gave in only after God performed an unusual miracle, how he took the message to Nineveh, and finally how he resented God's having compassion on the repentant people.

What was your friend's reaction? Is his or her reaction what you expected? Why do you think he or she reacted that way?

2. Read **1 Corinthians 3:6-8.** What were you supposed to do when you shared with your friend? What was God's responsibility?

_____

_____

_____

3. What convinced the people of Nineveh that they needed God?

_____

_____

_____

GIVING IN TO GOD

Though Jonah avoided doing what God asked, things became so uncomfortable that he finally gave in to God.

1. Why did Jonah run away from God **(Jonah 4:1-3)?**

_____

_____

What does the word *bigot* mean? Was Jonah a "bigot"?

_____

_____

2. Tell how you feel about being asked to share God's Word with someone. Is it hard to do? frightening for you? silly? annoying? Why?

_____

_____

_____

Did you share the story of Jonah with a friend? Why or why not?

_____

_____

Did you feel comfortable or uneasy sharing God's Word?

_____

_____

3. Sometimes our reluctance to share God's Word with someone else is hard to overcome. You might not be a religious bigot, but maybe you're a little overly concerned about yourself. What are some things you might pay too much attention to? What are some things that get in your way when it comes to sharing Christ?

_____

_____

4. One way to get over our selfishness (that's what it is, isn't it?) is to get more interested in someone else. Think of someone in your family, in your neighborhood, or in your class that God might be asking you to help.

Who do you think this might be, and what could you say to help him or her?

_____

_____

_____

BELONGING TO GOD

In the New Testament, the apostle Paul had to come down hard on the apostle Peter about his attitude toward Gentiles who believed in Christ **(Galatians 2:6-14).** And there were the Jews. Many of them had a real superiority complex **(Romans 2:17-24)** because of the religious and national identity God had established through them. Some were surprised that God actually *loved* people of other nations!

1. Many Jews (descendants of Israel) rejected Jesus Christ. The apostle Paul suggests that God then "grafted" Gentiles into the vine where these Jews had been cut off **(Romans 11:19).** Write one or two sentences telling what God did to make *you* His own.

_____

_____

_____

2. How do you feel about what God did for you in Christ?

_____

_____

3. Do you think God expects anything *from* you because of what He did *for* you? If so, what would God expect? _____

_____

_____

_____

(Read **James 5:19-20** and **Matthew 28:19-20** if you can't think of any expectations.)

[God] wants all men to be saved and to come to a knowledge of the truth.

1 Timothy 2:4

Session 87
Reviewing the Prophets

For this session you are to prepare a written report on one of the minor prophets. You may choose from **Hosea, Joel, Amos, Obadiah, Micah, Nahum, Habakkuk, Zephaniah, Haggai, Zechariah,** or **Malachi.** (The prophet **Jonah** was omitted because you studied him in the last session.)

Your teacher will have some specific instructions in addition to those that follow.

Your report must contain the following:

1. Your name, the date, and class period

2. Name of the prophet you have selected

3. Biographical data on the prophet (whatever is available)

4. Approximate dates of the prophet's activity

5. The kingdom where the prophet was active (Israel or Judah) and to whom the message was directed

6. The main purpose of the prophet's message (one or two sentences)

7. A summary of his message (several paragraphs)

8. The response of those to whom he spoke

9. What you learned from your study that has value for your personal life as a child of God (several sentences)

10. At least one passage that is worth memorizing and an explanation of its meaning

11. A bibliography (list of the books you used as references)

Your report is due on the day scheduled for this session unless otherwise announced by your teacher. It should be in your own words. Do not copy portions of another work unless quoting.

Be prepared to give a brief summary of your report in class.

Use the space below to write down any further instructions from your teacher.

_____

_____

_____

_____

The following activities will help you summarize and review some of the more important information about the other prophets in this unit and their messages.

1. List the four major prophets.

_____

_____

_____

2. What is the difference between the major and minor prophets?

_____

_____

_____

_____

_____

3. What lesson did you learn from Jonah?

_____

_____

_____

_____

4. To whom did God send Jonah?

_____

_____

_____

5. What lesson did God teach Jonah with the vine? _____

_____

_____

6. Whom does the prophet Isaiah talk about in **Isaiah 53:1-12?** _____

_____

7. Why was Isaiah so frightened when God called him **(Isaiah 6:5)?** How did God deal with Isaiah's fear?

_____

_____

_____

_____

8. What did you learn from Isaiah?

_____

_____

_____

_____

_____

9. Who was Jeremiah? (Give some biographical information on him.) _____

_____

_____

_____

10. What do you learn from **Jeremiah 1:5?**

_____

_____

_____

11. How did Jeremiah's personality differ from the other prophets you studied? _____

_____

_____

_____

12. Where did Daniel and Ezekiel live during their prophetic years?

_____

_____

_____

_____

13. What similarites were there between the calls of Isaiah and Ezekiel?

_____

_____

_____

_____

14. Why did Daniel prefer vegetables and water to the rich foods he was offered while in captivity?

_____

_____

_____

15. Which prophet presented God's message through symbolic actions and object lessons?

_____

_____

_____

_____

16. Which prophet came from a royal family in Judah? _____

17. Why was Daniel thrown into a den of lions? What do you learn from Daniel's experience?

_____

_____

_____

_____

18. Which prophet was appointed to be a watchman for God's people?

_____

Unit 13

The Exile and Return

Somewhere in the streets of a busy city, a street person named Zeb lives in a cardboard box. Like all the street people around him, Zeb gathers his daily food from alley dumpsters. He's careful to step over the hungry, cold, blanketless humans sleeping on the concrete. Once Zeb tried to keep warm by sitting in a pew in the back of an old city church. But some well-dressed usher not too kindly asked him to "move on, buddy." Once Zeb picked half-rotted tomatoes from a restaurant's trash container. But the manager caught him and warned him, "Don't ever steal our trash again!"

Do you think this "fictitious Zeb" is in exile? What do you think it means to be an exiled person? What kind of hope would you have if you were an exile? How does God protect the street people of the world? Do you think God expects us to somehow help people like this? How? What kinds of risks would you be willing to take to help Zeb know Jesus Christ if he didn't already?

Session 88

Esther

READING THE SCRIPTURES
(Esther 1—10)

Your studies of God's people in exile have been limited to the prophets and their messages. In the **Book of Esther** you'll discover some things about conditions in captivity as well as how God protected His people from annihilation.

Esther was a brave young woman who served God's people. Though God's name is not mentioned in the book you'll be able to see how God manipulated events for the sake of His people.

Try to imagine yourself in the position of Esther or her cousin, Mordecai. How do you think you would have reacted? Does God need people like Esther and Mordecai today? Why?

A THREAT TO GOD'S PEOPLE

1. Who was Esther, and how did she become queen to Xerxes **(Esther 1:1—2:18)?**

_____

_____

_____

2. Who was Mordecai?

_____

_____

3. Who was Haman, and what kind of a threat was he to Mordecai **(Esther 3)?**

_____

_____

_____

4. What risk did Esther have to take in order to fight Haman's plot **(Esther 4)?**

_____

_____

_____

_____

5. What was Esther's plan, and how did it turn out?

_____

_____

_____

6. Mordecai had done Xerxes a favor. How was he rewarded **(Esther 6** and **10)?**

_____

_____

_____

GOD'S WOMAN

Mordecai worked "behind the scenes" while Esther took many risks. Esther respected her guardian and her heritage.

1. At first Esther was reluctant to intervene on behalf of the Jews because of the risk involved. What was Mordecai's counter argument **(Esther 4:12-13)?**

_____

_____

_____

2. What was the relationship that Mordecai seemed to see between Esther's gifts of beauty and her royal position and the need of the Jews **(v. 14)?**

_____

_____

_____

3. Have you ever noticed that higher positions usually require greater responsibility for service? Who else do you know who was royalty yet became the servant of God's people **(Philippians 2:6-11)?**

_____

_____

_____

4. Have you ever been in a position to help someone, but you decided not to because of the risks involved? Tell about it.

_____

_____

_____

5. Does Esther give you the confidence to begin taking risks for others? Why or why not?

_____

_____

_____

_____

A ROYAL POSITION

You have studied **1 Peter 2:9** before. The passage describes you as a special person, a member of a royal priesthood, a person who belongs to God. Being a royal person carries responsibilities.

1. What is one of the royal purposes (privileges) God has for you according to **1 Peter 2:9b?**

_____

_____

_____

2. Another responsibility you have as one of God's children is recorded in **John 15:9-17.** What is that responsiblity?

_____

_____

_____

3. Jesus described another royal responsibility in **John 8:31-32.** What is it?

_____

_____

_____

4. **1 Peter 2:13** describes something that Esther did. What is it?

_____

_____

_____

5. Obedience isn't very popular, whether it's to our parents, to teachers, or to traffic laws. We naturally want to do just as we please. Esther took some risks that she described as disobedience. The law she vio-

lated had a special provision that allowed the king to show mercy if he chose to do so **(Esther 4:11).** This doesn't imply that in some situations it's ethical to disobey the law. If that were true, we would be constantly making decisions about obeying laws! What did Esther realize about her situation **(Esther 4:16b)?** Was she willing to accept the consequences?

_____

_____

_____

6. Obedience is always important but we must also remember who has absolute authority **(Acts 5:29).** To whom are we accountable in the end?

_____

_____

7. Is anything happening in your life that makes you want to disobey laws? Tell about it. (If you choose to keep your problems confidential, at least describe them to God.)

_____

_____

_____

8. What can you, as a royal child of God, do about those problems whenever you experience them?

_____

_____

_____

_____

9. Esther and Mordecai were able to talk with each other and ask for help or offer encouragement. Christians need that help from each other. To whom could you offer your Christian friendship?

_____

_____

_____

A project for people belonging to God: Sometime in the next week of school find one person who needs you as a friend. Support that person in your friendly conversations and pray for that person to experience life and joy in knowing Jesus Christ. Consider it your royal privilege!

You are a chosen people, a royal priesthood, a holy nation, a people belonging to God, that you may declare the praises of Him who called you out of darkness into His wonderful light.

1 Peter 2:9

Session 89

The Homecoming of God's People

READING THE SCRIPTURES (Ezra 1—10)

Let's go home!'' For most people that phrase has a happy meaning. For the exiles it meant that they were going back to their homeland, the land that God had given them. As with most homecomings, the people discovered that things had changed. Things were different from what they remembered and different from stories their parents had told.

What would it be like for you to buy an old, run-down house and try to restore it? New building codes and city zoning ordinances would tell you exactly what you could and couldn't do, but eventually you would finish the job. You'd make it home. And you'd feel good calling it "home."

In a way, that's what the Jews had to do when they returned to Judah and Jerusalem. Can you imagine some of the things they saw and heard as they worked to restore their homes and God's temple?

A PROMISE KEPT

1. The return of the exiles was no accident. God had predicted it through His prophets. Summarize the prophecies of
   a. **Isaiah 44:24—45:13**

   _____

   _____

   _____

   _____

   b. **Jeremiah 50:18-20**

   _____

   _____

   _____

   _____

   c. **Ezekiel 37**

   _____

   _____

   _____

2. God had even predicted who would release them. Compare **Isaiah 45:1** and **13** with **Ezra 1:1-4.** Whom did God choose?

   _____

3. Nations of the world have often believed that they were destined to achieve great things. Much of their confidence has been based on retrospect—that is, looking back over the years. Note that God first predicts the future and then He says, "You can believe Me because this is consistent and has happened this way in the past." Write down a promise of God in Scripture that will be fulfilled in the future.

   _____

   _____

   _____

   _____

4. About how many Jews returned to Judah in the first wave (Ezra 2:64-65 and 8:1-20)? Did all return? Why or why not? _____

_____

_____

THE TEMPLE REBUILT

Read and answer the following questions:

1. What did the exiles see as they returned to their home? (Review 2 Kings 25:13-21 and 2 Chronicles 36:18-21.)

2. What was the first thing the people had to do (Ezra 2:70)?

3. What was their first task in the temple (Ezra 3:1-6)?

4. Who took charge of rebuilding the temple (Ezra 4:1-5)?

5. Things didn't always run smoothly. How did the people of Samaria interfere (Ezra 4:1-5)?

6. How did God help His people (Ezra 5:1—6:18)?

A NATION RESTORED

By causing Cyrus to send the Jews back to Judah, God fulfilled half of His two-part plan. He also had to make sure His people would not make the same mistakes when they returned. In His wisdom God provided another person who was a good teacher of the Law. That person was Ezra.

1. Who was Ezra and what were his job qualifications (Ezra 7:1-6)? _____

_____

2. Have you ever thought that God placed your teacher in your classroom for a very special purpose? What assignment has God given your teacher?

_____

_____

_____

3. Ezra had boldly asked King Artaxerxes for help. What did Artaxerxes give him (Ezra 7:12-26)? _____

_____

_____

_____

4. How did Ezra begin the trip to Jerusalem (Ezra 8:21-23)?

_____

_____

_____

5. What problem did Ezra have to deal with when he arrived in Jerusalem (Ezra 9:1-2)?

_____

_____

_____

6. What was Ezra's response and why was it necessary (Ezra 10:1-17 and 9:10-12)?

_____

_____

_____

7. What evidence do you find of God's incredible love in the Book of Ezra?

_____

_____

_____

_____

OUR PERFECT HOMECOMING

What do you think it'll be like someday when God takes you to His perfect home in heaven?

_____

_____

_____

Read about our heavenly home in 2 Corinthians 5:1-10. Does this Scripture passage help you feel better about someday dying and going to heaven? Does just thinking about dying give you the creeps? It might help to talk about it with your friends, your family members, and even your pastor or Bible class teacher. Remember that God loves you, His Word is true, and He faithfully keeps *all* His promises!

Your word is truth.

John 17:17b

Know therefore that the Lord your God is God; He is the faithful God, keeping His covenant of love to a thousand generations of those who love Him and keep His commands.

Deuteronomy 7:9

Session 90
Secure in the Lord

READING THE SCRIPTURES
(Nehemiah 1—13)

A meaningful folksong from *Hymns for Now III* tells the theme of this session in its four verses. You can sing it if you know the melody, or make up a melody of your own! Its message reminds us of GOD'S INCREDIBLE LOVE FOR US and of His gifts to us—*strength, hope, love, and peace.*

God gives His people strength.
If we believe in His way,
He's swift to repay
All those who bear the burden of the day.
God gives His people strength.

God gives His people hope.
If we but trust in His Word,
Our prayers are always heard.
He warmly welcomes anyone who's erred.
God gives His people hope.

God gives His people love.
If we but open wide our heart,
He's sure to do His part;
He's always the first to make a start.
God gives His people love.

God gives His people peace.
When sorrow fills us to the brim
And courage grows dim,
He lays to rest our restlessness in Him.
God gives His people peace.

Written by Miriam Therese Winter © 1965 Medical Mission Sisters. Used by permission.

The account you are about to read in **Nehemiah** ends your study of the Old Testament. One person stands out in the account. Nehemiah's example shows us how we can be secure in the Lord. This person, chosen by God, lived a life of faith in the Lord God Almighty. He depended on the power of God. You can do the same.

LEADING THE PEOPLE

Nehemiah was another of the great leaders whom God had used so frequently to bless His people. His leadership style sets an example for all believers.

1. Read **Nehemiah 1:4; 2:4, 12; 4:4-5, 9;** and **6:9.** What was one of Nehemiah's first steps when he encountered a problem or challenge?

_____

_____

2. How do the following examples show that Nehemiah was a careful planner?

a. **Nehemiah 1:11—2:9**

_____

b. **Nehemiah 2:13-18**

_____

3. What do the following passages tell you about Nehemiah's attitude toward work?

a. **Nehemiah 4:6**

_____

b. **Nehemiah 4:23**

_____

4. What was Nehemiah's attitude toward God's law **(Nehemiah 5:6-13; 13)?**

_____

_____

5. To whom did Nehemiah give credit for his success? (Supply the passage that supports your conclusion.)

_____

_____

6. Describe Nehemiah's character and leadership style in your own words.

_____

_____

7. Do you know anyone like Nehemiah today? Tell about him or her.

_____

_____

_____

SECURING THE CITY

Nehemiah held an important position as cupbearer to Artaxerxes. The cupbearer was the official food taster. He was at the king's side constantly. Nehemiah had many opportunities to influence the king and could have continued to live in comfort. Yet he was concerned about his countrymen back in Judah. A new wall was essential to the security of Jerusalem.

1. How did Nehemiah convince Artaxerxes to let him return to Jerusalem **(Nehemiah 1:4 and 2:1-9)**?

_____

2. What was the condition of the wall in Jerusalem?

_____

_____

3. Nehemiah successfully got the people to work hard on the wall until some Samaritans tried to intimidate the workers and disrupt the building. What creative plan did Nehemiah think of to protect the workers and still accomplish the task **(Nehemiah 4:13-23)**?

_____

_____

4. Nehemiah had one more strategy to overcome the intimidation of his enemies. What was it **(Nehemiah 6:9)**?

_____

_____

_____

5. What caused Nehemiah's enemies to lose their self-confidence?

_____

_____

6. Nehemiah also had to take care of some spiritual problems. What were the problems, and how did Nehemiah deal with them?

a. **Nehemiah 5:1-13**

_____

_____

_____

b. **Nehemiah 13:1-28**

_____

_____

_____

PRAISING THE LORD

The **Book of Nehemiah** ends abruptly. It almost seems as though there should be a summary statement or acknowledgment. We must go back to **Nehemiah 8:9-18.** The people celebrated with *joy* over God's law!

1. Who was it that taught the Law to the people **(Nehemiah 8:2-9)?**

_____

2. Why were the people so willing to celebrate according to **Nehemiah 8:12?**

_____

_____

3. What did the people do in addition to reading the Law according to **Nehemiah 9:1-5?**

_____

_____

4. You've traced the history of God's people and His love for them from creation to their return from captivity. You've applied the lessons you've learned to your own life. What has God done with you and for you?

_____

_____

_____

5. Can you praise the Lord for something? What is it?

_____

_____

Praise the Lord!

The joy of the Lord is your strength.
Nehemiah 8:10b